the Unofficial Guide™ to Eldercare

Chris Adamec

Macmillan • USA

Macmillan General Reference USA
A Pearson Education Macmillan Company
1633 Broadway
New York, New York 10019-6785

ISBN: 0-02-862456-4

Manufactured in the United States of America

10 9 8 7 6 5 4 3 2 1

First edition

The book is dedicated to Maryam Banikarim, without whom it would not have been written.

Contents

The *Unofficial Guide* Reader's Bill of Rights

We Give You More Than the Official Line

Welcome to the *Unofficial Guide* series of Lifestyles titles—books that deliver critical, unbiased information that other books can't or won't reveal—*the inside scoop*. Our goal is to provide you with the *most accessible, useful* information and advice possible. The recommendations we offer in these pages are not influenced by the corporate line of any organization or industry; we give you the hard facts, whether those institutions like them or not. If something is ill-advised or will cause a loss of time and/or money, we'll give you ample warning. And if it is a worthwhile option, we'll let you know that, too.

Armed and Ready

Our hand-picked authors confidently and critically report on a wide range of topics that matter to smart readers like you. Our authors are passionate about their subjects, but have distanced themselves enough from them to help you be armed and protected, and help you make educated decisions as you go through your process. It is our intent that, from having read this book, you will avoid the pitfalls everyone else falls into and get it right the first time.

Don't be fooled by cheap imitations; this is the *genuine article Unofficial Guide* series from Macmillan Publishing. You may be familiar with our proven track record of the travel *Unofficial Guides*, which have more than two million copies in print. Each year thousands of travelers—new and old—are armed with a brand new, fully updated edition of the flagship *Unofficial Guide to Walt Disney World*, by Bob Sehlinger. It is our intention here to provide you with the same level of objective authority that Mr. Sehlinger does in his brainchild.

The Unofficial Panel of Experts

Every work in the Lifestyle *Unofficial Guides* is intensively inspected by a team of three top professionals in their fields. These experts review the manuscript for factual accuracy, comprehensiveness, and an insider's determination as to whether the manuscript fulfills the credo in this Reader's Bill of Rights. In other words, our Panel ensures that you are, in fact, getting "the inside scoop."

Our Pledge

The authors, the editorial staff, and the Unofficial Panel of Experts assembled for *Unofficial Guides* are determined to lay out the most valuable alternatives available for our readers. This dictum means that our writers must be explicit, prescriptive, and above all, direct. We strive to be thorough and complete, but our goal is not necessarily to have the "most" or "all" of the information on a topic; this is not, after all, an encyclopedia. Our objective is to help you narrow down your options to the best of what is available, unbiased by affiliation with any industry or organization.

In each *Unofficial Guide* we give you:

- Comprehensive coverage of necessary and vital information
- Authoritative, rigidly fact-checked data
- The most up-to-date insights into trends
- Savvy, sophisticated writing that's also readable
- Sensible, applicable facts and secrets that only an insider knows

Special Features

Every book in our series offers the following six special sidebars in the margins that were devised to help you get things done cheaply, efficiently, and smartly.

1. "Timesaver"—tips and shortcuts that save you time.

2. "Moneysaver"—tips and shortcuts that save you money.

3. "Watch Out!"—more serious cautions and warnings.

4. "Bright Idea"—general tips and shortcuts to help you find an easier or smarter way to do something.

5. "Quote"—statements from real people that are intended to be prescriptive and valuable to you.

6. "Unofficially..."—an insider's fact or anecdote.

We also recognize your need to have quick information at your fingertips, and have thus provided the following comprehensive sections at the back of the book:

1. **Glossary:** Definitions of complicated terminology and jargon.

2. **Resource Guide:** Lists of relevant agencies, associations, institutions, Web sites, etc.

3. **Recommended Reading List:** Suggested titles that can help you get more in-depth information on related topics.

4. **Important Documents:** "Official" pieces of information you need to refer to, such as government forms.

5. **Important Statistics:** Facts and numbers presented at-a-glance for easy reference.

6. **Index.**

Letters, Comments, and Questions from Readers

We strive to continually improve the Unofficial series, and input from our readers is a valuable way for us to do that. Many of those who have used the *Unofficial Guide* travel books write to the authors to ask questions, make comments, or share their own discoveries and lessons. For lifestyle *Unofficial Guides*, we would also appreciate all such correspondence, both positive and critical, and we will make best efforts to incorporate appropriate readers' feedback and comments in revised editions of this work.

How to write to us:

Unofficial Guides
Macmillan Lifestyle Guides
Macmillan Publishing
1633 Broadway
New York, NY 10019

Attention: Reader's Comments

The *Unofficial Guide* Panel of Experts

The *Unofficial* editorial team recognizes that you've purchased this book with the expectation of getting the most authoritative, carefully inspected information currently available. Toward that end, on each and every title in this series, we have selected a minimum of three "official" experts comprising the "Unofficial Panel" who painstakingly review the manuscripts to ensure the following: factual accuracy of all data; inclusion of the most up-to-date and relevant information; and that, from an insider's perspective, the authors have armed you with all the necessary facts you need—but the institutions don't want you to know.

For *The Unofficial Guide to Eldercare*, we are proud to introduce the following panel of experts:

Joseph Kandel, M.D. Doctor Kandel is a board-certified neurologist and a pain-management specialist. He treats many elderly patients and their families. He is co-author of *The Anti-Arthritis Diet* and *The Arthritis Solution*.

Marilyn S. Dlesk, M.S.W Marilyn received her master of social work degree from Ohio State University. She has practiced social work since 1989. Currently she is working as a home health and hospice social worker for The Cleveland Clinic and also Alliance Healthcare Network. She has a particular interest in educating patients about their healthcare options and empowering them to advocate for healthcare reform.

Suzanne G. Snyder, Ph.D. Doctor Snyder is a production editor for Macmillan General Reference. She is currently living with and is primary caregiver for her parents—particularly her father (a 70-year-old stroke victim). She gratefully acknowledges John V. Buffington's insights and advice concerning the first four chapters of this book.

Cheryl Primeau Ms. Primeau has worked as an eldercare giver at the Resurrection Nursing Home in Castleton, New York. She has also been a home care aide for more than 20 years. Her first client was her Aunt Margaret, an elder who lived with the family before moving to a nursing home. Ms. Primeau has organized and participated in workshops for the elderly at several senior citizen centers in the upstate New York area.

Christopher Florio, R.N., B.S.N. Chris Florio has worked with the elderly for the past five years. While attending Kent State University's School of Nursing, he was a nurse's aide at a facility that offered a full spectrum of eldercare: from adult apartments to assisted living and full

24-hour nursing care. Mr. Florio also worked as an R.N. at a skilled nursing facility for almost two years.

Mr. Florio currently works in the internal medicine/telemetry floor at the Cleveland Clinic Foundation. In this position, he deals with elderly people with chronic health problems.

Introduction

I f you find yourself in the position of caring for—or coordinating the care of—an elderly parent, you are most definitely not alone. Millions of others like you have assumed such responsibilities and are trying to make the best possible choices to provide the most appropriate care for their loved ones.

More than 34 million people age 65 and older are living in America at the close of the 20th century, a figure that's up from only about 3 million when the century began. Many of these seniors are fit, active, and living independent lives. But somewhat more than one-third report living with a disability severe enough to require assistance—and that assistance typically is provided by a family member.

By taking on the responsibility of providing eldercare for your parent, you are embarking on a sometimes difficult, often overwhelming task. It's easy to feel isolated, overburdened, confused—and just plain *tired*. And that's why this book was written—to provide you with a better understanding of what eldercare is all about and also to inform you of the help and hurdles before you.

This is not intended to be a handbook on the diseases of the elderly. It does not pretend to take on the subject of the clinical problems the elderly face, as that would require several highly specialized volumes to do the subject justice. Instead, this book provides you with the practical information you require to do *your* job as coordinator and caregiver. When you've finished, you'll have learned what you need to know to effectively act as the primary eldercare provider—from identifying your elder's specific care needs; to organizing his or her necessary financial, medical, and legal information; to discovering the wide variety of programs and services currently available to help you in your task.

The following sections detail what you can expect to find in the chapters to come.

Part One: An Eldercare Overview

The chapters in the first part of this book provide you with a basic understanding of the eldercare process. In Chapter 1, "The Growing Need for Eldercare," you'll learn about how and why eldercare has become an issue of increasing social, political, and economic significance. You'll discover the complex and wide-ranging problems and possibilities your elders—and you, as their caregivers—confront. You'll also learn just how diverse America's elderly population has become.

Chapter 2, "Who Needs Eldercare?," introduces you to the basic terminology, principles, and options of eldercare today. It breaks down the early warning signs that may indicate that your elderly parent may need some assistance. This chapter is intended to help you get started planning for your elder's needs *before* you're confronted with a crisis situation. After all, experts ranging from the federal government's

Administration on Aging to the American Association of Retired Persons all agree that the best way to guarantee a maximally comfortable and rewarding elderhood is to plan ahead—to anticipate what may need to be done *before* serious need arises. This way, you avoid the stress and possible panic that ensues when an emergency catches you by surprise.

Chapter 3, "Determining the Level of Care Required," takes the information of the earlier chapters a step further and moves into the practical realm of matching your elder's specific care needs to the broad range of options currently available. The focus of this chapter is to help you make the most appropriate choices based on your elder's preferences, resources, and level of need.

Part Two: The Human Side of the Eldercare Decision

The two chapters in this part of the book deal with the personal dimension—the emotional issues that we all bring to the concept of aging. Perhaps most significant of these issues is the problem of denial: None of us wishes to acknowledge that the passage of years means that we all eventually face a loss in vitality and independence.

For this reason, Chapter 4, "Denial and Other Emotional Issues," confronts the emotional aspects of aging. Denial is threefold: Understandably, your elder may prefer to deny the inevitable consequences of aging. After all, these are intimations of mortality. His or her denial also may make your own task of providing eldercare more difficult. Here, however, you will learn to understand what your elder is coping with and therefore can be better able to help your parent work through these emotional issues and participate as fully as possible in planning the best possible eldercare experience.

But your elder is not the only one who may have problems with confronting the concept of aging. Chapter 4 also addresses the issues you may personally be facing—issues that revolve around the recognition that your once vibrant parent may no longer be there for you in the same way. You also may find that your siblings, on whom you may be counting for help, are dealing with their *own* emotional responses to the fact that your parents are getting older. In reading this chapter, you will hopefully develop a better understanding of the reasons behind these emotional responses so that you'll be better equipped to cope with them.

This brings us to Chapter 5, "Strategies for Coping." This chapter is all about building an effective, coordinated family effort centered on the task of assisting your elder. Here you'll take a close look at the stress involved in eldercare, and learn ways to avoid or overcome it. You'll also learn ways to recruit help—from your family, of course, but also from outside services and agencies, if required. You'll learn about how to coordinate the elements of care your elder may need, and you'll learn about the resources available to *you*, when you need support.

Part Three: Getting Organized

Once you've faced the fact that your elder needs your help, you need to know what practical steps to take to make that help available. The two chapters in this section give you the lowdown on the preliminary steps to take. Chapter 6, "Organizing Your Elder's Finances," helps you get a grip on your elder's day-to-day issues of income and outflow. It's an important topic for two reasons: This is often one of the first areas where your help may be needed; and, without a clear understanding of your elder's finances, you cannot begin to determine the available resources for covering eldercare costs. A sound, baseline reading of your elder's financial situation helps you and your elder devise the best possible approach to care.

Chapter 7, "Organizing Your Elder's Medical Affairs," takes up an equally fundamental set of questions. This chapter provides you with the information you need when trying to establish an accurate reading of your elder's physical condition. As your parent gets older, his or her medical needs become increasingly complex. It's important that you get a firm sense of just what's been done (and prescribed), and what must be done to help your elder achieve the highest degree of physical health and comfort. Here you'll learn the practical steps you can take to bring order to the possible confusion of multiple diagnoses, medications, and treatments.

Part Four: Options in Eldercare

This is, arguably, the heart of the book. Once upon a time, very few options were available for the care of the elderly. Once an elder needed assistance, the choice was either moving him or her in with one of the children, or finding a nursing home. And that second option was sometimes one that inspired horrific Dickensian images of dark, depressing institutional settings and indifferent staff. Many improvements have occurred since then.

In the past three decades, the heightened social and political awareness of the needs of the elderly has prompted a broad range of choices in eldercare. One positive effect of this new awareness has been the growing belief that elders can—and should—be empowered to maintain as independent a lifestyle as possible for as long as they can. For many elders, this means "aging in place"—staying in his or her familiar surroundings.

Chapter 8, "When There's No Place Like Home," takes you on a tour of the ways in which you can help your elder make his or her home more "elder-friendly." With this information, your elder may be able to stay independent even when faced with some disability. You'll learn about the basics of modification and repair needed to elderize a home to accommodate increasing physical frailties, and you'll learn about community-based services that can cater to your elder's needs. These services include home meal delivery, transportation, domestic help, and in-home medical care.

Chapter 9, "It's a Family Affair," takes up some of these same issues—and more—as they apply to the situation of moving your elder into your own home. In addition to offering guidance about how your household can accommodate your elder's needs, it also addresses the interpersonal issues that you are likely to confront as you merge your family's needs with those of your parent. This chapter helps you identify the circumstances and situations in which personalities and living styles may come into conflict, and it offers suggestions on how best to overcome adjustment problems for your elder and for the other members of your household.

Chapter 10, "Assisted-Living Facilities," introduces you to a relative newcomer on the eldercare scene: transitional residential facilities. If your elder is no longer able to safely live alone but is unprepared to move in with you (and is not so disabled as to need round-the-clock care), the assisted-living facility (commonly known as an ALF) is often a good alternative. In this chapter, you'll get an introduction to this option—who it's best suited for, how to find one in your area, and the sorts of services generally offered to residents.

Of course, in some situations the only real answer is round-the-clock, institutionalized care. Chapter 11, "When Long-Term Care Is Needed," takes on the subject of the traditional nursing home and addresses the improvements in quality of care and services during the past three decades. While some institutions still live up to the negative stereotypes of "the old folks' home," progress has been made, thanks to increased public awareness and greater legislative responsiveness to the needs of the elderly. Here you'll learn how to evaluate the full-service facilities in your area so that you can choose a comfortable, compassionate, and caring place for your elder.

Part Five: The Financial, Legal, and Social Realities of Eldercare

These final three chapters take on some difficult but necessary realities of the eldercare process. Chapter 12, "Managing Eldercare Costs," acknowledges that care is often expensive, but it leads you through the steps to protect your elder's financial interests while covering the costs of care. From Medicare, Medicaid, and Medigap insurance, to alternative financing methods such as the reverse mortgage, you'll learn everything you need to know to handle expenses. When you're through here, you'll have a solid understanding of the resources available and the steps your elder must take to qualify for many programs and services designed to assist the elderly.

Chapter 13, "Protecting Your Elder's Legal Rights," faces the possibility that your elder may need your help at a very basic level if no longer able to act on his or her own behalf. This chapter tells you what steps you can take ahead of time to ensure that your elder's wishes are honored in such a situation. You'll learn about the concepts of the living will, the healthcare proxy, and the durable power of attorney, and you'll discover how these legal instruments can be employed to guarantee your elder full legal protection, regardless of his or her condition.

The final chapter, "Eldercare, Your Elder, and You," returns to the emotional territory first discussed in Chapter 4. Here, however, the focus is different. Eldercare is a difficult undertaking, but it is one that can be immensely rewarding, even in the saddest circumstances. This is a time when you and your elder can build a closer relationship than you ever had before—when you can share and grow together, constructively work through issues that have come between you in the past, and provide one another with comfort and caring during these latter years in your parent's life.

The role of primary eldercare provider is not an easy one: The responsibility is great, and the demands on your time and resources can be daunting. But this book is intended to help you find ways to make this a positive, affirming experience for both you and your elder. By taking on this responsibility, you are truly one of "the good guys"—one of the many adult children of aging parents who has chosen to help make your parent's elderhood as independent and enjoyable as possible.

An Eldercare Overview

GET THE SCOOP ON...
Eldercare terminology ▪ Demographics of aging
▪ Demands on caregivers ▪ Available resources

Chapter 1

The Growing Need for Eldercare

Eldercare: This is the umbrella term currently used to describe the physical, psychological, financial, and other forms of assistance provided to people over the age of 65. Sometimes this care is provided by the adult child of an aging parent. Other times the assistance may be provided by other relatives, or by healthcare specialists such as nurses or physicians. But no matter who provides the actual, day-to-day assistance, usually one person—most often a daughter, and sometimes a son of the elderly person—is entrusted with the tasks of decision-making and coordination of care on behalf of the aging parent.

In this chapter, you'll learn about how—and why—the changing demographics of American society have translated into a massive expansion of the eldercare industry in the United States, and you'll learn what that means for you. You'll discover how the combined impact of birthrate trends and improvements in healthcare technology has

3

changed the face of the eldercare industry dramatically over the course of the twentieth century. And you'll learn how these changes directly affect your choices when it comes to securing adequate eldercare for your own elderly parent. But first, let's take a moment to define a very important constellation of terms.

A brief terminological digression

The field of eldercare encompasses a broad range of issues and concerns. After all, even the target population for that care—the elderly—is not a homogeneous group in characteristics or needs. The term *elderly* refers to everyone from the still-active, newly retired 65-year-old to the "very elderly" population over age 80. It includes both people with minimal or no handicaps, and the bedridden and chronically ill. It includes people with substantial economic resources to cover their care, and people who are heavily dependent upon family or public assistance to cover their basic needs.

Just as the elderly themselves comprise a highly varied demographic group, so also do the services available for their care. Properly speaking, eldercare services can mean anything from home-delivered meals to long-term care institutions such as nursing homes. And eldercare issues can range from legislation for the improvement of wheelchair accessibility in public facilities to the guarantee of Medicaid coverage for essential medical treatment.

Cutting through the confusion

Finally, the term *caregiver* in the eldercare context covers a broad spectrum of people—so broad, in fact, that even a basic discussion of the topic can quickly get bogged down in confusion. So, in this book we're adopting a little shorthand.

> 66 Caregiving your elderly parent is not just love and a pot of chicken soup. It's a long-term commitment, and one you must learn and grow into. There is no caregiving gene.
> —David Levy, President of AdultCare, Deerfield Beach, Florida 99

We'll be discussing eldercare in the standard, broad sense of the term given at the start of the chapter, of course. But our focus is on the elder himself (or herself), and on the adult family member who shoulders the burden of securing and coordinating the whole eldercare experience. That's you, the ultimate caregiver, whose decisions and actions control the direction that the eldercare experience takes. When we talk about the *primary caregiver*, we're talking about you.

What's in a name?

This quibbling about terms may seem trivial, but it's not. Other people who provide services for your elder, such as doctors, nurses, and lawyers, are also giving care, but they have recognized, professional roles. You, as the adult child of an aging parent, have no such professional title to claim. And at times this simple lack of a recognized *title* can make you feel powerless. More importantly, it can make you feel intimidated when you need to speak up about the direction that the eldercare process will take for your elder.

By taking the responsibility of overseeing the care of your aging parent, you have assumed a real and important role in the caregiving process. Regardless of the type of eldercare you ultimately choose for your parent, you *are*, in the final analysis, the primary caregiver by virtue of this obligation you have assumed. To be effective, you need to recognize—from the very first moment of your eldercare experience—that your contribution to your elder's care is substantial. You are *not* on the sidelines in this process.

Adult children of aging parents who take on the role of at-home caregiver may have little trouble

Bright Idea
Most primary caregivers are juggling the responsibilities of caring for their aging parent, holding down a job, and raising children of their own. If that's you, don't hesitate to enlist the help of others—family members, neighbors, members of your church or synagogue, and professional service providers.

recognizing the centrality of their role in practical terms, but they can sometimes find themselves steamrolled into decisions that conflict with their own best instincts simply because they are intimidated by the formal authority of the professionally recognized caregivers. It's even harder for those who entrust their elderly parents to more institutionalized care facilities—from the operators of assisted-living facilities to nursing homes—to realize that the role they play is important.

But your role *is* crucial. And in the course of fulfilling that role, you need to feel secure in your authority as decision-maker (along with your elder, if he or she is capable of participating in determining his or her care needs) in the care process. If you need to ask about the reasons for a particular treatment, or if you need to challenge the decisions of other care providers, you must feel that you are doing so from a position of strength. Your choices will have a direct impact on the quality of life enjoyed by your elder in his or her later years. The responsibility you have taken on is a serious one.

Diversity among the elderly

That having been said, it's time to look at the many faces of the elderly in America. Here, too, we can quickly find ourselves lost in a bewildering variety of issues, problems, and concerns. Many of us have grown up with a stereotypical image of the elderly. We tend to unthinkingly lump this wildly disparate group of individuals into a single conceptual category of "old people" without recognizing the diversity within that category. Until we're faced with the actual need for eldercare for our aging parents, most of us think of "eldercare" as synonymous with "nursing home," not recognizing that the needs of our elders can range from something as simple as the addition of a few appliances (grab bars, wheelchair ramps) in the home to round-the-clock medical attention.

In the early decades of this century, the elderly comprised a small percentage of the population. They were few, and they were not particularly vocal, which meant that their issues rarely occupied a central place in the agendas of the political, legal, or medical professions. That has changed, however—and changed dramatically. In the remainder of this chapter, we'll take you on a quick tour of the changing—and aging—demographics in America and their profound effects on the burgeoning eldercare industry.

Watch Out!
Older women, the very old (over age 80), and the minority elderly are the most likely to have a high need for eldercare and to have the least ability to secure it for themselves.

The graying of America

Recent government and private studies have revealed that the numbers of the elderly in the United States—including the category of the very elderly (over age 80)—are growing at a rapid rate. According to the federal government's Administration on Aging (AoA), in 1998 43 million people were over age 60, with 3 million of those age 85 or over. The numbers of the elderly will only continue to grow: The AoA estimates that by the year 2030, those over 60 will climb to 85 million, and the number of people attaining or surpassing their 85th birthday will approach 9 million.

These numbers indicate the vast improvement in life expectancies in the United States since the turn of the 20th century. In 1900, only 3.1 million people reached or exceeded age 65, compared to today's figure of 43 million. The following table shows the steady increase in longevity for Americans

over the course of the century and illustrates how
that increase is likely to continue into the future.

Note! ➜
1997 is the last
year for which
U.S. census data
has been made
available.

Year	Persons 65+ (in millions)
1900	3.1
1920	4.9
1940	9.0
1960	16.7
1980	25.7
1997	34.1
2000	34.7
2010	39.4
2020	53.2
2030	69.4

Source: Based on data from the U.S. Bureau of the Census

Factors contributing to longevity

While it's true that improved healthcare for the
elderly has contributed to our overall increased
chances for living well into our 80s, that's only one
of the two primary factors that contribute to the
"graying of America." The other factor is birth rate:
For example, Table 1.1 discloses that the growth in
the elderly population hit a period of relatively slow
growth in the 1990s. That slow growth rate is projected to continue into the first decade of the 21st
century. After that, the growth rate is expected to
surge once again. These demographic trends are
matched by complementary birth-rate booms and
busts earlier in the century.

How does this work? Look at the slow-growth
period in the 1990s. Most of the people represented
by these numbers were born during the Depression
era, a time in which a relatively small number of
babies were born. Now look at what's projected for
the years 2020 and 2030: The elderly population is
expected to nearly double by the end of that period.

That's when the biggest demographic bulge in America's birth rate—the generation known as the baby boomers—reaches age 65.

How do these raw numbers translate into percentages of the total population? In 1990, only 4.1 percent of the population was age 65 or over. By 1997, that figure had tripled to 12.7 percent. Within that general population, there are more and more of the very elderly: Actuarial studies show that a child born in 1997 can expect to live to age 76.5. Compare this to the average life expectancy of a child born in 1900—that child could expect to live to only his or her mid-50s.

Aging in America, by the numbers

But the simple recitation of sheer numbers of the elderly in the general population tells us very little about the actual experience of aging in America—and even less about its implications for the availability of eldercare services. So let's take a closer look at how the raw population data breaks down.

Living arrangements of the elderly. Of the 34 million elderly in the United States in the late 1990s, only about 4 percent, or 1.36 million of them, lived in nursing homes. The majority of the noninstitutionalized elderly lived in a family setting: Some lived with a spouse, some with their children or other relatives, and some with nonrelatives. Gender is also an important factor in determining living arrangements, as the table below shows.

Clearly, a higher percentage of elderly men live with their spouses than is true for their female counterparts. Simply put, widows far outnumber widowers: In 1997, 46 percent of elderly women were widows, whereas only 25 percent of elderly men were widowers. This is due in large part to the

Unofficially...
The leading edge of the generation known as the baby boomers is being drawn into the need to provide eldercare, but many primary caregivers are themselves classified as elderly: The child of a very elderly parent (over age 80) is often over age 65.

LIVING ARRANGEMENTS AMONG THE ELDERLY

Sex	Living with spouse	Living with children or other relative	Living with nonrelatives
Male	72%	8%	20%
Female	40%	17%	43%

Source: Based on data from U.S. Bureau of the Census. See "Household and Family Characteristics: March 1997," *Current Population Reports.*

fact that women tend to live longer than men: Again looking at the data for 1997, women over age 65 made up nearly 59 percent of all the elderly. And as age increases, the gender gap widens: More than 2.5 as many women as men live to reach or surpass their 85th birthday.

This means that more elderly men *have* spouses to live with than do elderly women. And it means that the most physically vulnerable among America's elderly population—the over-80 group— is predominantly female.

Race and ethnicity among the elderly. One rapidly changing aspect of the demographics of America's elderly is the racial and ethnic composition of this population group. The figure below shows the breakdown as of the 1997 Report of the U.S. Census.

As the figure shows, the vast majority of the elderly today is white. This is largely due to the relatively greater affluence of whites and thus their greater ability to take advantage of regular medical care throughout their lives (and especially as they get older). But due to better health and living conditions and an increased life expectancy for minorities, the number of minority elderly is

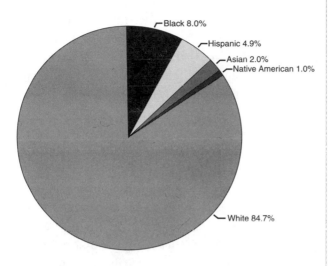

Black 8.0%
Hispanic 4.9%
Asian 2.0%
Native American 1.0%
White 84.7%

Race and
Ethnicity Among
the Elderly

expected to increase dramatically in the next few decades. By the year 2030, the AoA estimates that the elderly black population is expected to increase by 265 percent, and the elderly Hispanic population is expected to grow by a whopping 530 percent; the rate of increase for the white population is projected to increase by a comparatively low 97 percent.

These trends raise certain disturbing questions about the availability of adequate eldercare in the future. Income and ethnicity in America are strongly correlated, and as the minority population among the elderly grows, the income level represented by the elderly is likely to erode. More of the elderly may depend upon public funds or public programs to cover the costs of their necessary care. **Income issues for the elderly.** The U.S. Department of Health and Human Services (DHHS) set the poverty level for a single-person household in 1998 at $8,050, with an increase of $2,800 for each additional member of the household (the level and per-person increase are set a little higher for Alaska and

Watch Out!
America's most financially vulnerable elderly— women and minorities—are also the most likely to need high-cost medical care. Without increased public commitment to supporting this population's needs, many of these people may find themselves forced to face inadequate or substandard levels of care.

Bright Idea
Stay informed on
eldercare issues
when they arise
in your local or
state political
races. Most of
the improve-
ments in the
provision of
eldercare have
come from grass-
roots pressure.
Let your voice be
heard on issues
affecting your
elder's care.

Hawaii than for the rest of the country). The DHHS
defines "near poverty" as 125 percent of the poverty
rate, or a little over $10,000 for a single person. In
1997, 37 percent of all elderly persons reported an
income at or below the near-poverty level, with 10.5
percent falling below the poverty line.

A primary source of income for elderly
Americans is Social Security—91 percent collect this
monthly allotment. But of course many elders rely
on other income an assets. For example, 41 percent
collect a pension, 21 percent earn wages and six percent receive public assistance. In addition, about 12
percent of elderly Americans were employed in, or
actively seeking, part-time work in 1997. Yet while
it's true that there are many poor among the elderly,
the fact is that the elderly as a whole are substantially
better off, economically speaking, than ever before.
In households headed by persons over 65, the
median income in 1997 was $30,660, and the
median net worth of such households was $86,300.
This has had significant implications for the expansion of privately owned businesses that specialize in
serving the elderly community. In addition, the
financial clout of the elderly as a group, and the
high-profile advocacy of such organizations as the
American Association of Retired Persons (AARP),
have served to keep the issues and concerns of the
elderly high on the policy agendas of local, state,
and federal governments as well.

While we're on the subject of income, let's take
a moment to blow away a commonly held myth that
the elderly are largely helpless and generally idle.
The category of "elderly" includes everyone from
age 65 on up—that is, it begins at the same age that
has been set as standard for retirement. While it is

true that the majority of elderly are indeed retired, you'll recall that we cited a figure of 12 percent of all elderly Americans who were employed or were seeking full-time employment in 1997. That's 3.9 million older Americans, and this figure does not include the large number of casually (informally) employed elders. Even for the retired elderly, a large percentage are still active and fully capable of independent living.

Education and the elderly. As a group, the elderly are better educated than ever before. In 1997, 66 percent of all persons over age 65 had completed high school, and 15 percent had received at least their bachelor's degree. This has contributed to making them a much more aware and politically active group than at any other time in U.S. history.

Health issues and the elderly. We noted earlier that many of the elderly enjoy good health—fully 60 percent. But according to the U.S. Census, 52.5 percent report living with at least one disability (see Chapter 2, "Who Needs Eldercare?" for a discussion of the formal definition of disabilities), and a third of all elderly Americans reported having to cope with severe disabilities that restricted their lifestyles. the table below shows how these percentages compare to those for the rest of the population.

AMERICANS WITH DISABILITIES (BY AGE)

Age Group	% with any disability	% with severe disability
65+	52.5	33.4
15–64	18.7	8.7
0–14	9.1	1.1

Source: *Current Population Reports*. "Americans with Disabilities, 1994-95." August 1997.

Unofficially...
In 1995,
Medicare covered
the health and
medical services
for four out of
every five people
over age 65 (not
including those
enrolled in
HMOs), and the
annual average
payment for such
services was
$15,074 per per-
son. (Sources:
the U.S. Bureau
of the Census,
the National
Center of Health
Statistics, and
the Bureau of
Labor Statistics.)

As people age, they are more likely to need out-patient and inpatient medical care, and the care they require will probably last longer and cost more than for the rest of the population. When hospital-ization is required, the average length of stay in 1995 was 7.1 days for an elderly person (the figure was 5.4 days for the nonelderly). The elderly are twice as likely to have contacts with doctors than people under age 65, and their overall annual healthcare costs are likely to be more than twice those for younger Americans.

Implications for eldercare

How do the changing demographics of aging in the United States play out in the field of eldercare? More eldercare options are available now than at anytime in the past. Both the government and pri-vate industry have found it in their best interests to respond to increased demand for services and resources that meet the needs of the elderly and their caregivers. These responses include the follow-ing:

- More access to information and referral services
- More home-oriented services (personal care, visiting nurses, home-delivered meals)
- More "transitional" care options (assisted-living alternatives)
- More community-based services (senior centers, fitness programs, group meals)
- More access to the political process (through such groups as the AARP)
- More caregiver services (respite services, coun-seling, educational programs)

Each of these developments has contributed to the ever-expanding array of alternatives available in the field of eldercare. The increasing visibility of the elderly as voters and consumers, and the rise of advocacy groups for older Americans have made society as a whole more responsive to their specific concerns. But while the changing demographics of American society have increased the number of services available to the elderly, they have also added to the complexity of choices you face as you try to select the best eldercare for your aging parent.

Profile of a primary caregiver

Who are the people who assume the primary responsibility for eldercare? The profile of the typical primary caregiver is as follows:

- Female
- 46 years old
- Married
- Caregiver of at least one child
- Full-time worker

In real life, of course, the eldercare provider frequently breaks from the typical profile. Circumstances, local family or cultural norms, and sometimes just simple convenience often determine who takes on the task of caring for an aging parent. Often it's the eldest child, whether male or female, who assumes primary responsibility for the aging parent. Or it's the unmarried child—most frequently a younger daughter—who assumes responsibility.

The baby boomer impact on eldercare

The broad group from which many eldercare providers are drawn is the generation known as the baby boomers—those born between 1946 and 1964. This group, which makes up the single largest demographic group in the U.S. population, has

> 66
> I didn't expect to end up with the job of coordinating my father's care when he fell sick two years ago—it just happened that I was available at the time, since I worked at home and my brother and sisters had outside jobs. It certainly wasn't because I had any special knowledge or training—I had to learn as I went, every step of the way.
> —Linda, age 47
> 99

long enjoyed the greatest consumer clout in the country's history. As their needs have changed over time, the social, economic, and even political institutions of the country have been quick to provide the services they demand.

Education and involvement

Also contributing to the economic and political clout of primary eldercare providers as a whole is the fact that caregivers are generally well-educated. According to data released in 1997 by the National Alliance for Caregiving, AARP, and Glaxo Wellcome, 28 percent of all caregivers hold college or graduate school degrees, and another 23 percent have at least some college training. Only 9 percent lacked at least a high school diploma.

The high level of educational attainment on the part of primary caregivers means that, as a group, they are an active, engaged, and effective advocacy group for the elders in their charge. They are accustomed to keeping up with social and political trends that affect their lives, and they are willing to roll up their sleeves and get involved if an issue strikes them as important.

When the time for caregiving has come

Right now you may be simultaneously juggling practical concerns, personal knowledge about your own aging parent, and emotional reactions to the whole situation. You're trying to come up with the pragmatically "right answer," for the elderly person in your care, but you're also dealing with sleepless nights as you worry about whether your choices are going to upset or even alienate your parent. And you may be worried about how those same choices might affect the dynamics in your own household.

These fears are understandable. We all have been exposed to myths and stereotypes about the aging process—it's something that, as a culture, we find difficult to deal with rationally. And we rarely question our stereotypes until we're faced with a particular situation that contradicts them.

Breaking free from stereotypical thinking

As you can no doubt conclude from the demographic material offered earlier, no one stereotypical profile of the elderly is valid. Think of George Burns, who enjoyed an active career in films and television well into his 80s. Think of Sophia Loren, now in her 60s and still considered by some to be a major sex symbol. And think of Jack Palance, who was in his 80s when he dropped to the floor and did a series on one-handed push-ups on the 1991 Academy Awards show.

Many still tend to equate the idea of aging with decrepitude, even though we are surrounded by examples of vital, active, and immensely capable older people in our society. But by persistently clinging to outmoded beliefs about aging, we make it very difficult to face the concept of aging in our parents calmly. If we see that Mom's arthritis is really giving her trouble, we may leap to the assumption that she can no longer care for herself, when all she really needs right now are a few modifications to her home (see Chapter 8, "When There's No Place Like Home," on elderizing a home). But overreaction is never a useful response to your elder's needs.

Of course, under-reaction is equally a problem. It's hard to make the conceptual shift from viewing your parent as the strong, supportive person who was always there to help you to reach the realization that now it's your turn to be the supportive one.

Watch Out!
It is sometimes difficult to avoid the urge to assume that an elder is in need of intervention and care when we first notice a decline in physical abilities. But most elders prefer not to be rushed into dependence before it's truly necessary. Carefully evaluate your elder's situation and discuss it with him or her before you take unilateral action.

Once again, it's stereotypical thinking that makes clear judgment difficult.

Spotting the obvious—and not so obvious—clues

So, how do you know if your elder needs help? Sometimes the evidence is obvious: Your parent suffers a fall or debilitating illness, for example. Or he or she specifically mentions that it's getting tough to keep up a previously independent lifestyle. Or your elder's physician suggests to you that it's time to consider getting some help. But other times the signs are much more subtle. Here are the areas in which the first signs of a need for assistance might make themselves known:

- Failing health
- Increased safety concerns
- Nutritional problems
- Increased isolation

Obviously, monitoring all these potential trouble areas can be difficult. This is why, as your parent gets older, it's important to maintain regular contact. If you don't live near your elder, you may have to ask a friend, relative, or neighbor who lives near your elder to check in regularly and keep you apprised of your elder's health. When your elder is only gradually losing the capability to handle his or her day-to-day living activities, it's easy to overlook evolving problems. In the next chapter, we'll look more closely at the signs and symptoms you need to recognize so that you can provide your elder with the care he or she needs in a timely fashion.

Just the facts

- The elderly comprise the fastest-growing demographic group in American society.

- The eldercare industry has undergone massive growth in response to the increased demand for services and caregiving alternatives.

- As the primary caregiver, the adult child of an elderly person has an important role to play in determining—and securing—the care his or her elder requires.

- Stereotypical images of the elderly often make it difficult for a caregiver to objectively assess his or her elder's needs for assistance.

- Whenever possible, the primary caregiver and the elder should operate as a team to secure the most appropriate level of eldercare.

GET THE SCOOP ON...
Signs of aging ▪ Age-related illnesses ▪
Eldercare options ▪ Home care services

Who Needs Eldercare?

Aging is obviously an inevitable part of life. But there's a difference between getting older and needing eldercare. Sure, there's an inevitable decline in some of our abilities as we age. As time goes on, we usually lose a little visual acuity, and we lose a few of the other attributes of youth— perhaps that full head of hair or our previously accustomed sharpness of hearing. But that's not the same thing as needing eldercare.

As you'll recall from Chapter 1, "The Growing Need for Eldercare," the term *eldercare* refers to the assistance that some of the elderly need to manage the tasks of day-to-day living. At some point in life, nearly everybody will need at least a little assistance. But just because your parent has passed his or her 65th birthday doesn't automatically mean you must start shopping around for eldercare services.

This chapter is about recognizing when your parents may have reached that point in the natural aging process—increasing physical frailty, perhaps, or mental disability, or both—where they need your help. The following sections discuss the signs of aging that mean eldercare is something for you to consider, and they set forth some basic options and principles of eldercare.

Aging's early signs and symptoms

Eldercare comes into play only when an individual reaches that point when it becomes difficult to carry out some or all of the necessary tasks of daily life. An acute need for eldercare occurs when that person can't take care of the basic requirements of living, but a need for eldercare can also be indicated when assistance is required simply to make daily life more comfortable. So, right from the outset you should start thinking of eldercare as a continuum.

To establish the outer points on that continuum, it's helpful to think in terms of the definitions established by the Administration on Aging (AoA), which we mentioned in the previous chapter. Drawing on definitions included in the Americans with Disabilities Act of 1990, the AoA defines two types of situations in which eldercare may be needed. Because the AoA is a government agency, you won't be surprised to discover that these two types of situations were promptly assigned acronyms—ADL and IADL—and a full array of bureaucratic jargon. Both types are discussed in the following sections.

Alphabet soup: ADLs and IADLs

As your parent gets older, he or she may develop difficulties in performing certain activities necessary to day-to-day life without assistance. In the jargon of eldercare, these are *activities of daily living* (ADLs) and *instrumental activities of daily living* (IADLs). Table 2.1 sets out the activities covered by each of these categories.

TABLE 2.1: ACTIVITIES IN WHICH THE ELDERLY MAY NEED HELP

ADLs	IADLs
Eating	Meal preparation
Getting in and out of bed	Heavy housework
Getting around inside the home	Getting around outside the home
Dressing	Doing the laundry
Bathing	Grocery shopping
Using the toilet	Money management
Self-administering medications	Keeping track of medication schedules

Warning signs that help may be needed

When you're first faced with the possibility that your parent needs eldercare, unless you're looking at a sudden medical crisis, your elder's problem will probably be a loss in the ability to perform one or more of the activities listed under the instrumental activities category. This means that your parent has no trouble handling the basics, but certain more complicated tasks—such as managing the money, cooking meals, or coping with a complicated series of medications—have become difficult. How can you tell if these problems have arisen? Here are a few warning signs:

▪ The bills aren't getting paid on time. For example, Mom always used to pay them promptly, but now the kitchen counter is littered with overdue notices.

▪ Basic nutrition is being ignored. There's no food in the refrigerator and only a few canned items in the pantry. When you ask Dad what he's been eating, his answers are vague.

▪ Medications are not being handled carefully. The medicine cabinet is full of prescription drugs, but your parent can't tell you with certainty which pills are for what ailment, or when they're supposed to be taken.

■ Signs of emotional disturbance have begun to appear. Your parent seems depressed. Old pastimes or interests are forgotten, and nothing seems to make your parent brighten up.

■ Personal hygiene has deteriorated considerably.

■ The house or apartment that your parent always kept in apple-pie order is beginning to look decidedly unkempt.

Everybody has times when their standards slip in one or all of these categories—it's when the deviation from normal practice lasts for more than a few days or weeks that you should become concerned.

Physical and mental problems associated with aging

The risk of complications in many illnesses increases with age, as does the severity of their impact. In addition, the elderly are more likely than the general population to contract certain diseases. All these factors are significant to eldercare because, due to illness, your recently self-reliant elder may suddenly find him- or herself in need of help. Obviously, helping your elder maintain good physical health is important.

Physical illnesses affecting the elderly

Most diseases that afflict the elderly are present to some degree throughout the general population. However, some ailments hit older Americans in far greater numbers and with far greater severity than others. These illnesses include heart disease, arthritis, various forms of cancer, diabetes, high blood pressure, diseases of the eye (especially cataracts and glaucoma), prostate trouble, and osteoporosis.

▪ **Heart disease.** Between 2 million and 3 million Americans suffer from congestive heart failure—it's the number 1 cause of death in the United States. But the incidence of heart disease is disproportionately felt among the elderly: While only 1 percent of persons under age 50 die of the disease, the percentage increases tenfold for the over-80 population.

Fortunately, growing information on the link between heart disease and lifestyle factors such as exercise and diet, as well as diagnostic measures such as stress tests, may lead to a decrease in the incidence of heart disease.

▪ **Arthritis.** Arthritis is, in fact, a term that refers to a family of diseases, from osteoarthritis and rheumatoid arthritis to gout and lupus. While some form of arthritis strikes approximately 20 percent of the general population, a whopping 70 percent of the elderly live with some form of the disease. The steroid-based medications often prescribed for arthritis sufferers may ease pain, but unfortunately they can also contribute to liver problems and can speed the process of osteoporosis (see the section on osteoporosis).

▪ **Cancer.** A variety of cancers strike our elderly. Leaving aside the relatively easily treatable cancers, such as skin cancer, the most frequently occurring types of cancer among the elderly are prostate, breast, uterine, ovarian, cervical, lung, colorectal, and pancreatic cancer. Lung cancer is the leading cause of cancer deaths in women. Pancreatic cancer is difficult to diagnose, and very little treatment is available for it.

Moneysaver
The Pharmaceutical Research and Manufacturers of America (PhRMA) publishes a Directory of Prescription Drugs Patient Assistance Programs, which lists some 50 programs that provide medication to low-income people or people with no insurance. Call PhRMA's toll-free line: 800-762-4636.

■ **Diabetes.** Adult onset diabetes, or type 2 diabetes, in which the body does not properly use insulin to regulate the levels of blood sugar, is a significant concern. It strikes at a far higher rate among the elderly than the general population: Nearly 11 percent of Americans ages 65 to 74 have it.

■ **High blood pressure.** High blood pressure, or hypertension, directly increases the risk of coronary heart disease, heart attack, and stroke. It is particulary prevalent in the elderly. High blood pressure can be controlled through diet (particularly sodium reduction), exercise, and medication.

■ **Diseases of the eye (cataracts, glaucoma).** Cataracts, a clouding of the lens of the eye which causes blurred or dim vision, are a common problem for the elderly: More than half of all people over age 65 have some cataract development. Glaucoma is a condition in which increased pressure levels in the eye cause damage to the optic nerve. Glaucoma is the leading cause of blindness in the United States; approximately 80,000 people are totally blind from glaucoma, and approximately 1,200,000 more have some degree of vision loss from the disease. Because eye problems are so prevalent in the elderly, all seniors should have regular eye exams. If cataracts or glaucoma are diagnosed, laser surgery can be used to treat both conditions.

■ **Prostate trouble.** The prostate is a walnut-sized gland located in the male pelvis. Prostate cancer, which affects roughly 300,000 men each year, is the second most commonly diagnosed cancer and the second leading cause of death in men in the United States. Other ailments associated with the prostate, while not fatal, are also painful: Benign enlargement of the prostate can lead to urinary problems. Prostatitis, an inflammation of the prostate, can lead to pain in the lower back, testicles, lower abdomen, and rectal area.

- **Osteoporosis.** Although osteoporosis affects both men and women, it is far more prevalent among elderly females—70 percent of all elderly women live with the effects of this disease. Osteoporosis is a disease characterized by progressive loss of bone mass. Menopause speeds the progress of the disease, which explains why women suffer the effects of osteoporosis far more than do men. Unfortunately, the diagnosis of osteoporosis is frequently overlooked in its early stages, when there is a greater likelihood of successfully slowing the progress of the disease through diet and exercise. Osteoporosis can be identified early on by x-ray or bone density tests. For more information, contact the National Osteoporosis Foundation at 1150 Thea Street, N.W., Washington, D.C. 20036-4603; 202-223-2226.

All these ailments can affect your elder's ability to perform the activities of daily living. Most of them, however, can be alleviated to some degree by early and accurate diagnosis and treatment. Because of this it is crucial that your elder get regular physicals, as well as eye exams and dental exams.

Mental and emotional disorders affecting the elderly

Some elders are disabled by impaired mental functioning and its associated behavioral changes—this

Unofficially...
According to the American Heart Association, one in five Americans (and one in four adults) has high blood pressure.

Watch Out!
If your elder experiences any health problems, make sure they are not being caused by any medications she's taking. Incorrect dosages, medications that don't mix, or medications that cause unpleasant side effects can all cause physical ailments. Make sure your elder's physician is aware of all her medications, and be informed of the side effects they may cause.

condition commonly is referred to by the broad, general term *dementia*. An individual with dementia displays a significant deterioration from previous intellectual and cognitive capabilities. Dementia may occur in association with Parkinson's disease, depression, or other medical problems, or it can appear as a reaction to inappropriate levels of medication.

Of all the possible conditions associated with dementia, however, Alzheimer's disease is responsible for the greatest proportion of cases. Alzheimer's disease is a degenerative brain disease that strikes about 10 percent of all people age 65. The frequency of occurrence increases dramatically with age, and as many as 50 percent of individuals over age 85 have the disease. Alzheimer's disease may be easily confused with other conditions that cause mental impairment. The general symptoms include these:

- Forgetting how to perform simple tasks
- Forgetting the function or use of common items
- Getting lost in a familiar neighborhood
- Not recognizing friends or family
- Becoming extremely distracted or developing a tendency to wander off
- Developing an inability to communicate— becoming confused by language or having difficulty understanding what is being said
- Exhibiting general confusion

Because Alzheimer's disease is progressive in its development, early symptoms may be easily missed—after all, everyone is forgetful sometimes— but if your elder has frequent episodes of memory impairment and commonly exhibits certain specific signs (for instance, the inability to perform a simple task such as telling time, or not knowing the purpose of a watch), then you must consider the possibility of Alzheimer's disease.

Alzheimer's disease is frightening to both the elder and to his or her family. Because symptoms are usually gradual, an elder is often acutely aware of the slow erosion of mental abilities and becomes frustrated by his or her inability to anticipate or forestall episodes of memory dysfunction. The family of an Alzheimer's sufferer often lives in constant worry that the victim will wander off and be lost and vulnerable, when in the grip of confusion and memory loss. Perhaps most distressing of all for the family of an Alzheimer's sufferer is that ultimately sufferers lose the ability to recognize their own loved ones.

But Alzheimer's disease shares many of its symptoms with other conditions. Depression, for example, will frequently manifest itself in episodes of confusion and forgetfulness. Dr. Edgar Weiss, a geriatric psychiatrist and the medical director for the geropsychiatry program at Marshall I. Pickens Hospital in Greenville, S.C., notes that the misdiagnosis of Alzheimer's disease in a patient who is actually suffering from depression can needlessly prolong suffering for the elder. As Dr. Weiss states: "Depression is treatable, and it's not part of being old. Older people respond to psychotherapy in addition to medication, and it would be a tragic error to overlook depression in your parent."

Beyond depression, other conditions that cause symptoms of dementia include these:

- Parkinson's disease
- Huntington's disease

66
I have lost myself.
—Auguste D., the first person documented to have Alzheimer's disease, as diagnosed by Alois Alzheimer, M.D. Alzheimer diagnosed the disease in 1906, after performing an autopsy on Auguste D. and noticing a strange formation in the brain cells in her cerebral cortex (that part of the brain that controls reasoning and memory).
99

- Vascular dementia

- Brain tumor

- Heart disease

- Kidney failure

- Vitamin B-12 deficiency

- Alcohol or drug abuse

Because of the variety of conditions that can result in symptoms of dementia, it is important that your elder be thoroughly examined. Tests should include a complete blood count, tests of liver and thyroid function, and perhaps a magnetic resonance imaging (MRI) test to check for tumors of the brain. An accurate diagnosis of the underlying cause of dementia is crucial to ascertain the most effective treatment.

For example, it has been determined that people with Alzheimer's disease have a deficiency of the brain chemical acetylcholine. Two FDA-approved drugs, tacrine (brand name Cognex) and donepezil hydrochloride (Aricept), have been shown effective in inhibiting the breakdown of available acetylcholine in Alzheimer's patients, easing the severity of symptoms. But these medications are inappropriate for other dementia-causing conditions, such as depression, alcoholism, or kidney failure, and in those cases would provide no relief. By the same token, a vitamin B-12 deficiency is readily treatable with supplements, and depression responds well to a combination of psychotherapy and medication. An accurate diagnosis of the underlying cause of dementia, therefore, is crucial.

Effects of illness on the elderly

Physical impairments have the most obvious and direct impact on an elder's ability to perform the activities of daily living, but they are also often the most easily accommodated. Some simple remodeling—installing grab bars or a higher toilet seat—can make the bathroom easier to use. Mobility impairments can be offset with the use of canes, walkers, wheelchairs, or motorized scooters. Some physical impairments, however, are less easily accommodated. For example, the progressive bone loss associated with osteoporosis can result in an ever-increasing threat of bone breaks; massive loss of bone mass can mean that a simple act such as opening a window can result in broken bones in the hand.

Coping with problems of hygiene

Deterioration in personal hygiene is a common problem for the elderly and can be due to either physical or mental impairment. Fear of falling may make your elder unwilling to bathe or shower, and the aches and pains of severe arthritis may make it difficult to perform such simple tasks as washing the hair or even holding a toothbrush. In addition, persons suffering from dementia may forget to perform these tasks or may simply not care about them. Whatever the underlying cause for a lapse in hygiene, the problem can be resolved by assisting your elder in these tasks on a regular basis—or hiring a professional home care worker to come to your elder at least several times a week to help her perform these tasks. (We will discuss how to find and hire a home care worker in chapter 8, "When There's No Place Like Home.")

Even if your elder lives with you, personal hygeine may be one area where you find that outside assistance is necessary. For many elders, the need for help with such intimate activities as

Unofficially...
Some alternative health experts suggest that ginkgo biloba, an herb available both as a supplement and in tea, may help people who suffer from Alzheimer's disease, dementia, and short-term memory loss. You may want to discuss the efficacy of this herb with your elder's physicians.

bathing can be extremely embarrassing, and the helplessness such a need implies may be something they cannot comfortably expose to their children. This is particularly difficult when the parent is the opposite sex of the caregiver, and is most common for elderly men. Even if your assistance is welcome, or if your elder is beyond embarrassment, it can be difficult for an untrained caregiver to physically manage the task. All these considerations indicate the necessity of securing the services of a home care worker.

Coping with the wanderer

Dementia-related disabilities are more difficult to handle without constant oversight by a caregiver. Wandering behavior, for example, occurs in at least half of people with severe dementia. Such people easily becomes lost and agitated, and when found may be unable to provide any information on who they are and where they live. One way to forestall such a problem is to provide your elder with an armband or bracelet that provides identifying information and a phone number to call. These armbands and bracelets are fastened in such a way that your elder will be unable to take them off without assistance; thus you know that your elder will always have identification on him wherever he goes.

Another alternative is to join Safe Return, a national program sponsored by the Alzheimer's Association, which provides assistance with this particular problem. Safe Return offers wallet cards, clothing and jewelry tags, a national photo and informational database, a 24-hour toll-free crisis line, and local chapter support. If an elder wanders off, the program contacts the police and can create and fax photo flyers to area hospitals and law enforcement agencies. Conversely, if Safe Return is notified that a wanderer has been located, it immediately alerts the family. The program has located and returned more than 1,200 registrants since its inception in 1993. For more information, call 800-272-3900.

Coping with the distress of memory loss

In the early stages of Alzheimer's disease, and in many other forms of dementia, episodes of confusion alternate with periods of lucidity. Your elder is aware that, at times, he or she periodically becomes lost and confused, and quite understandably feels distressed and depressed at the likelihood that this condition will only worsen over time. In late-stage Alzheimer's disease, anxiety and paranoia are common even though your elder may no longer have lucid moments.

Paranoia, common also in memory-loss ailments other than Alzheimer's disease, presents a particularly difficult situation to the eldercare provider. When in the grip of the conviction that others are "out to get him," the elder will often actively work against the very people trying to provide him with help. If your elder exhibits paranoia, and is dependent upon healthcare or household assistance from strangers, it becomes especially important that you ensure that these services are provided by people with experience in coping with the problems of the elderly. Your elder's paranoia could be distressing enough to drive away otherwise perfectly suitable service providers.

Coping with sleep disorders

It's commonly said that you need less sleep as you get older. Whatever the truth—or falsity—of that old chestnut, it is truly the case that dementia can

Bright Idea
Some people are
especially sensi-
tive to the
sounds of noisy
neighbors or
street traffic. If
your elder com-
plains that noise
is disrupting his
or her sleep,
suggest earplugs.
Another option
is to try an envi-
ronmental sound
machine that
plays soothing
sounds, such as
a pounding surf
or a light
rainfall.

often causes an individual's biological clock to con-
fuse day and night. This is called "sundowning."
Arthritis, too, can throw off your elder's normal
sleep schedule, as can any other condition that
involves chronic aches and pains. Strategies for
helping your elder cope with sleep problems
include these:

- Medication to ease chronic pain.

- Activities for your elder during the day.
  Sometimes when elders participate in adult day
  services, they are tired enough at night to sleep
  better.

- Limited caffeinated foods and beverages
  (including coffee, colas, and chocolate).

- A quiet and uncluttered sleeping room.

- Soothing music at night.

- A friendly wake-up call or visit in the morning to
  make sure your elder gets up.

If, despite these suggestions, your elder continues to wander at night, make sure the house is safe.
Place night lights in key rooms (bedroom, kitchen,
bathroom, hallway) so your elder will be able to nav-
igate safely. Also, make sure that that the area
around the bed is clear from objects that your elder
might trip over at night.

Meeting nutritional needs

Your parent may experience difficulty at mealtimes
for either physical or mental causes. As noted earlier, osteoporosis sufferers may, in extreme cases,
have such a pronounced curvature of the spine that
the stomach and intestines are compressed. Small
amounts of food may be enough to make the patient
feel uncomfortably full so that she stops eating well
before she has had enough for proper nutrition.

This can be offset by switching from three large meals a day to several smaller ones.

But other eating disorders may manifest themselves in relation to physical or mental impairments. Your parent may have difficulty chewing or digesting many foods, she may have lost interest in food because of depression, or she may simply be too confused by the choices of foods and utensils confronting her at the table. In addition, the sensation of taste often becomes impaired as we age—foods lose their savor and aroma. Try these simple suggestions to make mealtimes easier:

■ Reduce the number of dishes and utensils used at the table.

■ Offer small portions of one food at a time. Clear away each course before serving the next.

■ Keep table talk simple and light—avoid difficult subjects that might cause distress.

■ Enhance the flavors of foods served: Use low-sodium flavorings and marinades, and vary the textures of foods served during a single meal. Bitter flavors may be heightened for the elderly, so you might want to avoid including bitter foods or flavorings.

■ If chewing or swallowing is a problem, try preparing foods that are more easily eaten and digested. *The Non-Chew Cookbook* by J. Randy Wilson (Wilson Publishing, 1985) provides a variety of appetizing recipes that require little or no chewing.

Many elders have health conditions that require them to follow special diets: Diabetes, high blood pressure, and high cholesterol are but three of the more common factors. Other conditions respond

Bright Idea
Many elders find that dental problems interfere with their ability to chew and enjoy the foods they love. To avoid painful tooth problems, make sure your elder gets regular dental checkups and cleaning. Also, if your elder has dentures, bridges, or other dental work, your dentist should periodically check to make sure they fit properly.

well to dietary changes—arthritis sufferers, for example, find that eating foods high in Omega-3 fatty acids (such as salmon and tuna) can yield a major reduction in the pain of their flare-ups.

According to a 1996 article in the *Journal of Nutrition for the Elderly*, a study of homebound patients between the ages of 58 and 93 disclosed that many failed to meet 70 percent of the Recommended Daily Allowances (RDA) for the basic food groups. One big reason for this problem may be that cooking has become difficult—the mere thought of dealing with the pots and pans may be overwhelming to your aging parent. This problem is easily remedied with many nutritious, pre-packaged microwavable foods that require little effort for preparation or clean-up.

Depression may have an effect on your elder's interest in nutrition as well. He may simply lose the desire to eat, or he may lack the motivation to prepare anything elaborate for himself and will settle for opening a can of peaches for dinner. In this case, he's eating regularly, but he's paying no real attention to balance in his diet—even though he's not showing signs of weight loss, he may actually be malnourished. Once again, the simplicity of microwavable meals can be helpful here. In addition, meal delivery services such as Meals on Wheels take away the problem of food preparation entirely and are available in most communities. (The drawback with such programs, however, is that they rarely offer weekend meal deliveries.)

Basic principles and options of eldercare

Earlier in this chapter, you learned about the activities of daily living (ADLs and IADLs) that are used

Watch Out!
Just because you stock your elder's fridge with healthy foods and meals doesn't necessarily mean he is eating them. If you suspect that your elder is not eating properly, you may want to arrange to take more meals together, so you can get a better sense of his true eating habits.

as criteria to judge disability. Beyond the provision of specifically medical treatment, *eldercare* essentially means finding ways to overcome those areas of disability that your elder faces so that these activities can somehow be accomplished. It means establishing routines and schedules so that someone is available to assume the burden of necessary tasks that your elder can no longer perform for him- or herself. Whether you assume that burden directly or take over the responsibility for organizing your elder's care through outside service providers or facilities, you are the primary eldercare provider. Therefore, you must become familiar with the options available.

In Part 4, "Options in Eldercare," you'll learn in detail the variety of approaches available for assisting your elder in coping with age-related disabilities. Here we'll just list the basic categories of care:

- **Aging in place**. The elder remains in his or her lifelong place of residence and receives assistance from outside service providers or from family members.

- **Living with family**. Your elder moves in with you so that you can more readily and conveniently provide the assistance he or she requires.

- **Assisted-living facilities (ALFs)**. These residential facilities combine some of the advantages of independent life with ready access to assistance in many activities of daily living. They also provide medical attention on both an ongoing and an emergency basis.

- **Long-term care nursing facilities**. Nursing homes provide round-the-clock care for individuals who cannot care for themselves and whose level of necessary care falls beyond the abilities of a family member or a limited-care facility such as an ALF.

Home care refers to services provided in the home by outside agencies, from housekeeping services to home health aides. It is an integral part of the eldercare experience, enabling elders to maintain full independence in the face of limited disability, providing support and relief services to the family member who has assumed responsibility for the parent, and augmenting the services provided in ALFs.

Home care and home healthcare agencies

Because most caregivers like you have multiple responsibilities—working outside the home, raising children, and caring for or organizing the care of an elderly parent—home care and home healthcare agencies are extremely important. Even with a well-organized network of other family members, friends, and neighbors contributing to the care of your elder, further assistance is often required.

Area Agencies on Aging (AAA). The first place to turn for such assistance is your Area Agency on Aging, the local arm of the federal Administration on Aging. These agencies provide information on homemaker and home health aide services, transportation, and home-delivery of hot meals, and they often help with information on home repair for the low-income elderly. They also provide information on other sources of assistance for the low-income elder, including subsidized housing, food stamps, Social Security, and Medicaid.

The AAA cannot provide direct assistance to higher-income elderly people, but can help you find for-profit agencies that will provide such assistance

Bright Idea
The Administration on Aging's Web site provides links to information on medical, legal, and financial issues that affect the elderly. Visit the site at http://www.aoa.dhhs.gov/default.htm. Or you can call at (202) 619-0724

in your area. In addition, your AAA can help you find volunteer groups that specialize in assistance for the elderly and the disabled. It also can direct you to senior programs (for elders with mild disabilities) and adult daycare programs (for elders whose disabilities may be more severe). An AAA also can provide referrals to home care workers and agencies, as well as medical supply houses if you need to purchase or rent health-related equipment such as wheelchairs or a hospital-style bed.

Home care agencies. Home care agencies can be run as either nonprofit or for-profit entities. They offer assistance in the nonmedical aspects of your elder's care, including housekeeping, meal planning, household management, companionship, and transportation. Before you contract for the services provided by these agencies, however, it's helpful to carefully assess how much and what kind of care your elder truly needs (see Chapter 3, "Determining the Level of Care Required," for a detailed discussion this topic). You pay the agency directly for the services you require. The agency recruits, trains, and pays the worker who assists your elder. Some agencies provide a nurse or social worker to help you draw up and coordinate an appropriate care plan and schedule for your elder. If your elder's physician has ordered home care in conjunction with home healthcare following a hospital stay, some services can be paid for by Medicare.

Home healthcare agencies. The medical side of your elder's care may be addressed by hiring trained health personnel (nurses, physical therapists) through a home healthcare agency. The AoA recommends that you ask the following questions of any agency you are considering:

Bright Idea
Check to see if the home health-care agency of your choice is Medicare-approved—even if your elder is not using Medicare to pay her medical bills. Medicare's certification program ensures that all hospitals, nursing homes, home health agencies, and other facilities providing healthcare services to Medicare and Medicaid recipients meet Federal standards for health and safety.

1. What type of employee screening is done?
2. Is the employee paid by the agency or directly by the employer?
3. Who supervises the worker?
4. What types of general and specialized training have the workers received?
5. Whom do you call if a worker does not arrive on schedule?
6. What are the fees, and what do they cover?
7. Is there a sliding fee scale?
8. What are the minimum and maximum hours of service?
9. Are there service limitations in terms of tasks performed or times of day when services are furnished?

Services provided by home healthcare agencies are eligible for coverage by Medicare if they are Medicare-certified and ordered by your elder's doctor. This is an important consideration, considering that the rates for private agencies can be very expensive. Some private health insurance policies also cover some of these costs, and the Veterans Administration (VA) may provide assistance as well. (See Chapter 13, "Protecting Your Elder's Legal Rights," for an in-depth discussion of how to handle healthcare costs.)

Private agencies

Agencies—both home care and home healthcare—typically charge higher fees than individual workers would charge if you hired them directly. This is understandable: Agencies recruit, train, and supervise of all their workers. However, you may prefer to go the private route, for cost considerations and to have the opportunity to personally screen individual(s) who will be working with your elder. You may get referrals from churches, your elder's physician, the local hospital, or through the AAA in your locality.

Hiring privately has its own risks. Fraud and theft have become a real problem in the caregiving industry, so take certain precautions before hiring an applicant. It is not enough to ask for references—check them out thoroughly. Request certificates or other proofs of licensing and training. Most states certify home healthcare workers; make sure any candidates you consider are state certified. Make certain that the care worker is fully apprised of all your elder's needs, and that the applicant is experienced in providing these specific types of assistance.

Your discussions prior to hiring the worker(s) should be clear on certain basic conditions of service:

- Salary
- Reimbursement for out-of-pocket expenses
- Vacations and holidays
- How to handle unscheduled lateness or absences
- Notice required (from both you and the worker) if the service is to be terminated

Other issues that should be addressed right from the outset, when applicable, include these:

- Dietary restrictions for your elder
- Schedule of medications
- Who to contact in case of an emergency
- Security concerns

Unofficially...
It is important to build a relationship of trust and mutual respect with your home healthcare worker. Your employee may be more caring with your elder if he or she knows that you are equally committed to your elder's care. On the other hand, if you are overbearing or difficult to deal with, your home healthcare worker may be turned off—and that could inadvertently lead to lesser-quality care for your elder.

Also, remember that by foregoing the use of an agency, you become responsible for dealing with Social Security taxes, unemployment insurance, and worker's compensation for the worker. You might consider securing the services of an accountant or payroll company to handle this.

Once a care worker has been hired, take a few simple precautions. Lock away your elder's valuables and personal papers. Monitor the caregiver's performance to make certain that your elder is receiving the appropriate care and that he or she is comfortable with the employee. You may want to make visits to your elder, both scheduled and unscheduled, to watch how your elder and care worker interact.

Caregivers for the caregiver. You, as the primary eldercare provider, may find that you also need assistance. Respite care is a limited care option that allows you to hire someone to temporarily take over tasks that you normally handle, but from which you may need a brief break. Respite care workers will come in to provide assistance with meal preparation; to help in dressing, grooming, and feeding your elder; and to do light housekeeping. You contract by the session, with a minimum of four hours being the usual period. There is generally an annual maximum number of hours you can use the service, which is typically 80 hours per year. Referrals for respite care may be available through your AAA.

In the next chapter, we'll take a look at how to pinpoint the specific level of care your elder needs. This evaluation is important: Some eldercare options are more appropriate than others, depending upon your elder's degree of disability and personal preferences. Once you have carefully assessed your situation, you are in a much better position to put together the best possible package of eldercare services.

Just the facts

- The need for eldercare is defined in terms of an individual's ability to perform for him- or herself certain activities of daily living (ADLs), including bathing, dressing, and other essential tasks of life.

- Milder age-related disabilities may result in an inability to perform instrumental activities of daily living for oneself such as heavy housework, meal preparation, and other common tasks.

- Physical ailments strongly associated with aging include heart disease, various forms of cancer, arthritis, diabetes, and osteoporosis. All these illnesses can result in or exacerbate your elder's need for care.

- Alzheimer's disease and other forms of dementia can render an otherwise healthy elder incapable of performing the essential activities of daily living.

- Eldercare options include aging in place, living with other family members, moving into an assisted-living facility, and moving to a full-service nursing facility.

GET THE SCOOP ON...
Identifying problems ▪ Taking an activities
inventory ▪ Getting physical ▪ Taking a
survey of choices ▪ Understanding
hospitalization issues

Determining the Level of Care Required

As you learned in Chapter 1, "The Growing Need for Eldercare," the elderly are an extremely diverse lot. Age alone does not directly indicate that a person requires assistance, nor does gender, or financial status, although all these factors do affect the likelihood of disability or impairment. Your concern is to determine not only *whether* your elder needs assistance, but also precisely *what kind* of assistance is most appropriate. That's the subject of this chapter—evaluating your elder's actual level of need. The sections that follow point you to the best resources or services to address your parent's needs.

Assessing the situation

Whether your elder's need for care is the result of a sudden crisis, or whether it arises from the gradual inevitability of the aging process, make certain that you do the right thing when the time comes that your help is needed. That means determining just the appropriate need for care—neither overreacting with excessive intrusiveness, nor ignoring needs that your parent may be unwilling to acknowledge. An inadequate assessment may mean that you prematurely reduce your parent's independence, or that you leave him in a situation that's dangerous to him or others.

Obviously, neither of these outcomes is desirable. Your goal is to ensure that your parent's quality of life is at its highest. Take special care to examine the whole picture, to truly understand the situation your parent is dealing with and to respond reasonably to it. Your first step is to determine the underlying cause of your elder's need for care.

The many faces of need

The need for eldercare can arise from a variety of situations. If your parent has been active and independent up to now, but recently suffered a fall or an illness that resulted in impairment, the cause of the need is obvious and abrupt. If, on the other hand, your elder seems as healthy as ever but has periods of extreme confusion or distress, your course of action is less clear. In the worst case, you could be dealing with the early stages of dementia.

It's also equally possible that you're dealing with something much less drastic and more easily handled—depression over the loss of friends or a spouse, for example, or a nutritional imbalance. Then, of course, there's the healthy and alert elder who simply refuses to face the fact that some activities are no longer safe—for example, Dad ignores his vision problems and insists on driving the car, or Mom really can't handle those big pots and pans anymore but insists on doing all the cooking.

Different problems, different solutions

The important thing to recognize is that the caregiving solution that is appropriate to some kinds of need is quite possibly inappropriate for others. Mom or Dad's unwillingness to recognize new age-related limitations would be ill-handled if you were to over-react—in fact, that would frequently make matters worse. On the other hand, mistaking the early stages of dementia for just a case of "Mom's acting a little moody today" could result in catastrophe.

So, what's a caring caregiver to do? Carefully evaluate all the information at your disposal, talk with your elder, and work together to arrive at a workable solution. Begin with an assessment of your elder's physical condition.

Taking an activities inventory

The concepts of activities of daily living (ADLs) and instrumental activities of daily living (IADLs) were covered in Chapter 2, "Who Needs Eldercare?" These criteria of disability provide you with a good starting place to determine the level of need your elder requires. In a nutshell, the following is a summary of the two sets of daily living activities outlined in the previous chapter:

INSTRUMENTAL ACTIVITIES OF DAILY LIVING

- Cooking for oneself
- Doing heavy housekeeping
- Getting around outside the home (driving, walking longer distances)
- Doing the laundry and similar household chores
- Grocery shopping

Bright Idea
Many elders who can see to drive perfectly well during the day suffer from "night blindness" (reduced visual capacity after dark). If this is the case with your elder, offer to drive him or her to evening activities, or find friends or other family members to act as his or her chauffeur.

- Managing money
- Keeping track of medication schedules

ACTIVITIES OF DAILY LIVING

- Feeding oneself
- Getting in and out of bed
- Getting around inside the home
- Dressing oneself
- Bathing
- Using the toilet
- Self-administering medications

Clearly, the activities on these two lists represent different degrees of disability, but they both break down into the same four broad categories:

Nutrition

Hygiene

Medical care

Mobility

Your elder may have difficulty in one category of activities (say, his arthritis has begun to affect his mobility) but be fine in the others. Or, she may be disabled on the ADL level when it comes to dealing with her medicines and mobility, but have only IADL problems in the area of nutrition and hygiene.

You should develop as careful an assessment of your elder's needs as possible. Use the lists above, and assign a relative scoring range of 1–4, with 1 being "mildly disabled" and 4 being "severely disabled." With this assessment, you can get a sense of just where assistance may be needed.

Considering causes

Once you have an idea of what your parent's basic problems might be, you should develop a clear sense about the underlying cause. If Mom's having trouble in the kitchen because her arthritis makes it difficult for her to open jars and lift pans, does she really need help cooking? Or would a re-evaluation of her pain medication resolve the problem? Is Dad having trouble keeping his bills in order? Maybe he's becoming confused—but maybe he just needs a new eyeglass prescription and a handy magnifying glass.

Your first order of business, then, is to make certain that there's no treatable underlying physical cause to deal with. Chapter 7, "Organizing Your Elder's Medical Affairs," discusses how to get your parent's medical situation in order, including ensuring that your parent has necessary checkups and that all medications are appropriate. It's useful here, however, to briefly touch on the basic areas to which you'll need to pay attention. Talk with your elder to determine his or her status in the following three areas:

■ **Vision:** When was the last time your parent had an eye exam? Does her prescription for lenses need to be revised? More seriously, has she been checked for cataracts and glaucoma?

■ **Hearing:** Has your parent been tested for hearing loss? Would a hearing aid be appropriate? If he already uses one, is it functioning properly?

■ **Mobility:** Is it time for a physical checkup to look for any underlying condition that may be causing your elder difficulty in getting around? If your parent has been diagnosed with such a condition, is it time to have her medications reviewed to see if a new dosage or combination of medications should be ordered?

Unofficially... According to the Administration on Aging, about one-third of Americans between age 65 and 74 and one-half of those age 85 and older have hearing problems. It's important to check your elder's hearing regularly; often, elders with undiagnosed hearing problems are considered confused or uncooperative, simply because they can't hear what is being said.

When you bring up these topics with your parent, keep in mind that it's not uncommon for people to be somewhat defensive about certain health topics. For example, Mom may be a little touchy about that hearing loss—many elders are sensitive about having to wear a hearing aid. If she's already supposed to be using one, you might want to check to make sure that she's using it regularly. And if Dad has been proud all his life of that 20-20 vision, he may be less than pleased to be forced to acknowledge that he doesn't see as well as he used to.

Check it out

Even if your parent has what seem to be only minor physical complaints, a good baseline understanding of his or her health status will give you and your elder the information you need to maximize his or her well-being. Don't stop with a general physical checkup, either. Headaches may signal vision problems that might be easily overcome with a rigorous eye exam and a prescription (or a prescription upgrade) for eyeglasses. Similarly, those troubling periods you've recently noticed when your elder seems inexplicably distracted or forgetful may stem from something as simple as hearing loss—she's not forgetting what you told her; she never really heard it. A good hearing aid can make all the difference in the world.

As you and your elder take the initial steps to assess the need for care, your first order of business is to encourage a discussion about the possible infirmities or disabilities he or she faces. Second, take steps to have them checked out by a physician or other healthcare specialist.

Offer checkup companionship

If your parent hasn't had a medical exam in some time, don't be too surprised. Many elders avoid medical attention because they fear having to face bad health news. This attitude may seem irrational, but it's perfectly understandable. After all, any serious condition may have a significant impact on your elder's continued self-sufficiency—and even relatively mild problems (such as vision impairment) may mean a loss of autonomy. As your elder gets older, the fear that physical discomfort or distress might indicate some life-threatening illness becomes stronger.

But if your elder is experiencing physical distress, it is essential to get a general physical snapshot of his or her current health status. Therefore, it's important to find a way to help your elder overcome any reluctance to going for a checkup. Be reassuring. Be understanding. Above all, let your elder know that you are there to provide support.

You may find that your elder is more cooperative about agreeing to get tests if you offer to accompany him or her to the doctor's office. This will also give you a natural opportunity to meet with your parent's physician and become more fully acquainted with the health issues involved. Chapter 7, "Organizing Your Elder's Medical Affairs," covers the issue of helping your elder organize his or her medical situation, from compiling a survey of past and current medications to dealing with the doctors. It also explains how you can involve yourself in the medical process without overly intruding upon your elder's own relationship with his or her physician.

Surveying the choices

Once you've got a good idea of both the limiting conditions your elder is facing and their underlying physical or emotional causes, you're better able to assess just what assistance your elder needs from you. In the best of all possible scenarios, you may discover that simply getting your elder in for a checkup has turned up a fully treatable condition. But ultimately, you are likely to be looking at one of four broadly defined circumstances in which care may be needed:

- When disability is minor

- When impairment is more pronounced

- When disability is extreme

- When urgent, short-term intervention, such as hospitalization, is needed

We'll take a closer look at these circumstances in the sections that follow.

Assessing choices when the disability is minor

If your elder faces only a few problems in coping with instrumental activities of daily living, numerous options are available to overcome the difficulties. They roughly coincide with three residential options—only you and your elder can decide which is best in your situation. The choices are listed here:

- Your elder remains in his home (also called "aging in place").

- Your elder moves into your home.

- Your elder moves into an assisted-living facility (ALF).

The aging in place option

Your elder may quite possibly be very comfortable maintaining his or her own household—with a little help. Chapter 8, "When There's No Place Like Home," discusses the concept of aging in place and explores resources available to elders who choose to remain in their own homes. Remember that if you are personally involved in providing the assistance your elder needs, you are also essentially facing the prospect of significant demands on your time and energy. After all, your parent may need to "elderize" his or her own home and may also need assistance with handling chores or tasks that are now too difficult.

But there is help—the dramatic growth of private and community-based service providers means that just about every city and town has some resources that your elder can use. For example, if your elder can no longer drive, but your schedule makes it difficult for you to provide transportation whenever he or she needs it, you might look into a local car or taxi service. Or, if his or her medication schedule has become overwhelmingly confusing, a home healthcare aide may be just what you're seeking.

Home: Where the family is

The second alternative is for your elder to move into your household. This arrangement has the advantage of keeping you in close touch with your elder and his or her needs, so you would not have to worry about how Mom or Dad is doing independently. But recognize in advance that you, your family, *and* your parent will be dealing with significant disruption to your normal routines. (See Chapter 9, "It's a Family Affair," for a detailed treatment of this option.)

Unofficially...
A recent study found that among those who say they are likely to need eldercare assistance, the services they are most likely to use are: Home healthcare—92%; assisted living—80%; general upkeep and care of home—53%; household finances—14%. Source: a nationwide survey conducted by Yankelovich Partners, Inc. for the AICPA Special Committee on Assurance Services, December 1996.

Make certain that you discuss this choice thoroughly with everyone in your family who will be affected—even your children are going to be coping with changes in their lives if Grandma or Grandpa comes to stay, and they'll handle those changes better if they're kept in the loop. Again, you'll also likely be looking at some home modification to make your home more elder-friendly.

Clearly, in this choice, your relationship with your elder—both current and past—will have an important impact on how well this choice works for all concerned. The essential factors in making this arrangement a success can be summed up as the 3-C's:

- Compassion
- Cooperation
- Communication

Compassion. No matter how well-adjusted a person might be to the *concept* of aging, it can be difficult to deal with on a day-to-day basis. The frustration of facing yet *another* reminder that we're not as young as we used to be can lead any of us to react with impatience or even anger. In addition, it may be even tougher to have to face up to some limitations *when you have an audience*. It's one thing to realize—in private—that you just can't hear the TV unless the volume is turned up high. It's another thing altogether to be watching the news and suddenly have your grandson (or daughter-in-law) complain about the TV blasting so *loud!* If your elder moves in with you, you and your family must try to remain firmly aware that your elder is facing some tough realities—respond accordingly.

Cooperation. You're all in this together—you, your spouse and children, and your elder. To make it work, you're going to need to pitch in and help one

another. So, your teenager should know that sometimes it'll be her turn to give Grandma a ride to the
senior center, and your spouse should recognize
that sometimes you'll be too tired for that night on
the town after you've spent a day at work and the
evening helping Dad sort out his medication schedule. And your Mom needs to understand that no
matter how much better music was in the 1940s, the
kids might deserve an opportunity to listen to their
favorite "noise" every once in awhile.

Communication. Nobody is happy when everyone
suffers silently, all feeling martyred and misunder-
stood. In fact, the "silent" part of that suffering
rarely lasts very long—but when it ends, it usually
does not end constructively. When you feel beset by
too many conflicting demands, find the courage to
talk about it *before* it builds into a resentment. So,
also, will your elder. There will be many little occasions for conflict, if you let them arise. From the
start, it's a good idea to create some mechanism to
air potential grievances—a regular family meeting,
perhaps.

It sounds difficult, but merging previously independent households always is. But it can be done—
and *is* being done by many households across the
country. What's needed, ultimately, is that everyone
involved approach the situation with love and good-
will.

ALFs: independence with a twist

A relatively recent option on the eldercare horizon
is the assisted-living facility (discussed in detail
in Chapter 10, "Assisted-Living Facilities"). Elders
who are relatively self-sufficient—in many
cases, fully self-sufficient—and who prefer to live
independently but want the reassurance of some on-

call services now have the choice of moving into an ALF. This is a particularly good choice for elders (and their primary caregivers) who have begun to find it too difficult to keep up their own homes, who don't feel comfortable about moving in with their children, and who would enjoy the social opportunity of living in a community with their peers. In addition, there's the reassurance of a regular, onsite healthcare worker and the convenience of access to a large number of services, from transportation to and from shopping malls and special events, to an on-site dining hall.

Assessing choices when the impairment is more pronounced

If your elder is having significant trouble with some of the more basic activities of daily living (ADLs), living independently may cease to be an option. It may be the case that your parent's house can't be effectively "elderized" (whether because the building won't support the modifications, or because the cost of making improvements is prohibitive), or it may simply be that living alone has become too emotionally difficult or distressing. Or, it may be that your elder needs more regular, day-to-day attention than you can provide in his or her own household. In this situation, you still have choices. If your household can handle the caregiving tasks (with some outside support from private or community-based services), that's one way to go. Otherwise, the ALF is a possible option.

Assessing choices when the disability is extreme

If your elder needs constant custodial care, your options are more limited. Some ALFs may require that their residents be capable of at least minimal levels of self-sufficiency, and these facilities are certainly not designed to address the needs of, for example, elders with advanced dementia (although some facilities do accommodate people with early Alzheimer's disease). Hospitals also are rarely an option—not only are they extremely expensive, but they are not available for long-term caretaking. Your choices are pretty basic—your elder stays with you or enters a long-term care facility.

If your elder stays with you, be aware that you should avail yourself of outside assistance—few families are prepared to handle the needs of the severely impaired on their own. Look into acquiring the services of home healthcare providers (see Chapter 8, "When There's No Place Like Home"). You'll also need to look into your community's respite-care providers—for your own sake. (See Chapter 9 for a discussion of respite care).

Coping with sudden catastrophe

Accidents and sudden illnesses can be devastating at any age, but they're more likely to occur as we get older. And the prospect of hospitalization often engenders fear in an older person—for lots of reasons.

Even when you're young, going into the hospital is generally a scary experience. The accepted wisdom holds that there's no such thing as "minor" or "risk-free" surgery. But in addition to the expected fears, elders bring a few extra ones to the mix. Elders, who are already dealing with the slow erosion of physical abilities that comes with age, now face the prospect of a sudden, major diminishment of capabilities. Many elders also belong to a generation that viewed hospitals as places where you went to die if you were elderly. In addition, medicine

Bright Idea
Your elder should take extra care to be in the best health possible prior to surgery: in the weeks before the surgery he or she should eat well, exercise moderately, get plenty of rest, drink lots of water, and cut back on cigarettes and alcohol.

today is sometimes overwhelmingly high-tech; it's often hard for a layperson—your elder *or* you—to understand just what's going to happen, when, and how.

Foiling the fears

If your parent is going into the hospital, don't simply dismiss his or her fears—even if you don't understand their origins, these fears are very real. Instead, it's a good idea to help your elder confront those fears head-on.

Fear of the high-tech unknown. If your elder is scheduled for major surgery or a complex procedure, ask the physician for pamphlets you can share with your elder—better yet, inquire about videos on the procedure. Get all the information you can about the recovery process ahead of time so that if there is pain or a difficult follow-up therapy, your elder will know what to expect.

Fear of diminished capabilities. Here, again, enlist the cooperation of the physician. A clear, concise explanation on the reason for the proposed treatment will help your parent realize that the surgery or procedure is intended to forestall a further loss of abilities, not provoke it.

Fear of going in, and never coming out. If at all possible beforehand, bring your parent to the hospital. Let her see the facility, speak to the staff, and otherwise demystify the experience. Avoid the temptation to focus all conversations on the illness or condition and the procedure—talk as much about what will come *afterwards*. That means talking about post-procedure therapy and also about plans for post-recovery. Provide your parent with material to construct a hopeful outcome

However, if your elder is facing a terminal illness or a significant post-op disability, don't lie. If your elder is mentally competent enough to handle all the other discussions on the surgery, its consequences, its post-op therapy, then your elder is also competent enough to hear the real-world truth. After all, this is your parent's life that's under discussion here. He or she deserves to know what is going on.

Taking action when hospitalization is unavoidable

Beyond addressing your elder's possible fears, be supportive on more pragmatic levels. Learning that hospitalization is imminent is often overwhelming, whatever your age, but it's easier to face with supportive family.

Going in prepared

Find out what your elder needs ready beforehand— prior medical records, insurance forms, and so forth. Also find out what he or she needs to do before the procedure. Should he skip meals prior to going in? Are there medications she normally takes that should be discontinued prior to surgery?

If your elder has executed a living will or health-care proxy, bring this to the attention of the hospital staff. (These documents will be discussed further in Chapter 13, "Protecting Your Elder's Legal Rights.") Most will request this information as a matter of course, but don't wait for them to bring it up. Your elder has the right to know in advance that his or her wishes will be respected, no matter *what* happens later.

If your elder doesn't have a living will or health-care proxy, and isn't up to executing one, you

Bright Idea
If your elder is from a foreign country, it is especially important to take him or her to the hospital, view the facilities, and meet the staff before a procedure. He or she might have a very different conception of what to expect from a hospital stay. Also, if your elder does not speak English well (or at all), try to have an interpreter available if you have to leave him or her alone in the hospital.

should discuss the options with other family members so you can present the doctors with a unified position, if possible.

Here are some other issues to consider before your elder begins a hospital visit:

■ Choose your hospital carefully. Is its location convenient to you? Is it well-credentialed? Does it specialize in the type of procedure your elder requires? While teaching hospitals have the most highly-qualified specialists for life-threatening or exotic conditions, community hospitals often have better nurse-patient ratios, and a friendlier environment. Which is most important to you and your elder?

■ Choose your elder's specialist and medical team carefully. Don't just consider the doctor you pick for primary care; consider the others in the practice, because when they do rounds, your elder will be visited by whomever is on duty for the day, not necessarily by your primary physician.

■ Your elder's primary care physician should have visiting privileges at the hospital(s) where your elder is staying.

Staying for the duration

You can go a long way toward reassuring your elder about both the surgery and the recovery if you stay close by. No one relishes the idea of going into the hospital alone—this is the time to contact your siblings and inform them of your elder's condition. Arrange for visits, both in the hospital and later, wherever he or she goes for post-hospital recovery.

Making a graceful exit

Every hospital has social workers on staff whose job is "discharge planning." These staffers try to ensure that the patient will receive adequate care upon leaving the hospital, so they may arrange for follow-up care and may recommend the services of physical or occupational therapy. In some cases they may even make an onsite visit to your home or your elder's home to help make certain that the necessary equipment (grab bars in the bathroom, for example) is installed. They'll also put you in touch with home healthcare services, if needed.

Back at your elder's home, you can make sure that your elder's recovery is as comfortable as possible by doing the following:

- Keeping key phone numbers (doctor, pharmacist, hospital, close friends and relatives) by the phone or programmed into auto-dial.

- Setting up a handy bedside tray with tissues, water, medications, lotion, towels, and anything else that may be needed.

- Having extra pillows, blankets, and compresses (if needed) on hand to make bedrest more comfortable.

- Stocking up on books, games, or hobby materials that your elder can enjoy during convalescence.

You may also want to rearrange the household somewhat so that your elder has an easier time getting around: for example, you can move the bed closer to the bathroom door, if possible. You can also make sure that everyday kitchen and bathroom items are in easy reach so your elder doesn't have to stretch or strain to get them.

Bright Idea
Try to use your elder's primary physician for admitting, if at all possible. If your elder is admitted through the emergency room, the admitting doctor will be in charge of his case throughout his stay, and your family and primary care doctors may not be fully apprised of his case. Take control of your medical care before an emergency arises.

Just the facts

- The first act of a primary caregiver is to correctly assess the level of care your parent requires.

- An activities inventory will help you to pinpoint those areas in which your elder needs special help.

- With a clear understanding of the needs that must be addressed, you can make appropriate choices among the many options of eldercare, from aging in place to full-service institutional care.

- Elders frequently avoid seeking medical attention—your support is key in determining physical causes for the disabilities associated with aging.

- When hospitalization is required, your involvement may be instrumental in securing good care before, during, and after surgery.

The Human Side of the Eldercare Decision

GET THE SCOOP ON...
Signs of denial ▪ Ways to help your elder overcome denial ▪ How to cope with your emotions
as a caregiver ▪ How to accept the facts of
aging ▪ Tips on sharing eldercare with siblings

Denial and Other Emotional Issues

A ccepting aging as a normal part of living can be difficult for all of us. After all, our culture places a high premium on youth and strength. We subscribe to the creed of rugged individualism and have little patience for people who don't pull their weight. But aging *is* a fact of life, and all the tummy tucks, hair dyes, hearing aids, and corrective lenses in the world can only cover up the simple fact that, as we get older, we lose a little hair or go a little gray at the temples, lose some sharpness of vision or hearing, get a little slower...in other words, we start showing signs of our age.

But even those who forgo the cosmetic cover-ups available in the local pharmacy and instead embrace their advancing years still find it difficult to accept the first signs that the independence and self-sufficiency of their youth is gone. And that perfectly normal urge to deny the consequences of aging can make it difficult to secure the cooperation of your aging parent in the search for appropriate eldercare.

Chapter 4

65

Your elder is not the only one who is facing the inevitable consequences of aging. You, too, may have trouble accepting the passage of the years and what this means for your parent—and for you. Your siblings and other family members may be indulging their own versions of denial of this difficult fact of life as well.

This chapter explores the common dimensions of denial, explains how and why it occurs as part of the aging process, and provides some insights into how to work through this phase to help your parent, your family, and you take an active, constructive role in the eldercare process.

I'm not getting older, I'm getting better

For all the social and technological advances of modern Western society, our culture does not view its elderly favorably. You don't have to be very old to notice this: Just ask your 40-year-old neighbor who recently found himself "downsized" out of his or her job how hard it is to find another. Or talk to people approaching their 60s who love their work but are beginning to look forward to their birthdays with dread because each one signals another year closer to mandatory retirement—whether they're ready for it or not. And how positively do most Baby Boomers greet their invitation to join the AARP on their fiftieth birthday?

Hey! Don't shove!

Elders often, and understandably, feel that through no fault of their own, they are being muscled aside—to make space for "kids" to take their jobs, forced to acquiesce to the interests and needs of the younger generations, and expected to just get out of the way. This isn't a comfortable spot to be in, and elders often deal with it by simply refusing to

acknowledge the first signs that they are indeed getting older. They may refuse to recognize that their
old eyeglass prescription is no longer adequate to
correct their declining vision, or they might insist
that "there's nothing wrong with *my* hearing—you
just mumble too much!"

Denial may place your elder in difficult or even
dangerous situations. Dad may insist that he can still
handle all his own yard work, when it clearly has
become a task beyond his ability or stamina—his
pride may place him at risk for a stroke. Mom may
insist that everything is "fine, just fine" when she's
having serious trouble putting her finances into
order because she's lost track of who gets paid what
and when.

Signs of denial

The need for eldercare can begin with a bang—a
sudden, massively disabling illness or accident—or a
whimper—the slow and slow-to-be-recognized
degeneration of one or more physical or mental
function. But regardless of which of these scenarios
applies to your elder, it is likely that you will be dealing with some form of denial. The denial may play
out in a wide range of ways, depending on the
disabling circumstances. Here are some common
elements to look for:

- Anger
- Frustration
- Refusal of assistance
- Excessive risk-taking

A closer look at denial

Let's take a close-up look at the behaviors listed in
the previous section and see how they may relate to
the issue of denial.

Anger. The children of aging parents commonly complain that their elders are frequently angry—for no good reason that they can see. But a little careful digging can turn up perfectly understandable reasons. First is the simple anger that many elders feel at the sense that the world has passed them by—that their opinions, experience, and concerns don't matter to anyone anymore. Anger is a response to the sense of powerlessness that arises from feeling that life has simply moved on without them. Anger arising from this source is perhaps the easiest to redress—simply taking the time to ask your elder for his or her advice or opinions can go a long way toward making your elder feel included again. Plus, this is a way to show respect.

But other times the anger has less obvious causes. As we noted already, one aspect of the aging process is its *gradualness*. True, a broken hip can render a normally active elder housebound overnight, but other disabilities make themselves felt only slowly. Take hearing loss, for example. It's easy to ignore the first stages of encroaching deafness. People just seem to be mumbling more softly than usual, or they're keeping the TV or the radio tuned irritatingly low. If your elder is denying signs of the aging process, he may respond to such irritations with anger. Similarly, as his or her eyesight dims a little more each year, your elder may start complaining about the increasingly small type the local newspaper insists on using. It must be the typeface—admitting the alternative is unthinkable.

Frustration. The emotional expression of frustration is closely related to anger, but it stems just as surely from denial. For example, if your elder has been experiencing a slow loss of visual acuity—and is denying it—it's easy to understand how long-established patterns of behavior can become increasingly frustrating. An elder who has taken life-long pride in keeping up with the journals and publications of his or her career suddenly finds that the print is difficult to read. A house-proud homemaker whose rheumatoid arthritis is gradually worsening finds that one day-to-day chore after another is too difficult to do on her own.

In both cases, the loss of ability is clearly evident, but your elder's desire to continue as always remains strong. So your elder may keep trying to carry on as if nothing has changed—with predictable, unsatisfying results. That makes for a guaranteed source of frustration. This also can be difficult to address because any effort you may make to help out runs head-on into the third common expression of denial: refusal of assistance.

Refusal of assistance. A big part of denial is pride. When your elder encounters difficulty with handling once-normal tasks, it's only natural for you to want to leap in and take over—to open the jar that she's not able to grip strongly anymore, or to take over certain chores that have become too much for him to handle. But by doing so, you are also directly challenging your elder's ability to pretend that nothing has really changed. As a result, he or she may angrily reject your well-meant attempts to help out.

For a formerly fiercely independent elder, it can be deeply wounding to have new incapacities held up for the world to see—which is the way your instinctive attempts to help may be perceived. Until your elder can find a way past his denial, it will be difficult for him to accept your help gracefully. In fact, your repeated attempts to provide unwelcome assistance may cause your elder to respond in potentially dangerous ways, as he seeks to prove to himself that he is, indeed, still as strong and capable as he ever was.

Excessive risk-taking. An elder who needs to prove that he's as fully competent as always may take excessive chances with his health and well-being—and may well put others at risk. For example, if Dad is in denial about his loss of vision, he may insist on driving, even though he can no longer see well enough to avoid hazards. Mom may wish to deny that her memory is not what it should be and insist on continuing to cook, although she's likely to forget that pot on the burner and could start a potentially disastrous kitchen fire.

Until you can break through the denial, there's little you can do to help your elder, short of arbitrarily stripping some or all of his autonomy. The problem is that that response may be excessive. It's far better to try to understand the roots of this denial and work with your elder to help overcome it.

Aging as a subjective experience

Aging is not merely an objectively visible process; it's something that your elder experiences subjectively as well. Sure, the calendar may provide proof positive that he or she is now 70 years old—but *subjectively*, the last 10 years may *feel* like they've passed in the blink of an eye.

No one likes to admit that life has moved on past youth and middle age. When you recognize that we all—not just our elders—resist accepting the passage of the times of our lives, you'll find it easier to understand some of your elder's denial-based behaviors.

Ways to help your elder overcome denial

It's obvious that you cannot simply demand that your elder face the facts of aging. If it were that simple, there'd be no problem. Besides, unless your parent suffers from dementia, he is no doubt excruciatingly aware at some level of the inevitability of the aging process. He is simply not yet ready to acknowledge this.

How can you help your elder work through his or her denial? Here are a couple of basic strategies:

▪ Whenever possible and appropriate, turn to your elder for advice and assistance. This will go a long way toward reassuring her that she still has an important contribution to make to her family and her world.

▪ Rather than leaping in to take charge of tasks that your elder can no longer handle on his own, begin with conversation. For example, if he is insisting on handling heavy yard work that would better be handled by someone else, talk with him about the landscaping job he's kept up over the years. Tell him about how difficult you find some of the tasks so that there's no shame—and certainly no age-specific admission required—in admitting that, yes, perhaps some chores are very taxing. This gives you an opportunity to float the proposition that you've been considering getting someone in to help out in your own yard. By carefully and tactfully leading the conversation, you may be able to get your elder to accept help without wounding his or her pride.

▪ Realize that your elder may avoid asking for help not because she is in denial, but because

> 66
> My parents, both physically handicapped to an extent from their infirmities (father: stroke, mother: arthritis), teach English to elderly Russian immigrants three mornings a week. The volunteer work gives my parents the needed feeling that they can still make a positive difference in others' lives. The Russians, in turn, love it that their teachers are people their own age!
> —Suzanne Snyder, a caregiver for two elderly parents
> 99

she simply doesn't want to impose on you. You can overcome this by assuring your elder that you can and will find the time to help her with things that aren't easy for her any more—and that you actually enjoy being able to help her out.

By now, the underlying principle should be clear: You can best help your elder overcome her denial of aging by addressing some of her fears. But you may not be able to address all her concerns on your own. If your parent finds solace in religion, suggest that she speak to her priest, minister, or rabbi. If she's likely to be receptive to the suggestion, you might offer to take her to a counselor or therapist.

Avoid feeding into your elder's fears that he is obsolete or unimportant. Whenever possible, work *with* your elder to map out an eldercare plan, rather than simply taking over and imposing your ideas or choices upon him. Obviously, this is not an option when your elder is incapable of cooperating due to severe medical or mental disability, but in such circumstances your elder is likely to be beyond caring about participating in care decisions. Even in such situations, however, try as much as possible to make decisions consistent with what you think would have been his or her preferences.

Emotions and the caregiver

It's easy to see that your own issues regarding your elder's aging process can cloud your judgment when you are faced with making decisions regarding care. If you are having difficulty with simply facing the fact that he is becoming frail, you may miss the early signs that he needs help. And if you respond with some of the same denial-based reactions such as anger and frustration, you are setting the stage for confrontation that will benefit no one.

More likely, however, you are dealing with much more than just denial. Many primary caregivers deal with a broad range of emotional responses to the unmistakable signs of aging in their parent, and to the responsibility that they must assume their elder's care.

Common emotional responses to your elder's need for your care include:

- Denial
- Over-reaction
- Fear
- Anger and resentment
- Guilt

We've already dealt with the problem of denial. In the paragraphs that follow, we'll consider other common emotional responses and their possible effects on your ability to effectively handle the role of caregiver.

Over-reaction

Discovering that your parent has a previously unrecognized need for care can prompt you to jump to unnecessarily drastic conclusions or solutions, especially if the triggering event for this discovery is an accident or other crisis situation. But this is also precisely the time when a cool head should prevail: Decisions must be made that are best for your elder. That means trying your best to ensure that your response to the situation—whatever it may be—is carefully thought out and is in the best interests of your elder.

> 66
> I love my mother, but I feel like I really don't have a life anymore. I work full-time and come home and clean and cook and care for Mom. Whatever's left goes to my husband and kids. There's no me anymore.
> —Pat, a 48-year-old primary eldercare provider
> 99

Unofficially...
Eldercare can be a richly rewarding time of sharing between you and your elder—one that strengthens your relationship, rather than puts a burden upon it. Your attitude (easily communicated to your elder!), can make the difference between your eldercare experience being a cross to bear or an opportunity for closeness and growth.

One way to guard against over-reacting to a specific triggering event is to plan well ahead of any actual need for eldercare decision-making. Involve allies—your fellow siblings—in any caregiving you may find yourself taking on. Chapter 5, "Strategies for Coping," provides some insights in how to initiate such planning. Part 3, "Getting Organized," provides concrete information on organizing your elder's resources so that you are ready with all the information you need to make reasoned choices about your elder's current needs.

Fear

Concern for your elder is perfectly normal, not only in an emergency situation but also as a simple response to the sudden recognition that your parent is getting older and more frail. But fear can be crippling, inhibiting your ability to adequately provide for your elder's needs.

Still, fear is an understandable response. Up to now you've probably seen your parent as a stable anchor in your world. Now, you must recognize that the tables have turned and your parent relies upon *you*. This is a difficult new reality. You may find yourself beset with self-doubts and feelings of inadequacy in your new role. If you have the foresight to pre-plan, however, you can dispel most of your fears about your ability to fulfill your obligations to your parent. And if you make a point of educating yourself on eldercare, the prospect may well seem less daunting than you originally thought.

One common fear many caregivers face is the feeling that they are all alone with the problem of providing care. At such times, it is immensely reassuring to have access to a support group made up of others like yourself, who can help you with advice, information, and the knowledge that you are not alone.

Anger and resentment

As mentioned earlier, anger is a natural offshoot of denial—and of guilt (see the next section). But it is also a close relative of resentment, which is a normal reaction to the sudden realization that you are suddenly responsible for the care of your aging parent. The fact that you are thrust into the role of caregiver is often a simple fact of happenstance: You are the nearest, or oldest, or the one with the fewest outside responsibilities.

It is easy to give way to resentment if you feel that the eldercare burden fell to you unfairly, but you can take simple steps to reduce this sense of unfairness. First, involve the rest of your family—not just your siblings, but also your spouse and children. A shared burden is one less likely to inspire feelings of resentment, and one more likely to be handled with grace and compassion.

Guilt

Guilt may be the most debilitating emotional response of all. It is also the one least appropriate. You are performing a compassionate and noble task, providing your elder with the care he needs at a time when he needs you most. You may be consumed with guilt that you can't do enough, or the more irrational guilt that you should somehow have foreseen and forestalled your elder's need for care in the first place. These are not constructive or even realistic responses to your current situation.

If you have had strained relations with your elder in the recent past, guilt is particularly likely to rear its ugly head now that your parent is vulnerable. We all have unresolved issues with our parents, and such issues can color our reactions in any number of negative or destructive ways. But in your role of caregiver, you now have an opportunity to work through these issues—privately and perhaps even with your elder. If you need further assistance, do not hesitate to seek counseling. Sometimes talking your problems through with a trained third party can help you put things into perspective.

Once again, you may find enormous help in overcoming such emotions as guilt through the advice and counsel of others who have stood in your shoes. Contact local support groups and share your feelings with others. For additional coping strategies, consult Chapter 5.

Intimations of mortality—your own

Many baby boomers (the population from which primary caregivers often are drawn) seem to have considerable difficulty in accepting the aging process. The general culture also doesn't help us accept the inevitability of aging gracefully. No wonder, then, that when we are confronted with our elder's undeniable aging, we find it unsettling, at best, and frightening, at worst. Their mortality is a reminder of our own.

As contradictory as it may sound, however, by acting as your elder's caregiver, you may find that you slowly learn to accept aging as a natural process. And this benefit may not accrue solely to you—your siblings and even your children may gain important insights into aging. They may also discover a new understanding of compassion, empathy, and the concept of caring for others.

Unofficially...
Experts suggest that members of the "sandwich generation" — people who are raising their children and caring for their aging parents simultaneously—are particularly conflicted by guilt because they feel they cannot devote enough time to *either* generation. Many members of the sandwich generation find that they need outside help to care for their elders.

When your siblings can't accept the situation

When your siblings first learn of your elder's need for care, they too may wrestle with issues of denial and guilt, as well as fears of their own mortality. Siblings who live far from your elder's home may be particularly susceptible to these responses—it's a common reaction when an individual recognizes that his or her parent needs help but they cannot provide any. If they've been away for a long time, they may have an even greater problem with some of these emotions than you do, because they haven't personally observed the gradual warning signs of an impending need for care.

Ironically, you may find that siblings who are least involved in the day-to-day provision of care resent your more central role in the process. One way to help your siblings overcome these problems is to make a point of including them in the overall process. This is why the next chapter strongly recommends that you involve all siblings in a planning conference to map out a care strategy. Be certain to call on them if they have particular expertise that might be helpful in providing assistance—whether financial or practical—in the ongoing aspects of your elder's care.

Most of all, however, recognize that their responses are similar to your own. Share information with them and urge them to organize their own support networks. They may become your best allies in this whole experience.

Just the facts

- Your elder's denial of the aging process may lead him to reject assistance or indulge in risky

Unofficially...
In a unique study published in a 1977 issue of *The Gerontologist,* researcher Diane L. Beach describes the positive impact of adolescent relationships with their families when an elderly person was in the family's care. The teens experienced greater empathy for older adults and developed a greater understanding of aging.

behavior in an effort to prove to himself that he really isn't changing.

▪ Tact and compassion are essential tools to help your elder overcome her denial and actively participate in the eldercare process.

▪ Do not let negative emotions hinder you in fulfilling your eldercare responsibilities. Seek counseling or the advice and counsel of support groups.

▪ If you can help your siblings overcome denial and guilt, they can become your biggest allies in the eldercare process.

GET THE SCOOP ON...
Stress and stress-relief ▪ Ways to recruit family
support ▪ Support groups ▪ Internet resources ▪
Professional help

Strategies for Coping

R egardless of the specific approach you take
to provide eldercare—from helping your
parent maintain an independent home to
having her admitted to a nursing facility—one thing
is certain: Acting as primary caregiver is extremely
stressful. The simple fact of assuming responsibility,
along with the pressures of meeting your obligations
(to your elder as well as the rest of your family), is a
stressor. Add to that the likelihood that you may be
operating on less than optimal sleep and losing a
great deal of what once was your leisure time, and
you've got a recipe for trouble—if you aren't prepared.

This chapter explores the stresses you might
encounter when shouldering the responsibility of
primary eldercare provider. It identifies the sources
of this stress and points out how, if left unchecked,
such stresses can damage your health and relationships. But this chapter also provides you with strategies for dealing with stress, from building practical
and personal support networks to getting professional help.

79

Stress and caregiving

Think of eldercare as encompassing two distinct types of stressors. First is the stress associated with a crisis situation: Your elder is diagnosed as having a catastrophic illness or suffers a sudden, disabling accident. The stress of coping with such crisis situations is undeniable, but at least you know what caused the stress, and just about everyone understands why the situation might cause you to shut down on your other responsibilities while you leap in to handle this problem.

Long-term or chronic stress is the second type of stressor often associated with eldercare, and is far more insidious than crisis stress. There is no one triggering event to point to as its cause; rather, it is the cumulative result of any number of small, seemingly mundane pressures.

You Know You're Stressed When...

- You eat the tuna out of the can because you're just too tired to bother mixing it with mayo in a bowl.

- You keep losing track—is it Monday or Tuesday?

- It's 3 a.m. and you're wide awake—again!

- You're normally an avid reader, but you haven't even looked at a book or newspaper in a week.

- Even the simple plot lines of a sitcom lose you after a few minutes.

You may not even notice that you are operating under stress at first. After all, you're just taking on a few extra responsibilities to help Mom, right? So you'll drop by her home every day on your drive home from work to make sure she's okay and visit with her awhile. And you'll take on a little of that yard work that Dad just can't handle anymore. Oh, and then there's that promise you made to spend next Saturday sorting out Mom's bills and insurance. Surely there'll still be time as well to make your daughter's Halloween costume and whip your house into shape, and you certainly can fit in the work you need to do to meet the deadline for that report you have to finish. You'll just stay up a little later a few nights this week, and maybe cancel that movie night you had planned....

Stress usually begins with a whimper of creeping exhaustion, not the bang of an exceptional crisis. When you finally notice that something is wrong, you may already have done serious damage to yourself. Make certain that you are not ignoring warning signs that stress is making inroads on your health. Here are a few signs that you are suffering from stress:

- You are not getting adequate amounts of sleep on a regular basis.

- You are not eating enough (or are eating too much), or your mealtimes have become chronically irregular.

- You are no longer permitting yourself time for leisure activities.

- You no longer see friends or family outside the home—you are becoming socially isolated.

Watch Out!
Experts have created a name for the stress associated with caring for those who are unable to take care of themselves. *Compassion fatigue* (CF) commonly affects those who care for others for a living (doctors, nurses, counselors, and others), but it also may affect you as a caregiver. If feelings of anger and exhaustion threaten your ability to take care of your own needs—or your elder's—you may need to rethink your arrangements.

Watch Out!
If you don't think getting a full night of sleep is important, consider the consequences of a lack of sleep: irritability, depression, anxiety, decreased cognitive function, decreased motor skills, and an impaired immune system.

Sleep, that ravels up the sleeve of care

Not everyone needs the proverbial eight hours of sleep each night—some people get by quite nicely on far less. Think about Benjamin Franklin and Thomas Edison—both were legendary for working long and hard on minimal amounts of sleep. But they are the exception, not the general rule. Sleep experts agree that the average person requires somewhere between seven and eight hours of uninterrupted sleep per night, preferably on a regular schedule.

That kind of sleep may sound like a luxury to you in your role as caregiver. You may be up late trying to catch up on your own chores to make up for time spent on errands for your elder. If your elder is living in your home, her own sleep problems may keep *you* up nights. Or maybe you simply can't sleep because you have too many worries on your mind. In each of these cases, you may inadvertently disrupt your sleep/wake cycle and set yourself up for a more long-term sleep disorder.

Food, glorious food

Unfortunately, when we're stressed we tend to let bad things happen to our good nutritional habits. Stress can take us to either of two extremes: We either forget to eat, running the risk of compromising our nutritional health; or we overeat because we turn to food for comfort. In either case, we are not paying careful attention to maintaining a balanced diet. If you find that you're relying on quick-to-get, quick-to-consume junk foods or are skipping meals altogether, you're heading for trouble. Likewise, if you find that the dish of ice cream you promised yourself as a reward after a hard day is consistently turning into a quart-sized serving, you're using food to cover up other unmet needs.

In either case, renegotiate the way you are approaching mealtimes. Pay attention to the number, frequency, and content of your meals. Make certain that you eat plenty of fresh fruits and vegetables and drink lots of water. Consider taking a vitamin and mineral supplement to boost your nutrient intake (although a supplement alone can't make up for a poor diet). Stress depletes your body of energy, vitamins, and minerals—by slipping into poor nutritional habits, you're only exacerbating an already bad situation.

Time out—to get a life

When you work at a full- or part-time job, as most caregivers do, and then come home to care for your family and put in a full shift as an eldercare giver, it's no wonder if you wake up one day to realize that you have no life. With all the demands on your time, it may seem that the easiest way to cope is to cut back on the time you would normally give yourself. You might think that taking from anyone else's claims on your hours would mean making excuses or explanations that are just too tiring to contemplate. Besides, with all this work to be done, you can easily feel that grabbing an hour or two to yourself is downright selfish.

But depriving yourself of leisure time is a bad idea. Just as you need adequate regular sleep and nutritious meals, you also need "unwind time" to recharge your batteries, so to speak, and to restore your perspective on life. Yes, you are needed by others—pretty much all the time, it can sometimes seem—but you can be of very little help if you drive yourself too hard. And consistently depriving yourself of leisure time can also lead to depression.

Bright Idea
Music may indeed soothe the savage breast, but it can also be extremely therapeutic for reducing your stress. If you need to mellow out, listen to your favorite slow-dance tunes. If you need an energy boost, put on some high-energy music.

How to get back into the social swing

One insidious problem that caregivers face is the ease with which they can become isolated—it seems to happen without even trying. You cancel one event because Mom has a minor crisis, then another because you're just too tired to make the effort to go out. After enough canceled engagements, your friends stop inviting you because they assume you're too busy to join them, and you find that you've boxed yourself into your caregiver's role with no social life to break the routine.

Socializing with friends and family is a major de-stressor. You need periodic contact with people who don't represent just one more obligation or chore. You need reminders that there is more to life than your daily round of responsibilities—and, frankly, you need a few rewards to make the work worthwhile. There is no reason to feel bad about seeking a few hours of help each week so that you are free to meet friends for lunch or a movie. Ask other family members if they can take over for a couple of hours on a regular basis, or look into enrolling your elder in a community-based service such as an adult day-care service or senior center—she, too, will probably benefit from some contact with people outside the home.

Factors that increase your stress

The day-to-day stressors of providing eldercare can be complicated by the particulars of your elder's condition. Caregivers who are dealing with severely disabled or impaired elders—and particularly those who care for a parent with Alzheimer's disease—tend to be the most stressed out of all.

Guilt is another contributor to your stress levels. No matter how much you care for your elder, it is easy to fall into thinking that this burden will never end—and to then feel guilty for harboring such thoughts. But this is needless guilt: You are only human if the task you've taken upon yourself sometimes seems more than you're willing to continue to bear. You need to give yourself permission to acknowledge the sometimes less-than-heroic feelings we're all prone to. These feelings can be useful reminders that you need some help and support, too. And there *is* help available, if you are willing to find it and use it.

Strategies for stress-relief

You can take steps to keep your emotional side in good working order. Acknowledging that you actually *have* a problem is probably the hardest step you'll have to take—once you recognize that it's there, you can choose from a number of different ways to alleviate your stress and to reduce the amount of stress you face in the future. Common effective self-help strategies for coping with stress include these:

■ Relaxation techniques

■ Meditation/visualization techniques

■ Exercise and physical activity

You can learn relaxation techniques through any number of books or tapes, but they are all based on a single, simple set of exercises. Essentially, you lie down on a comfortable mattress or mat in darkened room and consciously attempt to isolate, tense, and then relax one part of your body at a time: first your toes, then your feet, then your ankles, and so on up to your scalp. Take your time, and linger on one body part as long as it takes to feel it fully relax before moving on up to the next.

Unofficially...
A 1996 study of 500 caregivers by the Alzheimer's Association found that caregivers of elders with Alzheimer's disease spent an average of 69–100 hours per week providing care. Three-quarters of caregivers in the survey said they were depressed. Half lived with the person with Alzheimer's disease, making theirs a round-the-clock job.

Some people find it helpful to combine relaxation techniques with meditation or visualization exercises. While lying comfortably, close your eyes and visualize a peaceful scene. Try to imagine each detail of that scene as vividly and realistically as possible: Feel the warmth of the sun, hear the sound of water running in that imagined stream, smell the newly mown grass.

Finally, exercise can be an enormously effective stressbuster. For some people, just *going* to the gym is a release. And the physical exertion of using exercise equipment or participating in exercise class provides a definite boost to the spirit. There's a perfectly good biochemical reason for the stress-reducing effect of exercise: Physical activity releases brain chemicals called endorphins, which are your body's own antidepressants. They alleviate your stress and elevate your mood—and also offer the bonus of reducing pain and increasing your normal energy levels. If organized exercise venues such as a gym aren't your style, you can get the same benefit by taking a long walk every day.

If your elder is physically capable, you might want to explore activities you both can enjoy together, such as walking, swimming, hiking, gardening, or taking a gentle exercise class. Not only will you both reap the physical benefits, but you'll also have a chance to bond in a relaxing setting.

Bright Idea
If high-energy exercise isn't your speed, consider taking a yoga class. Regular practice of yoga decreases stress, improves the function of your immune system, and promotes a profound feeling of relaxation and well-being. (It's a great workout, too.)

Networking: organizing a support system

Eldercare providers like you can often succumb to the feeling that they are all alone in the world facing problems that no one else could possibly understand. The highly stressful and time-consuming task of providing care for your elder—especially if he or she is particularly frail or suffers from a debilitating condition such as Alzheimer's disease—can easily make you feel isolated and alienated.

But there is no reason to feel you have to go it alone when facing the sometimes difficult and even overwhelming responsibilities of caregiving—not if you take the time and care to put together a broad-based support system. There is help available on all sides: in your community, within your family, sometimes in your workplace, and even on your computer over the Internet. You just need to know where to look.

Help within the family

The sibling who lives closest to the frail elderly parent is usually "it." When an older adult is sinking fast and someone has to arrange for assistance *now*, there is usually no time for a family meeting. Instead, the job falls to the one who is most readily accessible.

It would be far better—and fairer—if all the siblings were able to get together *before* a crisis arises and they could work out a reasonable, workable plan to meet all contingencies when Mom or Dad is no longer able to remain independent. This is the ideal way to approach handling your elder's future care needs, but it is an ideal rarely achieved in real life. If your elder is currently in relatively good health, consider organizing just such a meeting with your siblings and other family members.

There are many benefits to arranging a proactive meeting. You have the opportunity to address important caregiving decisions without the pressure of a crisis situation to cloud your judgment. You can give your siblings a fuller understanding of the care issues that may arise in the future. Your siblings will get the chance to take an active role in contributing to that care in ways that best fit their abilities. You also can determine what your parent would prefer while he is still able to communicate his wishes.

Keep in mind that the success of such a meeting really depends on your elder's attitude. If your elder doesn't like to discuss the issues associated with aging and eldercare, a formal family meeting might make him feel uncomfortable. If that's the case, perhaps a series of informal discussions (such as a one-on-one with your elder over dinner or coffee) might be an easier way to broach the subject.

If you do have the opportunity to organize a family meeting in advance of an emergency, you can take certain steps to make it go smoothly.

▪ Hold the meeting in or near your parent's home, since the decisions you'll be making are on your parent's behalf. Because this planning session is occurring while your parent is still capable of participating and expressing his or her preferences, you want to make it as convenient as possible for him or her to fully engage in the process.

▪ Prepare an agenda of issues ahead of time, and provide written copies to all participants at the start of the meeting. This will help you keep the discussion focused. Some items you will want to include are these:

The budget: Identify resources available for present and future care; list who can contribute if funds are needed beyond your elder's own resources.

Scheduling issues: Determine who, besides you, will have the time and ability to provide caregiving support when needed; what kind of support can they provide; and how frequently you will be able to count on that support. (Obviously, scheduling is an issue that may need to be revisited from time to time as things change; if you or your siblings move, change jobs, get married, have children, or get divorced, your abilities to provide eldercare may be affected.)

Care needs and options: What tasks does your parent currently need assistance with? What further assistance is likely to be needed in the foreseeable future?

Living arrangements: Here you really want to have your elder's input—after all, this decision will determine where and how he or she will live for the next several years. You might assume, for example, that because Mom is still quite comfortable handling her activities of daily living, she would prefer to age in place. But she may actually prefer something on the order of an assisted-living facility (see Chapter 11, "When Long-Term Care is Needed") for the convenience and greater possibilities of social interaction. You may be willing to have Dad move in with you, but he may have a strong resistance to "becoming a burden" and may prefer some other alternative instead.

Emergency planning: If your elder is at risk for a crisis situation in the foreseeable future (especially if he or she is exceptionally frail or shows the earliest signs of dementia), now is the time to talk through a plan for handling it. You can allocate responsibilities among your siblings—one assumes the job of

Unofficially...
The SPRY Foundation recently conducted a study to find out how caregivers make long-term decisions about eldercare. They found three major influences on consumer decision-making: 1) decisions are most often made in response to crises; 2) real or perceived limits of available options hinder consumers from seeking information; 3) emotions such as fear, guilt, and denial often hinder consumers from making informed decisions.

securing emergency assistance, another takes on the task of contacting and informing family members, and so on. With an emergency plan in place ahead of time, you can face the prospect of a sudden crisis or accident much more calmly.

■ If you can afford it, arrange to have a geriatric care manager or therapist in attendance who is familiar with your elder's condition and likely needs. (See Chapter 7, "Organizing Your Elder's Medical Affairs," for more on the cost of care managers or therapists.) This is useful for two reasons: First, the subject of a meeting such as this one is inherently difficult for many families. A disinterested third party can defuse tensions. Second, a professional in the field of eldercare will be able to provide on-the-spot, authoritative answers to questions that arise in the course of the meeting, such as these:

Where are assisted-living facilities in your area?

What is known about the reputation of the local nursing home you might be considering?

How can we get access to the government services for which our elder is eligible?

How can we connect with agencies that provide transportation or other specialized services for the elderly?

How to make the meeting work

Recognize in advance that this meeting may be difficult for all concerned. It may be the first time some of your siblings actually face up to the fact of your elder's aging. But the potential benefits are enormous. Your siblings are much more likely to be willing to volunteer their assistance if they are brought into the process early on. The possibility of resentment or rivalry among siblings (with one sibling feeling as if she's stuck with all the work, and others feeling left out) is greatly reduced. Your elder is reassured that her wishes are known and will be respected; and—most of all—you can radically reduce the possibility of bad decisions made under the duress of crisis.

When you draw up the list of people invited to attend this meeting, you will immediately face one issue that causes problems for many families: Should the spouses of the immediate family be included? Some families choose to restrict the meeting to siblings and other close kin who might conceivably participate in providing care (younger brothers or sisters of your elder, for example). This meeting will, after all, address matters that your elder may prefer to keep "in the family."

On the other hand, the spouses of your siblings are likely to be affected by your decisions. (In fact, many families report that female in-laws are often the ones co-opted into the caregiving process.) If, for example, it is decided that your elder will be moving in with you, your partner surely deserves a say in the discussion.

Your actual family dynamic will determine whether in-laws should be involved. But one thing is certain: In-laws attending such a meeting should be respectful of the fact that this is *your* elder whose care is under discussion, and should restrict contributions to helpful suggestions or practical advice.

When a meeting is impossible

Of course, a family meeting is an ideal way to pre-plan the eldercare process, but as noted earlier, many families do not have the luxury of such advance planning. It is still possible to recruit support and assistance from your family, even if the need for eldercare decision-making arises out of an emergency situation for your elder. The secret is simple: Keep communications open with your siblings; encourage them to stay aware of and involved in your elder's day-to-day life; and by all means make sure that they are aware of any illnesses or other conditions that may make increased levels of care necessary in the future. If some or all of your siblings reside near you and your elder, turn to them for help once in a while—ask your sister to spend an evening with Mom so that you're free to attend your son's Little League game. Ask your brother if he can take Dad to the pharmacist to pick up his prescriptions. Consult your siblings if you need help working through your elder's finances and they have the expertise to assist you.

❝
I always tell people that their primary contact should be their local senior center because [the center] will be aware of all services to the elderly in their area.
—Jerry Whitley, director of Kentucky Division of Aging Services
❞

Support options outside the family

These days it seems that there is a support group for just about every problem or passion you can think of—there's even one for people who have been struck by lightning! All you really need to know is where to look for the group that suits your needs.

Finding a suitable support group

When looking for support groups, it's good to have a clear idea of just what kind of support you're seeking. If your elder suffers from Alzheimer's disease, for example, you may find that a group specializing in this problem is more in tune with your needs than a more general-interest eldercare support group. Try to find a good fit, particularly if you're looking for support and advice on handling a specific, disease-related caregiving issue.

Your best first line of inquiry for local support is probably your Area Agency on Aging. This agency will likely be able to provide, at minimum, information on referral services for support groups and may be able to make some referrals. Also contact the Eldercare Locator (tel: 800-677-1116) and get in touch with your local senior center, which should have some idea of most, if not all, elder-related services in your area.

Don't be afraid to let your fingers do the walking, either. Your local White Pages will provide listings for the local offices of governmental agencies and support services, and the "Social and Human Services" heading of your Yellow Pages will provide you with promising leads to many more in the private sector. In addition, your local newspapers may include listings of support group meetings.

Don't neglect the support that might be available through your employer. Although most companies don't yet have comprehensive eldercare programs, many larger companies are beginning to offer services in the form of counseling and helplines. It's not sheer altruism that's motivating this trend—studies have shown that companies lose billions of dollars in productivity because of employee absenteeism directly related to the need to provide eldercare for their parents.

Screening local support groups
When you're faced with the overloaded schedule of a typical eldercare provider, you don't have much time to spend running from meeting to meeting to find a support group you can feel comfortable in joining, but that is often the best way to go. After all,

Timesaver
You can search the Eldercare Locator database online to quickly find the available eldercare options in your area. This nationwide directory assistance service is administered by the National Association of Area Agencies on Aging and the National Association of State Units on Aging. To view the database, go to www.ageinfo. org/elderloc/ elderdb.html.

a support group is made up of people who provide comfort, counsel, and rapport. They face problems and issues similar to your own. You're selecting a support group for *your* sake—this is one time when it's truly worth taking the time to find the group you feel is best suited to your needs.

When checking out a support group, take these steps to gain the most from your initial visit:

- Be on time—or, better yet, be a little early. This way you'll have an opportunity to meet a few of the regular members.

- Check to see if there are any informational pamphlets or newsletters available for the taking.

- Choose a seat that gives you a good view of what's going on.

- Listen! At this first meeting, get a feel for how regular members interact, the protocols of participation, and the types of issues discussed. Of course, if you are invited to speak up, and you feel comfortable about it, then do so, but keep your remarks brief. You are here at this first meeting to evaluate the group's fit for you, and you can do that only if you keep the focus on *them.*

- Stick around after the meeting formally adjourns. Introduce yourself to other members and talk a little about the subjects brought up during the meeting. Do individual members seem open and congenial to you, the newcomer?

If you simply cannot schedule visits to every prospective support group on your list, you can call the groups for information that might help you eliminate some from consideration. Here are some

Unofficially...
Children of Aging Parents (CAPs) is an organization with chapters throughout the country that provides education, information, and support. To find the nearest chapter, call 800-227-7294, or write to CAPS, 1609 Woodbourne Road, Suite 302-A, Levittown, PA 19057-1511.

useful questions to ask when you do your fact-finding by phone:

- Who is your group geared to provide support for?

- What are the main problems that your group is interested in?

- When and where do you meet? How often?

- Do you have a newsletter or other informational materials you can send me?

- Do you have guest speakers? How often? What topics have they covered?

Even if the support group you've called turns out to be inappropriate for your needs, don't hang up the phone with a polite "thank you." Instead, ask if they know of other groups more directly involved in your particular area of interest. Often they will be able to suggest a few likely groups to try.

Support groups, cyber-style

There's plenty of useful information available on the Internet. A simple Web search using the word "eldercare" will bring up literally thousands upon thousands of hits. It's easy to get overwhelmed by this much available data, but there are some good sites with helpful links that will give you a good start. You can take it from there on your own. A selection of useful sites includes the following:

- EldercareWeb is a site run by a CPA with a strong interest in all aspects of eldercare. The Web site provides links to financial, legal, social, health, and other informational sources. You'll find it at www.elderweb.com/about.htm.

- The American Association of Retired Persons (AARP) is another rich source of information on all aspects of aging. This site is particularly useful for keeping yourself informed of legislation affecting the elderly. Find AARP at www.aarp.org.

■ The Administration on Aging (AoA) runs a very helpful site that provides access to statistics, fact sheets, and informational booklets that can be downloaded or ordered directly from the site. (The organization also provides a telephone contact number for use when ordering some materials). You can reach AoA's main page at www.aoa.dhhs.gov/aoa/pages/aoa.html.

■ The National Senior Citizens Law Center provides a wealth of information on issues in elder law and on legislation affecting the elderly in America. Contact this organization at www.nscic.org.

In addition, a wide range of other sites are devoted to eldercare issues, including several that deal with disease-specific topics:

ADEAR Center (Alzheimer's Disease Education and Reference Center)
    www.cais.com/adear

American Heart Association
    www.americanheart.org/

American Cancer Society
    www.cancer.org/

Healthcare and Financing Administration (Medicare and Medicaid)
    www.hcfa.gov/medicaid/mc9icnsn.html

Senior Citizens Information
    www.etpb.com/VEBE/pages/communityinfo/seniors/
    FrontSenPg.html

Older Adult Resource Center
    www.healthanswers.com/health_answers/
    ha_homepage/index.hem

Family Caregivers Alliance Resource Center
www.caregiver.org/resource.html

Mental Health Net, Disorders and Treatments, Aging
www.cmhcsys.com/guide/aging.htm

See Appendix B for a list of other Web sites you may find helpful.

In addition to Web sites with informational materials, there are many special interest bulletin boards, chat rooms, and discussion groups that allow you to participate in e-mail or real-time cyber-communication with others around the world who share your issues and concerns.

The therapeutic solution

Who'll take care of the caregiver? That can become a serious issue, when the eldercare burden becomes overwhelming and there seems to be no relief in sight. When you find that you're approaching real burnout, it's time for a time-out to tend to your own needs. After all, you can be of little use to your family—especially your elder—if you are driven into depression or a stress-related physical illness.

If you've called in help from the family troops, joined a support group, and investigated respite care and still find that you're having trouble shaking your stress, consider seeking professional help. This is especially true if you find yourself exhibiting symptoms of depression, which include these:

▪ A lack of interest in activities that you formerly enjoyed

▪ A lack of appetite (or, conversely, a great increase in appetite)

▪ Chronic insomnia

▪ Frequent headaches or stomachaches

Watch Out!
While the Internet can be an incredibly useful resource, not all Web sites contain current or accurate information. Also, some sites may promote specific agendas that you do not agree with. When you visit a site, try to find out who sponsors the site, how reliable the sponsor is, who provides the content, and how often the information is updated.

- Unshakable feelings of sadness
- Worsening chronic medical problems

Depression is not something to treat lightly. It can render you incapable to help yourself *and* others who depend on you. If you think you might have a problem with depression—as millions of other Americans do—be sure to get help. Depressive patients generally respond very well to therapy, and medications such as Prozac or Zoloft may provide you with the mood stabilization you need to continue your caregiving tasks.

Just the facts

- The role of primary caregiver is a demanding one that increases your risk of stress and stress-related disorders.

- It is not selfish to reserve time for yourself when the stress of caregiving threatens to be overwhelming.

- A family meeting held *before* your elder enters a crisis situation can help minimize the strain of handling difficult eldercare situations and can provide you with willing recruits to share the caregiving role.

- Local support groups can help you find information and assistance for just about any aspect of eldercare that interests you.

- The Internet provides access to a broad range of information, services, and support.

- When the burden of eldercare is causing you serious distress, consider seeking professional therapy.

Getting Organized

PART III

GET THE SCOOP ON...
Bringing up the subject ▪ Working together ▪
Discovering the data ▪ Getting financial relief

Organizing Your Elder's Finances

Chapter 6

When you first contemplate your parent's need for eldercare, one of the many issues you'll need to address is your elder's financial situation. This is important for two reasons: First, your elder's physical or mental condition may mean that he or she has been unable to keep up with financial obligations and may, in fact, have lost control of this aspect of life. Second, you need to get a sense of the resources that will be available to cover eldercare-related costs.

Involving yourself in your elder's financial matters can be a delicate undertaking. Many elders are uncomfortable with sharing the details of their financial lives, and some may be suspicious of anyone who inquires too deeply into such a private matter. You too may find it awkward or difficult to bring such matters up with your parent. Still, it must be done at some point, and this chapter helps you approach the subject with tact and sensitivity. The sections that follow will give you a good idea of what you need to know and what you need to do to get your elder's financial situation on track. When you're done here, you'll be in a far better position to judge the kinds of care your elder can afford and assess his or her eligibility for outside assistance. You'll also learn what you need to do to optimize your elder's financial resources.

Broaching the subject of finances with your elder

As mentioned just above, the subject of finances can be a touchy one. Your elder may not be eager to share the details of his financial life with you—or anyone else, for that matter. The reticence may simply be a generational issue—many elders grew up with the attitude that money issues are simply not a fit subject for discussion. But it may also reflect a deeper fear. Consider these words of Konstantin Bernasche (of the Vancouver chapter of the Canadian Association of Retired Persons) in a 1997 article published in *BC Business:*

> Seniors fear that once they have lost control of their finances, they will be pushed aside by their children, or will be put into an old folks' home.... [But i]t's so important that they and their children talk about the subject. Both have to identify what each other's plans are and share their ideas and desires and needs. But it has to be done subtly, maybe even with a neutral person present, so that it doesn't become a fight.

Recognize that discomfort with talking about finances cuts both ways: Adult children of elders are also often uncomfortable bringing up the topic. Even financial experts aren't immune to this reluctance. Financial columnist Linda Stern, writing in

Unofficially... In his book Estate Planning for Baby Boomers and Retirees, author and financial advisor Stewart Welch lists the five common personality types he encounters in elders who are making financial decisions: the Prudent Planner, the Giver, the Scorekeeper, the Worrier, and the Controller. Understanding which type best describes your elder can help make financial discussions easier.

the Winter 1997/1998 issue of *Family Money*, put it
this way:

> I'm a financial journalist who specializes in
> these matters. But we never discussed details
> because I didn't want to seem like I cared more
> about Dad's money than about him. That's no

excuse. Most adult children want their parents
to enjoy their last dime before they die, but it
doesn't hurt to organize the inheritance, just in
case.

The only way you can effectively step in to help
your elder with finances in times of crisis or distress
is by clearly understanding the income and outflow
ahead of time. In addition, you'll need an awareness
of your elder's other assets and resources if you try
to help him or her cover—or qualify for assistance
to cover—eldercare costs.

Focus on the practical

You may first get involved in your elder's finances in
response to a problem: Mom is having trouble keeping up with her bills, or Dad needs a little help collecting his benefits. If your parent asks for help, you
have a perfect opportunity to begin with practical
assistance and move to a more general discussion of
broader financial issues.

If no such request for assistance arises, consider
approaching the subject obliquely, by offering to
help your elder establish an overall *lifeplan*—offer to
help your elder sort out his or her general legal,
medical, and financial affairs to create a general
plan for all major contingencies.

Such an approach is likely to be less threatening
than a blunt inquiry specifically focusing on your
parent's finances, because it is general in scope and
is aimed at your elder's practical concerns. A direct

request that your parent disclose his or her bank account balance and investment information might come across as intrusive and even self-serving. Conversely, an offer to help your parent sort through all his or her affairs in order to achieve a desired goal (such as how to calculate whether he or she can afford to move into a new house) makes it clear that you're asking for this information so you can help your *parent*—not yourself.

Start with the basics

In fact, this approach has more going for it than simply providing cover for your inquiries into a potentially delicate topic. It's frequently true that your parent really *does* need some help in sorting out the confusing details of pension benefits and the like. (If he doesn't, it's probably because his affairs are already in good order.) Of course, if one of the signs that your elder is in need of care is that he or she is having trouble keeping on top of the bills, your offer to pitch in and help sort out these day-to-day concerns gives you a natural opening for a broader inquiry into his or her financial affairs.

Similarly, if your elder is concerned about securing insurance or retirement benefits, offer to help with this narrowly focused problem and move logically into sorting out the broader financial picture. (See Chapter 13, "Protecting Your Elder's Legal Rights," for a look at the practical issues of managing eldercare costs).

In other words, some elders who would bridle at an inquiry into their assets will be far more receptive to your offer to help sort out their liabilities. Once you've gained their approval to provide such help, however, it becomes only natural to ask for asset information as well. An alternative approach is to ask your elder to advise *you* on your own finances. If you are willing to share such information with him, he may be more comfortable in reciprocating.

Looking at the overall budget

Assuming that you've managed to get your elder to accept your assistance, start by determining his or her current financial situation. You need a general idea of his income and expenses.

Establishing budget basics

To establish a good sense of your elder's ground-zero financial picture, first sort out his or her general expenses. This is a basic information-gathering process: pull together information on all your parent's regular (monthly and annual) bills and obligations, including these:

- Mortgage or rent payments
- Utility bills
- Car payment
- Insurance premiums
- Licensing or registration fees
- Prior year tax records (for income and property taxes)
- Credit card or other consumer credit obligations
- Regular health-related bills (for example, recurrent payments for ongoing prescription medicines)

Once you've gathered together the records or statements for your elder's regular financial obligations, you need to know the resources available to cover them. Now is the logical moment to request that your elder show you this regular income information:

- Regular monthly income (Social Security check, pension check, wages, and so forth)
- Income from retirement and pension plans (drawdowns from a 401(k) or IRA, certificate of deposit, or other such investment instruments)
- Savings account balance
- Stocks and bonds

It's important that this initial data-gathering phase be as thorough and accurate as possible, so you might find it helpful to approach the task with a checklist, much like the one in Figure 6.1 (reprinted with permission from AdultCare, Inc., a Fortis company). Use it to identify and locate all pertinent records—it will reduce the risk of overlooking important records or information.

Organizing the information

If organization is not your elder's strong suit, you may find that once you've accumulated all the budgetary paperwork, you're still faced with a nightmare of tangled forms and statements. Consider computerizing the information—there are many software programs designed to help with financial planning.

As you organize the information, you'll also be in a better position to identify gaps in your parent's records. If, for example, your elder's tax information is in a tangle, your elder can contact the IRS (tel: 800-829-3676, or visit their Web site: www.irs.ustreas.gov) and request copies of prior year tax returns.

If your elder is reluctant or unable to contact the IRS, you may have to handle this yourself. This may involve getting power of attorney over your elder's financial affairs. See Chapter 13, "Protecting Your Elder's Legal Rights," for more information.

FIGURE 6.1: FINANCIAL AND LEGAL INFORMATION

Name _____

Social Security # _____

Accountant _____ Phone: _____

Attorney _____ Phone: _____

Financial planner _____ Phone: _____

Insurance agent _____ Phone: _____

PERSONAL PAPERS   LOCATION

Birth certificate _____

Children's birth certificates _____

Passport _____

Adoption papers _____

continues

← **Note!**
Use the information in this table when working out your elder's legal and medical affairs (see Chapter 7, "Organizing Your Elder's Medical Affairs," and Chapter 8, "When There's No Place Like Home") as well.

FINANCIAL AND LEGAL INFORMATION (cont.)

PERSONAL PAPERS　　　　　　　LOCATION

Naturalization papers _____

Marriage certificates _____

Divorce decree(s) _____

Military records _____

House deed(s) _____

Auto title(s) _____

Social Security card _____

Insurance ID cards _____

Location of and access to safety deposit box _____

DOCUMENT	ACCOUNT # (IF APPLICABLE)	LOCATION
Will		
Living will		
Power of attorney		
Finances		
Health decisions		
Pension		
Checking account(s):	ACCT. #	BANK
Saving accounts:	ACCT. #	BANK

continues

FINANCIAL AND LEGAL INFORMATION (cont.)

Mortgages and notes: _____

_____

Tax records: _____

Canceled checks: _____

	ACCT. #	TYPE

Credit cards: _____

_____

_____

Certificate(s) of deposit: _____

_____

Checkbook: _____

_____

	ACCT. # (IF APPLICABLE)	TYPE
Bonds	_____	_____
Mutual fund shares:	_____	_____
	_____	_____
Annuities	_____	_____
	_____	_____
IRA(s):	_____	_____
	_____	_____

continues

FINANCIAL AND LEGAL INFORMATION (cont.)

Records of payment

Medical bills _____

Utility bills _____

Telephone bills _____

Tax bills _____

Other _____

Insurance

Life _____

Property _____

Liability _____

Medical _____

Dental _____

Homeowners _____

Automobile _____

Medigap _____

Long-term care _____

Pre-need contract _____

Other _____

_____

_____

Handling first things first

One reason elders are reluctant to share information on their financial condition is a fear that they will lose control. You can go a long way toward relieving this concern by keeping your parent well-informed of what you're doing every step of the way. You want this to be a joint effort, insofar as your elder is able to participate—you most definitely should not insert yourself in her financial affairs in a high-handed or authoritarian way. Besides, working together cooperatively will make your task much easier

If your parent is beginning to have trouble keeping his financial affairs in order, here's what you may find:

▪ Crucial bills have gone unpaid.

▪ Credit card interest is piling up.

▪ Important correspondence has gone unanswered.

▪ The checking account is overdrawn.

▪ Insurance policies are in danger of lapsing for lack of payment of premiums.

▪ Receipts needed for taxes or to back up an insurance claim are lost.

Before you become involved with long-term or estate planning (a subject we take up in detail in Chapter 13), your initial concern must be to stabilize your parent's current financial situation. The best way to determine just what needs to be done is to collect the last several statements for each of your elder's recurrent bills. But if your elder has been having trouble keeping such accounts current (as is often the case), have him contact the creditor, bank, or utility to which payment is owed and request that

they send a current billing statement. As the creditor or customer of record, your elder will have far
less difficulty eliciting such information than you
might if you try to do it in his or her behalf.

Bringing order to chaos

For many elders, all you'll need to do is impose a little order on their financial records—after all, they
have been handling their own affairs for a lifetime.
But if your parent has gradually lost control of this
aspect of his or her life, you may find that you must
make arrangements to clear past-due balances. If
you notify most creditors of the situation, they will
work with you to set up repayment plans. Before you
call, however, make certain that you fully understand just what is available in your elder's budget to
handle such a plan—you don't want to commit your
parent to a repayment agreement that he can't follow through with later.

If your elder's affairs are in serious disarray, you
may want to consider calling in professional help.
Hiring an accountant or financial planner might be
your best bet—and your elder might also be less
reluctant to work through his or her finances with
you if there is a professional third party involved in
your discussions. If you're looking for a financial
planner, you can get a referral by contacting:

The Institute of Certified Financial Planners
3801 E. Florida Ave., Set. 708
Denver, CO 80210
800-282-7526

If you need a certified public accountant, referrals can be obtained by contacting:

The American Institute of Certified Public
Accountants
Personal Financial Planning Division
1211 Avenue of the Americas
New York, NY 10036
800-862-4272

Outsmarting the scammers

It's a sad fact of life: Many businesses and con artists
target the elderly. Stories of phony roofing or drive-
way paving jobs abound. Less direct types of cons
and scams include selling products at highly
inflated prices, and "gift" offers or sweepstake
"prize" notifications that conceal a commitment to
purchase products in the fine print of the acceptance form.

The elderly are particularly vulnerable to scams
and cons—even a parent who could once spot a
scammer from a mile off can be taken in by the
urgency of an offer in the mail marked "OPEN ME
NOW!" or "YOU ARE A WINNER."

Not all of the companies that target the elderly
are readily identifiable as fly-by-night con artists,
either. Even the phone bill can contain false or
unauthorized charges. Unethical financial advisors
may suggest unsafe retirement investments or insurance plans. The problem is a serious one: Elders are
routinely bilked of their estates by fraudulent
schemes. If you have reason to believe that your
elder is being victimized by an unscrupulous company, contact your local Better Business Bureau and,
if appropriate, your local police department.

Working *with* your elder on finances

Keep your parent involved in her own financial
planning as much as possible. If you take over too

Bright Idea
You can limit the
amount of junk
mail or telemar-
keting pitches
your elder
receives at home.
To get less junk
mail, write to
the Direct
Marketing
Association, P.O.
Box 9008,
Farmingdale, NY
11735-9008. To
get fewer phone
solicitations,
write to the
Direct Marketing
Association, P.O.
Box 9014,
Farmingdale, NY
11735-9014. In
both cases, send
a letter request-
ing that your
elder's name be
removed from all
mail and/or
phone lists. Be
sure to include
your elder's
name, address,
and home tele-
phone number in
the letter.

many duties that your parent can still handle, you simply confirm her fears that she is being shouldered aside and is losing her independence.

Making it a cooperative effort

Even if your elder is no longer able to handle all her affairs on her own, she may still be able to participate to some extent. Don't assume that just because she's having trouble keeping things in order you should leap to suggest that your name be put on her account. You may eventually have to do that (see Chapter 13), but for as long as possible, respect your parent's desire for autonomy. Can she write checks? Then you can work together by organizing her bills and presenting them in a tidy pile for her to pay. Even if she can't handle that much involvement, she may still be able to sign the checks that you prepare for her.

Here are a few "dos and don'ts" to help you keep your parent actively involved:

WORKING ON FINANCES WITH YOUR ELDER

Problem	Do	Don't
Mom needs general help paying her bills.	Offer to help by balancing the checkbook.	Insist on being made cosigner on her checking account or summarily take over the task.
Dad can't balance the checkbook.	Suggest he get (or better yet, present him with) a good, large-button calculator	Demand he hand over the account records and do it yourself.
Mom doesn't understand her financial statement.	Sit with her and explain it, item by item.	Take it away, check it out on your own, and simply announce that you've dealt with it.

Dad's having trouble dealing with the mail.	Go through the stack together— he may be having trouble reading the small print.	Take the pile and announce that you'll decide what's important.
Mom can't find important papers.	Offer to help her track them down.	Search the house for the papers.

Of course, in crisis situations, or if your parent is seriously impaired, you may have to resort to a more intrusive approach to sorting out your elder's finances. But the goal is to temper your involvement so that you are offering only as much help as is needed—not overstepping your bounds.

Dealing with creditors

If your parent has fallen into arrears in some or all of the bills, she may welcome your help in getting creditors off her back. Many people—not just the elderly—find it extremely uncomfortable to deal with dunning letters or calls from collection agents. Most creditors are quite happy to work with you to retire the debts—they'd rather collect some of the money they're due than end up having to write off the total amount. Many utility companies, in particular, have programs in place that will allow you to pay off a large overdue balance over time, but even credit card companies are likely to help—and some may be willing to reduce the total amount owed in return for a lump sum payment now. Just be careful not to commit your parent to a repayment schedule that will leave her without enough money in the budget for necessities.

If your parent's bills have fallen seriously into arrears and you are forced to deal with collection agents, don't be put off by their sometimes aggressive tactics. Even they must work with you if you demonstrate that you are trying to discharge the debt in good faith. Furthermore, there are legal limits as to what they can do in the process of collecting a bill. Collection agencies are not allowed to do any of the following:

- Use abusive language.

- Threaten to disclose your elder's indebtedness to a third party.

- Call before 8 a.m. or after 9 p.m.

Unfortunately, some agencies routinely violate these regulations—they know that many debtors are too uncomfortable about their financial condition to file a complaint. If you think your elder is being harassed by a creditor, report the situation to your state Consumer's Protection office—and make sure that you send a copy of your complaint letter to the offending agency. That is usually enough to make them pull in their claws and work more cooperatively with you.

Finding more help for your elder

If your elder needs inexpensive (or possibly free) credit counseling, call the Consumer Credit Counseling Services (CCCS) at 800-388-2227. This organization can advise you of the branch of their service nearest you. But beware! Many other companies out there claiming to "repair your credit" exist merely to strip their clients' assets.

Your elder may benefit by consolidating his or her debts. However, this is something to think about long and hard. Banks have recently stepped up their offers to extend second—and even third—mortgages for the purpose of paying off other indebtedness. Unfortunately, some people who have taken advantage of such "easy access" loans have wound up losing their one major asset—their home—when

Watch Out!
Think carefully before deciding to go with an equity conversion mortgage—it does provide a steady monthly income, but your parent *does* have to give up his interest in the house. If this is likely to cause financial hardship down the line, you might want to look at other sources of funding to cover the remodeling expenses.

they found they couldn't keep up their new mortgage payments. On the other hand, your elder might benefit from securing a *reverse mortgage* (discussed in detail in Chapter 12). The regular monthly income he or she would realize from such an arrangement may be just what's needed to cover expenses.

Taking action if the money has run out

If your parent has exhausted his financial resources, he may be eligible for a number of assistance programs. By all means, he should look into Medicaid (see Chapter 12), but don't stop there. Your Area Agency on Aging can refer you to other sources of public assistance and might provide a list of local eldercare providers that offer low- or no-cost services to the poor.

Seeking more help

The Internet contains a number of financial-information sites that you might find useful as you try to pull your elder's finances into order. Here are just a few:

- American Express Financial Advisors
  www.americanexpress.com/advisors
- Investor Guide
  www.investorguide.com
- Microsoft Network
  www.investor.msn.com
- Metlife
  www.metlife.com
- Insurance News Network
  www.insure.com
- Family Money
  www.familymoney.com

In addition, the Administration on Aging and the American Association of Retired Persons both include financial information, advice, and advisories of interest to elders and eldercare providers.

Just the facts

- Helping your elder organize his or her finances is an important early step in planning for his or her overall eldercare.

- You may meet resistance from your elder when you ask for information on his or her finances.

- Including your elder in the financial organization and planning process will go a long way toward securing his or her cooperation.

- If your parent is in debt, notify her creditors of the situation—they can usually be convinced to work with you to resolve the situation.

- Beware: Scammers and con artists often target the elderly

GET THE SCOOP ON ...
Identifying ailments ▪ Handling medications ▪
Working with providers ▪ Patient's Bill of
Rights ▪ Handling insurers ▪ Family and
Medical Leave Act

Organizing Your Elder's Medical Affairs

Whcn putting together a viable eldercare plan for your parent, one very important area to get a full understanding of is the level of medical care required. Whether your elder is attempting to continue living independently or is entering a long-term care facility, make certain that his or her current and future medical needs will be appropriately addressed. In this chapter, you learn about the information you need to collect and how best to contribute to your elder's ongoing medical care.

Identifying areas of concern

Helping your elder organize the healthcare aspect of his or her life involves paying attention to the following two major areas of concern:

▪ Identifying your elder's current physical condition

▪ Organizing current medication(s) and evaluating their appropriateness for your elder's current state

Get started in familiarizing yourself with the people and paperwork involved in your elder's care. Do this by:

- Making yourself known to your elder's physician and other healthcare providers
- Sorting through your elder's healthcare coverage, and enrolling him or her in any programs for which he or she qualifies

Depending on your elder's likely needs, you may wish to get started early on assessing your own resources, because you may need to help with payments for your elder's medical needs.

Establishing your elder's current medical needs

In Chapter 3, "Determining the Level of Care Required," you learned the importance of gaining an understanding of your elder's health status when establishing an overall eldercare strategy. The value of becoming involved in your elder's medical care is important for a second reason as well: The time may come when you must take charge of his or her medical care due to a sudden crisis situation. Certainly, if you want to help your elder pull together his or her medical insurance to cover ongoing health costs, you need a solid sense of the treatments that are generating them.

If you haven't yet sat down with your elder (and/or her physician) to discuss the overall health picture, now's the time to do so. If your elder is in crisis and hadn't previously given you a durable power of attorney on medical issues, you may need to look into being named guardian by the courts (see Chapter 13 for a discussion of both powers of attorney and guardianships). In either case, it would be wise to request copies of your elder's medical records so that you have a clear idea of past medical attention and can better assess what may be needed in the future.

Getting a grip on the meds

Many elders deal with a variety of major or minor physical complaints, each requiring some degree of medication or therapy or treatment. It is very common for an elder to have several medications prescribed by different providers, and for each of these providers to be in the dark about the prescriptions ordered by the others. But some medicines have dangerous—even deadly—interactions with one another and with certain over-the-counter products.

You need a sense of the combinations your elder is currently taking, and you also need a list of current medications to avoid problems with drug interactions when any new prescriptions are added. It's also a good idea to get all of your parent's medications through one pharmacy, so the pharmacist can help track any potential problems.

This issue of keeping an accurate record has achieved greater urgency in this era of managed care. Today, your parent may see one primary care provider for general evaluation and then be sent off to a variety of specialists for particular treatments or therapies. The primary physician is supposed to keep centralized records of all treatments and medications ordered, but that record-keeping function is sometimes a bureaucratic enterprise handled by the administrative staff, not the doctor. It is very possible that incompatible drugs can be ordered with no one the wiser—until your parent has a bad reaction.

Bright Idea
Many pharmacies now offer information sheets on various drugs, their side effects, and their possible interactions with other medications. Ask your pharmacist for such information whenever your elder gets a new prescription or a refill. You may also want to keep a copy of the latest edition of *Physician's Desk Reference* on hand.

Watch Out!
Many seniors heralded Viagra as a wonder drug when it was first introduced. However, those who take heart medications such as nitroglycerin should not take Viagra because a combination of the two can result in heart attack, stroke, and even death. This is one example of why all your elder's medications should be discussed with the primary physician.

One helpful tool for organizing the sometimes confusing variety of medications is a simple survey chart, like the following, which was reprinted courtesy of AdultCare, Inc., a Fortis company.

Begin by taking an inventory of your elder's medicine cabinet, and fill in the gaps by talking with your parent and his or her physician. Make certain to collect full details on dosages—both amounts to be taken and the frequency and conditions under which they are to be taken (such as, "three times daily, with meals").

Make your survey as exhaustive and detailed as possible, and include all over-the-counter or alternative medicines your elder may be using. Too often, people assume that non-prescription items are by definition "harmless" and don't understand that a widely used cold medication or health-food store supplement may be very dangerous when taken in combination with other drugs.

Getting involved in the medical care process

Meet with your elder's doctors for two reasons. First, whether or not your elder is currently in crisis, you may someday face an emergency situation and will need to be well-enough informed to make sound decisions on her behalf. That means knowing—and being known by—the physicians and other health-care specialists who have been involved in her ongoing care. Second, you need to feel confident that her current providers have been appropriately chosen and are giving your elder the highest possible level of care right now.

Meeting the providers

Most doctors and medical care providers are sensitive, competent, and caring. Then there are the

TABLE 7.1: GENERAL MEDICATION SURVEY

Condition	Name of medication	Dose/How often?
Sleeping		
Arthritis		
Pain killers		
High blood pressure		
Diuretics		
Cardiac		
Chest pain		
Blood thinners		
Insulin		
Diabetes		
Depression		
Stress/Nerves		
Anti-inflammatory		
Antibiotics		
Vitamins		
Eye drops		
Thyroid		
Cold/flu		
Stomach		
Cholesterol		

Do you self-administer your drugs? ____ Yes ____ No

If not, who does?_____

Do you routinely use:
    Laxatives? _____ Yes ____No
    Antacids? _____ Yes ____No

Do you take medications as prescribed?
    _____ Yes ____No

Do you ever skip doses?
    _____ Yes ____No

others. Some doctors can be intimidating or less-than-forthcoming with information. Others do not willingly accept or treat patients who receive public assistance for the payment of their medical costs.

The doctor-patient relationship is an intimate one best maintained in an atmosphere of mutual trust and respect. Whether your elder is privately insured or has coverage provided through Medicaid or some other assistance program, quality care is a right. Meeting with medical providers will give you a good understanding of the personal connection between your elder and the medical personnel upon which he depends.

This is also a good time to evaluate the degree to which your elder's physician will welcome your involvement and possible intervention. This can become a crucial issue in a time of crisis: If the physician balks at including you in decision-making on your parent's behalf, you may have problems later when you're trying to ensure that your elder's wishes are respected if he or she is not able to make those wishes clear.

Most doctors, however, will welcome your involvement. They recognize that you are an ally in their efforts to ensure that your elder follows the recommended treatment, diet, or medication regimen. They understand because they share your motivation to make certain that your elder enjoys the best possible health.

Following examination etiquette

If you have succeeded in obtaining your elder's approval to accompany her to necessary medical examinations or treatment, keep in mind that your role is primarily a supportive one (unless, of course, your elder is in crisis or otherwise cannot speak for herself). Stay in the background—avoid the temptation to take over the conversation or otherwise marginalize your parent from the process. Do take notes, however— make certain that you have a good record of all recommendations and/or diagnoses to refer to later.

One complaint voiced by many elders is that their physicians don't take them seriously. Often, this is simply because the elder doesn't know how to present his symptoms or questions in an organized manner. You can help by meeting with your parent before any appointments and offering to make a list of symptoms or complaints. That way, no important points will be forgotten, and the doctor will have an easier time addressing your parent's concerns.

Spotting the need for a change

When there's a bad fit between patient and doctor or other healthcare provider, it is definitely time to consider making a change. However, many people—and this is perhaps particularly true among the elderly—find it intimidating to switch physicians. Here are some indicators that a change in providers is a good idea:

▪ Appointments are difficult to get.

▪ Not enough time is scheduled for a meaningful exam during appointments.

▪ The doctor doesn't seem to take your elder's complaints seriously.

▪ The physician is unwilling to explain the reasons for treatments or medications he or she orders.

▪ The staff treats your elder disrespectfully.

Some of these circumstances arise when your elder's medical coverage is provided through

Medicaid or other assistance programs for the low-income elderly. Some doctors and facilities limit the time and space they will allocate to patients enrolled in such programs because they object to the levels at which reimbursements are set and they resent the amount of paperwork required when filing claims. As medical care becomes more "corporatized," it has become a sad fact of life that concerns for the bottom line have assumed great importance in the field of healthcare. But neither you nor your elder need accept cavalier treatment from healthcare providers. Advise your elder that the majority of doctors and other healthcare workers are dedicated and compassionate people, and suggest that he or she seek one of them.

But do keep in mind that this ultimately is your *parent's* choice. If your elder is comfortable with his or her current physician and there is no reason for a change beyond your own personal preferences, gracefully acquiesce to your parent's decision. Unless your elder is incapable of making such choices personally, do not impose your own opinions on her.

Deciding to switch or not to switch

If there are real, identifiable problems in your elder's relationship with her healthcare providers, the first step is to notify the doctor of the issues. Very often, communication difficulties between a doctor and a patient arise because the patient is intimidated about bringing issues out into the open. A simple conference could clear the air and bring the relationship back on track. Sometimes, however, there is no simple solution, and changing providers is the only viable option.

Once upon a time, when fee-for-service care ruled the medical profession, changing physicians was simple. You asked around among friends, checked out the Yellow Pages, and called your local hospital for referrals. But with the prevalence of HMOs and other managed-care programs, it's not quite so easy—subscribers are required to choose their physicians from a preapproved list of providers. Check references and credentials thoroughly, and schedule a preliminary appointment so that your elder has the opportunity to see whether she is comfortable with the new physician.

Filling in the information gap

It is far too easy for an office staff or previous care provider to forget to send key information to a new physician. When your elder changes providers, get copies of his medical records, test results, and so on from the previous physician. These records are legally the property of the patient, not the doctor, so your elder is perfectly within his rights to request them. Then, when it's time to meet with the new physician, pass a copy of these records along—in this way you are assured that the new doctor has a complete history of your elder's condition(s).

Remember to bring along a completed copy of the medications survey you filled out earlier in this chapter. Your elder's over-the-counter or other non-prescription medications will not appear in the formal records from the previous provider.

Organizing coverage and benefits

Chapter 12 provides a basic introduction to the principal sources of coverage for medical care costs, from Medicare and Medicaid to Medigap and long-term care coverage. Turn to that chapter to learn how these programs and policies work. Here, however, we are more concerned in simply getting the information you need into some sort of order so that when the need arises, you can quickly get your hands on the necessary documents and data.

Gathering your elder's medical paperwork

To expedite payment of your elder's medical care costs, you need three pieces of information:

- Insurance policies and contracts

- Identification/claim cards

- Any contracts with healthcare facilities in which your elder is enrolled (if applicable)

Bright Idea
For a helpful listing of healthcare information, arranged by region, see the ElderWeb site (www.elderweb. com/insure.htm).

If your elder has private insurance, gather all policies and descriptions of coverage issued by the insurer. These should be kept in a readily accessible but secure location so that you can get your hands on them whenever the need arises. Some people keep these sorts of records in a safety deposit box in the bank, but that may not be the best idea: Access is restricted to the bank's business hours, and in a crisis situation you might need them at night or over the weekend. You are better off keeping the originals in a safety deposit box, but keep a full set of copies in a secure, fire-resistant box in your elder's (or your) home as well.

ID/claim cards are another important piece of documentation that you'll need to keep handy. Make certain that you know where your parent keeps these cards for private insurance, for Medicare and Medicaid coverage, for VA insurance, and for any prescription coverage or discounting programs to which he or she belongs.

If your elder resides in an assisted living facility or a full-service care facility, make certain that you have copies of your elder's agreement-for-care or contract-for-services issued by the facility. Your elder is paying for the services stipulated in these contracts, and your familiarity with these documents will go a long way toward ensuring that the services are provided. Make sure these documents are stored in a safe place. Keep a file of all medical treatments and referrals ordered by your elder's physician. This material will be required as back-up documentation if your elder ever needs to contest a decision by the insurer to deny coverage.

Forestalling or resolving problems with the insurers
No matter how clearly your elder's insurance policies or programs seem to spell out what is and is not covered, it is very common for disputes to arise. Insurers are in the business of making—not paying—money and will challenge claims if they feel there are appropriate grounds. Medicare has its own set schedule of fees, beyond which it will not pay—no matter what a physician feels is an appropriate charge for a given procedure.

Perhaps the most common complaint voiced by Medicare patients is how difficult it is to keep up with the unending flow of paper generated by the government: updates on fee schedules, changing tables of covered procedures and treatments, and so forth. This tide of data can easily reach overwhelming proportions. ElderServe, Inc. (Web site: http://www.elderserve.com; phone number: (800-234-2507) is one of the many organizations which can help you with medical claims processing.

In any billing dispute, take the following steps:

▪ Have ready the date of the service, your elder's insurance number, and the name of the provider before you make the claims call.

Watch Out!
Many older people habitually pay their bills upon receipt. With medical bills, however, this is not a good idea, because you could end up overpaying. Medicare decides what a doctor can charge and will not reimburse for anything above that amount. Submit the bills and wait—give the system a chance to work.

- Make certain you know the claim number assigned by the insurance company.

- Make a list of the important points you need to address during your call—you want to present your information clearly and logically.

- Take down the name(s) of anyone with whom you discuss the claim.

- Maintain your cool when talking to the claims department—if you receive no satisfaction from your original contact person, calmly request to speak to a supervisor.

- Take notes throughout the call—you may need them for later follow-up or to take your claim to a higher level.

Follow up your phone call with a formal letter confirming the details of your claim and the claim-handler's response. If you expect a continued dispute on the claim, send the letter certified, return-receipt requested so that you have evidence of your mailing. You may also wish to send a copy of this correspondence to the provider or facility to whom the money is owed so that they know you are attempting to settle the claim and secure their payment.

If, after all this, you or your elder still receives dunning letters from the provider demanding payment of the bill, find out who is in charge of the billing organization. Inform that person of the situation, the steps you're taking to address it, and when you expect to achieve resolution. Often, even if the facility or provider is willing to work with you to resolve billing problems, the demands for payment are still cranked out by a computer. You may need someone in authority to intercede to get this annoyance to stop.

Finally, if your elder is having trouble reaching specialists or securing reimbursement, you and your elder may wish to contact Physicians Who Care. This 3,500-doctor advocacy group provides assistance to people who are having problems with their HMOs or other managed-care providers. Contact the organization through their complaint hotline (800-800-5154). Note, however, that this group does not answer personal medical questions regarding treatment.

The Patient's Bill of Rights

It is impossible to organize your elder's medical care and treatment if you are unaware or unsure of his or her rights. The American Hospital Association (840 North Lake Shore Drive, Chicago, Illinois, 60611; tel: 312-200-6000) has developed a Patient's Bill of Rights that stipulates what everyone has a right to expect when receiving medical care. The following excerpt from the Patient's Bill of Rights presents just a few of the 12 points addressed in those rights—a full reproduction of the Bill of Rights appears in Appendix D.

Getting help at *your* end

Although eldercare has yet to achieve the degree of recognition among employers as childcare has reached in the last few decades, more major corporations are beginning to include some provision in their employee benefits packages. Hewitt Associates, a consulting firm in Lincolnshire, Illinois, surveyed the work and family benefits offered by 1,050 major employers in 1996. Of these businesses, 30 percent offered eldercare benefits—up from only 17 percent in 1991. Members of the International Foundation of Employee Benefit Plans predicted

TABLE 7.2: SELECTED EXCERPTS FROM THE PATIENT'S BILL OF RIGHTS

1. The patient has the right to considerate and respectful care.

2. The patient has the right to and is encouraged to obtain...relevant, current, and understandable information concerning diagnosis, treatment, and prognosis.... The patient also has the right to know the immediate and long-term financial implications of treatment choices, insofar as they are known.

3. The patient has the right...to refuse a recommended treatment or plan of care to the extent permitted by law and hospital policy, and to be informed of the medical consequences of this action....

4. The patient has the right to have an advance directive (such as a living will, healthcare proxy, or durable power of attorney for healthcare) concerning treatment...with the expectation that the hospital will honor the intent of that directive to the extent permitted by law and hospital policy....

5. The patient has the right to every consideration of privacy. Case discussion, consultation, examination, and treatment should be conducted so as to protect each patient's privacy.

7. The patient has the right to review the records pertaining to his/her medical care and to have this information explained or interpreted as necessary, except when restricted by law.

11. The patient has the right to expect reasonable continuity of care when appropriate and to be informed by physicians and other caregivers of available and realistic patient care options when hospital care is no longer appropriate....

that the number of companies offering eldercare resource/referral services would rise to 64% by the year 2000.

The benefits of eldercare benefits

The trend to provide eldercare benefits is increasing, and this is a matter of simple good sense: According to *The MetLife Study of Employer Costs for Working Caregivers*, the decreased productivity of employees with eldercare responsibilities costs businesses nearly $22.5 billion per year. These costs are incurred through absenteeism, interrupted work days, and, of course, employee turnover when a worker finds that juggling work and caregiving simply gets to be too much.

Even without the problems of turnover and absenteeism, companies that don't provide benefits to their employees lose big. Employees may make themselves unavailable for job-related relocations, for example, or may turn down promotions if these changes are perceived as likely to interfere with their ability to provide care for their elders. In addition, an employee who is carrying a heavy caregiving burden is likely to be working under extreme stress—which can, in turn, lead to accidents and errors on the job.

But the stresses faced by eldercare providers are not dissimilar to those (already recognized in childcare benefits programs) encountered by parents. The average eldercaregiver provides 18 hours of care per week, performing tasks that range from providing transportation and handling the elder's household chores to helping a parent bathe, dress, or eat.

Some employers do understand

Companies are drawing from the lessons they have learned in the development of childcare benefits. Often the help they provide takes the form of toll-free numbers that employees can call for advice on aging issues and for information on senior or adult day centers, nursing homes, assisted living, and more. In addition, they may provide informational brochures, financial help, and counseling. Some allow employees with eldercare responsibilities the option of working on a flextime or job-sharing basis.

Many employers are turning to outside contractors to provide the advice-and-referral services their employees need. One such contractor is the Boston-based company Work/Family Directions, which advises employees of Fortune 500 companies across the nation on elder- and childcare-related issues. Other large companies have set up their own specialist divisions to handle the same issues through over-the-phone advice and referrals. AdultCare Service, a division of Fortis Long Term Care in Milwaukee, Wisconsin, is one such benefit provider—it was established in 1997 to respond to the eldercare concerns of Fortis's 6,500-plus employees.

The Family and Medical Leave Act

Most people associate the Family and Medical Leave Act (FMLA) of 1993 with childcare benefits—the law guarantees a parent time off to care for a sick child. But the law also covers employees with elderly parents in their care. If you're a full-time employee who has worked for at least a year at a company with 50 or more employees, you're covered under the provisions of this act. The FMLA provides for covered employees to take 12 weeks off per year, but keep in mind that this is *unpaid* leave time.

Organizing care when you can't be there

Part 4, "Options in Eldercare," discusses in detail the kinds of eldercare residence choices to address your elder's care needs, whether he or she lives independently, with you, or in a partial- or full-care facility. One other way to organize and address eldercare needs—particularly as they pertain to your parent's medical condition—is to turn to professionals in the care-management field. These are known as *geriatric care managers.*

A geriatric care manager (GCM) assists you and your elder by assessing the overall situation, drawing up a plan for medical care, and (frequently) monitoring the plan once it is in place. The GCM has expertise in the practicalities of eldercare: determining the best residential option for the individual elder, identifying the need for—and securing access to—specialized services, and overseeing other aspects of your elder's care needs. These managers don't come cheap: Fees can be $50 or more per hour, and their services are not covered by insurance. For more information, contact the National Association of Geriatric Care Managers at 520-881-8008.

Watch Out!
As with other areas in the rapidly growing eldercare industry, some individuals have set themselves up as care managers with no real experience or expertise. Check credentials thoroughly before retaining anyone for these services.

Organizing on the home front

Whether your elder is living independently, with you, or in an assisted-living facility, he or she may be using the services of home care and home healthcare workers. This, too, is something that you should touch upon when you are organizing your elder's medical situation. You need the contact information for each person upon whom your elder depends. It is equally important that you gather information on the agency or agencies through which this assistance is provided. Should circumstances arise where you need to change or discontinue some services, this information will be key.

Just the facts

- Many elders avoid medical attention; begin by getting a full checkup to establish baseline medical and other health needs.

- Medications can become confusing—and some interact dangerously. A full inventory of your elder's medication needs will be useful for you, your elder, and his or her medical provider.

- The doctor-patient relationship is an intimate one—assist your elder, but don't intrude too deeply.

- The myriad contracts, IDs, and documentation booklets can easily get lost—store them in a safe, convenient place.

- Your employer may provide eldercare assistance ranging from referrals to counseling.

Options in Eldercare

PART IV

When There's No Place Like Home

A ccording to the Administration on Aging, "The type of housing and the community in which people live are critical factors in assuring independence as they age." This finding, echoed throughout the professional eldercare industry, has had significant influence in the development of a broad array of home- and community-based services, all aimed at making aging in place a viable, safe option for as many of the elderly as possible.

This chapter provides you with a solid understanding of the issues that elders—and their families—may need to address if they wish to make the choice of remaining in the home a safe and convenient one. You'll learn why aging in place for as long as possible is generally regarded as the best all-round option for most elders. In addition, this chapter explores the professional and personal services available to elders who maintain an independent household. The upcoming sections examine ways to make that home elder-friendly by removing the common household hazards and obstacles that can inhibit your elder's independence.

Aging in place

It's easy to understand why an older person would prefer to remain in the home that he or she has known for years. By remaining home, an elderly person may maintain long-standing relationships in a familiar community, avoiding the disruption that relocating would entail. And, if your elder can keep his or her own home, there is no need to give up personal belongings, pets, or comforting routines. They all contribute to a strong sense of security and quality of life.

As a person becomes more frail with age, however, the ability to perform the necessary or instrumental activities of daily living (see Chapter 2, "Who Needs Eldercare?") may decline. As vision or hearing becomes less reliable, or as age-related aches, pains, and illnesses set in, living independently may entail increased risks. For this reason, home- and community-based services are critical elements in the aging in place option. Basic concerns of safety and convenience *can* be addressed if you take careful stock of your elder's specific needs and seek out ways to accommodate them.

If you or a family member lives near your elder, it will be easy for you to assess your elder's ability to live alone, and make adjustments or improvements where necessary. However, if no family member lives close to your elder, you may have to rely on a neighbor, social service worker, church member, or someone else in your elder's neighborhood who can keep tabs and let you know when your elder needs assistance.

Unofficially...
According to the Association on Aging, nearly 84 percent of all elderly Americans are fully capable of living independently if they so choose. Even among the very oldest—those over age 85—a full 51 percent have no physical limitations to prevent them from remaining in their homes.

Exploring the basics of home care

For aging in place to be a viable option for an elderly person, two broad categories of concerns must be addressed. First, the home must be made safe and accessible enough for your elder to get around with ease. Second, your elder's individual needs for medical, social, and daily assistance must be addressed. The first problem can be handled through "elderizing" the home—making basic repairs or modifications to its physical structure. The second generally requires that you or your elder engage home care services from outside providers.

Home modification and repair

More than 5 million American elderly remain in their homes, whether by choice or because finances overrule other living arrangements. Most houses and apartments, however, were never explicitly designed to accommodate the specific safety and accessibility needs of the elderly. With increased physical frailty, that once comforting home can become a very dangerous place. The AoA identifies the following as typical safety problems faced by elderly people who live at home:

- Difficulty getting in and out of the shower
- Slipping in the tub or shower
- Difficulty turning faucets, appliance knobs, and doorknobs
- Difficulty gaining access to the front door or upper floors of the home
- Difficulty controlling the heating or ventilation

Later in this chapter you'll learn specific ways to elderize your parent's home to fix these and other problems of physical safety.

Bright Idea
Next time you are at Mom's home for a meal, observe the inconveniences she faces when getting around the kitchen. Sometimes it's the little, easily remedied things—shelves set too high for convenient access, faucets too tight for arthritic hands to turn, that cause the most frustration in day-to-day living.

Home care services

In addition to the basic problems of physical safety, elderly people living at home often also need help in taking care of some medical needs and performing some of the basic or instrumental activities of daily living (see Chapter 2). For these problems, a broad range of home care services has become available over the last several years. The care provider(s) fall into one of the following categories:

- **Housekeeper (chore worker):** Helps with basic household tasks and light cleaning

- **Homemaker (personal care worker):** Provides personal care, meal planning, household management, and medication reminders

- **Companion (live-in):** Provides a broad range of assistance, from light housework to companionship and medication reminders

- **Home health aide (certified nurse assistant, nurse's aide):** Provides personal care, assistance with or administration of medications, and physical therapy, when required

The home health aide differs significantly from the other categories of home care workers. He or she has received specific training in the medical aspects of care, is supervised by a registered nurse assigned to your elder, and makes regular status reports on changes in the patient's condition to both you and his or her supervisor.

Elderizing the home

No matter how much outside assistance you bring in for your elder, your first concern must be the physical safety of the home. More than 60 percent of all older persons living at home occupy residences that are 20 years old—old enough that they lack many of the modern safety features commonly found in newer buildings. As your elder becomes more frail, he or she is increasingly vulnerable to accidents—particularly falls.

Home modification and repairs planned with the specific physical limitations of your elder can accommodate the changes in lifestyle and ability that go along with aging. And these modifications can really make a difference in the safety of your elder: Research by the AoA suggests that one-third to one-half of all home accidents among the elderly can be prevented by making basic modifications and repairs to the home.

Take a quick look around your elder's home. At first glance, you probably won't notice much that needs changing—after all, this is familiar territory to you. There's the carpet that has always graced the living room floor, there are the good dishes in the kitchen cabinets, there are Mom or Dad's toiletries in the bathroom—everything looks more or less as it always has. But each familiar room presents possible dangers to your parent as his or her abilities diminish with age. Take another look around, this time with a more critical eye.

Bathroom basics

The bathroom presents the most potential hazards for any elderly person. Precarious balance can lead to slips on a wet floor or shower tiles; arthritic fingers can have difficulty with sticky faucets so that water runs too hot and causes scalds or burns; fixtures set too low can make it difficult for your elder to rise from the toilet. Many of these situations can be fixed with relative ease. Here's a list of some basic alterations that will greatly improve the safety of the bathroom:

Watch Out!
Many elders have accumulated a lot of memorabilia over the years. Make certain such things are carefully stored, not blocking hallways, doorways, or stairs. If an accident occurs and your parent needs to get out of the home quickly, these collectibles can suddenly become life-threatening obstacles.

■ Install a support rail by the toilet, or install a raised toilet with arm rails to make getting up easier.

■ Install a ceiling heat lamp so your elder doesn't get chilled when getting out of the bath or shower.

■ Install grab bars in the tub or shower.

■ Install an in-tub bathing chair or a transfer bench on the edge of the tub.

■ Install a long-corded, handheld shower head.

■ Install a nonskid bath mat or decals in the tub or on the shower floor.

■ Replace faucets with lever handles.

■ Install non-skid strips or a firmly anchored mat or carpet on the bathroom floor.

Slips and falls are the single most common cause of bathroom injuries among the elderly, and most of them happen while getting in and out of the tub. That's why the transfer bench and handheld shower is such a convenience. The bather sits on the bench and slides from there into the tub itself; to exit the bath he or she simply reverses the procedure. The bench removes the need for the bather to ever have to stand up on the slippery tub floor. Similarly, a combination of bathing chair and handheld shower head enables your parent to shower while sitting.

Scalds and burns from excessively hot water are also common. Installing levers in place of the more conventional faucets make it far easier for even arthritic fingers to grasp and to control the flow and temperature of water into the bath or shower. This modification can be enhanced when used in conjunction with a transfer bench, which allows your parent to ease into the bath slowly.

How to case out the kitchen

The kitchen also ranks high on the list of potential danger areas for your elder, so check it carefully for hazards. Here, too, slips and falls are common, but there are other safety concerns as well. For example, many elderly have problems with weakened or aching joints that make it difficult to maintain a sure grip on glassware or knives, so cuts are common. And forgetfulness, whether or not it is caused by early-stage dementia, is also a concern: Many kitchen fires are caused when a pot or kettle is left on the stove and forgotten. Here are a few basic changes to consider to make it safer:

- Purchase unbreakable glasses and dishes for everyday use.

- Make certain that any mats or carpeting are securely anchored.

- Install a smoke detector—and make certain that it is kept fully charged.

- Keep a portable fire extinguisher near the stove.

- Make sure that no curtains, towels, or other flammable items are too close to the stove.

- Place bright, easy-to-read labels on the stove dials—and mark the "off" setting clearly.

- Reorganize the cabinets so that all items are easily reached without using a stool.

- Replace stove-top appliances such as tea-kettles with the kind that have an automatic shut-off feature.

- Make certain that oven mitts are within easy reach and are fire resistant.

Timesaver
Fire extinguishers and smoke detectors are of little use if they're not properly recharged, or if the batteries have died. Set aside a single regular maintenance date so you can check all such household safety features and bring them up to speed in one visit.

The rest of the house

While the kitchen and bathroom present particular safety problems, your safety tour shouldn't ignore the rest of the house. Look out for several potential problems:

- **Carpets and rugs.** Are they well-secured? Loose carpeting is a common cause of falls.

- **Electrical cords.** Are they secured against the wall or otherwise tacked down? These, too, can easily cause your elder to trip and fall.

- **Closets.** Are items stored within easy reach? Everything should be stored low enough so that your elder can reach things without standing on a stool or chair.

- **Furniture.** Are the chairs or sofa so low that your elder has trouble getting up? Are there exposed sharp edges that could exacerbate injury in case of a fall? Are there too many items obstructing the major walkways?

- **Lighting.** Is it bright enough that your elder can clearly see where he or she is going? Are the switches within easy reach and logically placed? Are there nightlights in the hallways, bathroom(s), and kitchen?

Many elderly people have difficulty climbing stairs. If that's the case for your parent, consider moving his or her sleeping area to a ground floor. If there is no way to avoid using rooms on the upper floor(s) of the home, make certain there are secure, sturdy handrails. If the home's floor plan includes step-up/step-down features between rooms, install a sloping ramp at those places. If the home has sliding glass doors, affix brightly colored decals at eye height so that your elder can easily tell when the door is closed and avoid a nasty bump or fall.

Bright Idea
If your elder is beginning to have trouble with stairs but the bedroom is on the second floor, consider converting a downstairs room into a sleeping area.

In the bedroom, you might consider replacing the conventional bed with one that has an adjustable mattress, so that your elder has less trouble getting up. A good nightlight here is also an excellent idea. And, it is wise to make certain that there's a telephone extension in the bedroom within easy reach of the bed, just in case of emergencies. You might even consider preprogramming some emergency numbers into its speed-dial feature.

Upstairs and down

Two easily overlooked danger areas are the attic and basement. In many homes, these areas—and the access to them—are left unfinished, with no handrails for the stairs, unfinished flooring, inappropriate or inadequate lighting, and exposed pipes.

The simplest way to remove danger in these areas is to reduce or eliminate the need for your elder to enter them. Unfortunately, that's not always possible—particularly in the basement, where the furnace and fuse box are commonly found. Now's the time to make certain that basic access is rendered safe: Install stair rails or a ramp, and get light switches installed at the top of the stairs (even better, install the switches beside the basement door but within the main portion of the house). Install suspended ceiling tiles to cover exposed pipes and wiring, and make certain that uneven or broken flooring is repaired.

While you're at it, check that the home is adequately weatherized—the elderly are more susceptible to extremes of temperature. Check that the house is properly insulated, that storm windows are installed during cold seasons, and that adequate

Bright Idea
If your elder isn't ready for a walker or wheelchair, but does need assistance moving around, consider getting a special cane such as a quad cane. This can help your elder stabilize himself and move around more easily.

cooling is available during the hot months of the year.

Outside the home

Unofficially...
Here's a plan that benefits both young and old—find a reliable and responsible teen in the neighborhood who is willing to mow your elder's lawn regularly and shovel snow when necessary. Set up a schedule and a system of payment. The same teen may be happy to help with other yard work (raking leaves, for example) or home repair for additional pay, as well.

As elderly people become more frail, the outside world can become a dangerous place. Icy walkways, steep steps, insecure handrails, and inadequate lighting can contribute to a frightening environment and keep your parent indoors against his or her will. Here, again, it's wise to install ramps and sturdy handrails. While you're at it, check to make sure that all garden tools and equipment are stored within easy reach, and that shrubs and trees are pruned so that they don't obstruct the walkway. Make certain that exterior lighting is adequately bright and that the control switch is easily accessible.

If your elder still wants to do yardwork, look into purchasing equipment that may make the tasks easier: a riding mower, electric hedge trimmer or leaf blower, and most certainly a riding snowblower (if you live in the Snowbelt). Even very fit individuals can easily overtax themselves doing some of the heavier outdoor chores.

How to make modifications affordable

Several local and federal agencies, which have recognized that there are real and measurable benefits to the elderly *and* to the community when older people are able to remain at home, have made funding available for use in home modification and repair. Here's a partial list of the resources currently available:

▪ **Farmers Home Administration (FHA):** The FHA provides loans and grants to rural, low-income elders.

▪ **Local Community Development Department:** Some, but not all, municipalities administer block grants for home repair and improvements through their community development departments. These are not specifically earmarked for the elderly, however. Check with the department to find out how to qualify.

- **Low-Income Home Energy Assistance Program (LIHEAP) and Weatherization Assistance Program (WAP):** The U.S. Department of Energy has established these two programs for low-income persons to help subsidize the costs of repairs and modifications that improve the energy efficiency of their homes.

- **Older Americans Act (Title III):** Funds from this act are often available through your local Agency on Aging for use to modify or repair your elder's home.

- **Medicare/Medicaid:** If your physician or healthcare provider prescribes the installation of medically related equipment, your elder may qualify for Medicare or Medicaid assistance to defray the costs.

In addition, if your elder is a homeowner, he or she may qualify for a Home Equity Conversion Mortgage (HECM). This type of mortgage allows your elder to convert the equity value of the home into cash. The bank essentially purchases the home from your elder, but pays for it in regular monthly installments over time until the payments total the value of the home. During the payment period, your elder retains his or her right to remain in the house as usual.

Most resources mentioned here are geared to the homeowner elder, but some are also available to renters. If your elder rents a home, keep in mind that the landlord is required to permit reasonable

Moneysaver
If you or another member of the family is handy, you can install many of the common elderizing appliances in your parent's home yourselves, saving the expense of hiring a contractor. You might even organize a family day of it, calling your siblings in to work on the modifications as a team.

modifications, as long as the tenant assumes responsibility for the expense. This is mandated by the Fair Housing Act of 1988, which requires certain safety features in all dwellings with four or more units built after the law was passed. Those features include many of the safety features discusses previously, as well as wheelchair accessibility, easily reachable electrical outlets and thermostats, and reinforced bathroom walls that support the installation of grab bars.

Calling in reinforcements

As mentioned earlier, more professional home care services exist than ever before, from one-day-a-week cleaning help to live-in companions. You can choose among these professional providers to tailor a combination of services to suit your elder's specific needs.

First, however, you need a clear understanding of those needs. Chapter 3, "Determining the Level of Care Required," discussed the activities of daily living—both basic and instrumental—with which an elderly person may need assistance. The checklist you filled out in that chapter will come in handy now, as you sort through all the home-care options to find those choices best suited to your elder.

Help with instrumental activities

You'll recall that there are two categories of activities of daily living, known as ADLs and IADLs. If your elder needs only instrumental assistance, he or she still handles most of the necessities of daily life well enough on his or her own. Tasks such as heavy housework, or perhaps getting around town (if vision problems preclude driving) might prove more difficult.

These are obviously the easiest services to acquire—there's no special "elder" aspect to them.

Unofficially...
A study conducted by the Seniors Research Group found that over 80 percent of grown children are concerned about their parents' security. When asked what they would do to improve security, about 40 percent of respondents said they would buy a cellular phone, 39 percent said they would like more outdoor lighting around the elder's home, and 37 percent said they would install a home security system. Over a third of respondents would choose a personal emergency response device.

But carefully screen any potential service providers for reliability and quality of performance. Check into whether or not a particular company offers a senior discount to customers over age 65 (62, in some areas). Make certain that your elder and the worker who comes to the house can get along comfortably.

When more basic disabilities are involved

Impairments in the more basic ADLs are a bit more difficult to address. You may consider hiring a home health aide to provide assistance of a more personal nature: bathing and dressing, physical therapy, and administering medications. Here you face two primary concerns:

- Strong credentials and references
- A comfortable rapport between the caregiver and your elder

The need to check credentials and references is obvious: You want someone with the appropriate level of training and experience for the assigned jobs. But the ability of the service provider to establish rapport with your elder is also crucial: It can make a big difference in the quality of your elder's day-to-day life—and in yours, as Evelyn can attest:

> We couldn't fault the aide's abilities—she was well-trained and obviously competent. And I got along with her just fine. Unfortunately, she just rubbed Dad the wrong way. He complained about her attitude and couldn't wait until her visits were over. He refused to cooperate when she tried to bathe and shave him, so I ended up doing half of what we originally hired her to do. Obviously, she had to go.

Bright Idea
Make certain
your elder
participates in
interviewing
healthcare aides
or live-in help.
Your elder is the
only one whose
feel for the
worker's person-
ality really
counts. No mat-
ter how much
you might like
Candidate X, if
your elder feels
more comfortable
with Candidate Y
(and if both
have good cre-
dentials) you've
got to go with
Ms. (or Mr.) Y.

Sometimes you just have to keep trying until you find the right personality match for your elder. In Evelyn's case, it took three tries, but in the last home health aide she—and her father—struck gold. Within a couple of visits, this aide was singing old big band tunes along with Dad during his bath; by the end of the first month, he was introducing her as his "long-lost other daughter." Life for all concerned became decidedly more pleasant. As Evelyn goes on to say:

> It was tedious, having to go through all the interviewing three times over. And sometimes I just lost patience with Dad— I thought he'd just never stop finding fault, no matter who we hired. But you know, it was worth the effort once we saw how much a difference it made to Dad to have someone he was happy with. After all, he's the one who has to see her three times a week.

Make no mistake about it—when your elder has had a lifetime of self-sufficiency and independence, adjusting to the need for regular assistance from a stranger is difficult. Among the quality of life concerns that matter most to the independent elderly is the sense that he (or she) still "rules the roost," to some degree. No matter how many concessions to the aging process he has to make, he is not going to happily accept the intrusion of a caregiver with whom he cannot get along.

These issues become more important when you're seeking a live-in companion. This is a person who'll be with your elder day in and day out. Whoever you hire must suit your elder's personality. Whether Dad prefers someone who's "seen but not heard" or Mom wants a companion who'll join her in a game of Gin Rummy, your best bet is to try to find somebody who'll fit the household well.

Just the facts

- Most older persons prefer to remain in their own homes as they grow older.

- More elders are able to retain home-based independence for far longer than ever before, thanks to the proliferation of home-based eldercare services.

- Discuss with your elder the modifications and repairs that might be needed to make the home safer and more convenient to carry out the normal ADLs.

- Much recent legislation protects your elders right to make necessary modifications to his or her household, even if the home is rented.

- Assistance to cover the costs of home modification is available to low-income—and many middle-income—elders through local, state, and federal programs.

GET THE SCOOP ON...
Living with your elder ▪ Merging households ▪
Addressing caregiving issues ▪ Preparing the
space ▪ Getting help ▪ Scheduling ▪ Checking
out senior and adult care centers

It's a Family Affair

When your parent can no longer maintain fully independent living but does not need (or does not want) to make the move into a long-term care facility, one alternative is to hire a live in companion (discussed in some detail in Chapter 8, "When There's No Place Like Home").

If your elder remains able to care for him- or herself, a second option is to make the move to an assisted-living facility (ALF), as described in Chapter 10. But it is still the case that many people—both among the elderly and among the adult children of the elderly—prefer to keep much of the responsibility for eldercare within the family. In such circumstances, you may decide that your purposes are best served by moving your parent into your own family home.

This chapter discusses the positive and negative aspects of the decision to move your elderly parent into your home. We'll talk about the impact that such a move may have on your parent, on you and your spouse, and on your children. And we'll talk about the things you'll need to do to make such an arrangement work with as little friction and stress as possible—for all concerned.

And parent makes three (or more)

If you fit the typical profile of the primary eldercare giver, you've got a home and family of your own and probably a job that takes you out of the home at least part-time several days a week. You've built up a lifestyle and family routine that feels comfortable and appropriate to your interests, and to the preferences and interests of your spouse and children. This routine and this lifestyle will necessarily undergo some fundamental changes when your elder moves into your household.

Whether or not the changes are positive or negative will depend upon how realistic you are about your abilities to cope with your elder's needs, how flexible you and your family can be about the necessary changes that this choice entails, and how much cooperation you, personally, receive from your spouse, your children, and your elder.

Before you leap...

It's easy to succumb to emotions when deciding if you should move your parent in with you. After all, this is someone who put years into raising you, caring for you, supporting you through the childhood joys and fears, and perhaps putting you through school. Often, adult children of an elderly person feel a profound sense of obligation, a deep desire to personally see to their parent's comfort and safety in the later years. And this is a noble desire. But keep in mind that the choice to move your elder into your household is a difficult one. As much as possible, you need to move beyond your initial emotional

Bright Idea
Before moving your parent into your home, have a family meeting. Explain to your spouse and children why you feel you need to take on this responsibility, and be honest about the inconveniences it may entail. Let everyone, even the youngest, express their concerns. The situation will go more smoothly if everyone feels involved.

reactions to a clear understanding of the task you are really taking on.

While considering how such a choice may affect you and your own family, remember that your parent has preferences, too. Many elders find the idea of moving in with an adult child deeply distressing—they perceive it as "becoming a burden." An elderly person who has, up to now, maintained an independent lifestyle may not relish giving up that autonomy to anyone. Instead, it may seem easier to rely upon outside service providers. After all, relying on an "outsider" places the elder in the non-dependent position of employer, whereas relying on a family member gives no such sense of continued autonomy.

Evaluating the issues

Consider five key areas when you and your elder are thinking about merging households:

1. Are you and your household prepared to cope with the current and likely future needs of your elder?

2. Do you have a home large enough to comfortably accommodate your parent?

3. Is your household appropriately outfitted so that his or her needs and safety can be met?

4. Does your work or school schedule (and the schedules of other family members) leave enough time for you to assist your elder in those aspects of daily living for which he or she needs help?

5. Is your family supportive of the idea that your elder will be moving in? Is your elder happy with the choice?

Watch Out!
When asking your family how they feel about caring for your elder in your home, don't just listen to what they say. Be attentive to unspoken cues of acceptance or resistance as well.

An honest appraisal of your family's ability to handle caring for your elder in your home requires that you carefully consider the following essential questions:

- What level of medical care does your parent require? Can this be provided within the context of your household?

- In case of an emergency, will medical care workers have adequate access to your house and room to help your elder?

- What is your elder's emotional and mental capability at this point? Can your family cope with the problems presented by advanced dementia, if your elder suffers from it?

- How, specifically, must you alter the physical space of your home and its allocation to accommodate your elder's need? Will one of the children have to give up a room? Will your spouse have to turn over a personal space (den or workroom)? Are all family members comfortable with these adjustments?

- What day-to-day changes in your family life will you face—scheduling, meals, and other elements of your routine?

- How much assistance do you expect from other members of the household? Are they prepared to make that kind of commitment to your elder's care?

Can we cope with the medical issues?

If your parent's medical care requirements are profound, you need to be certain that you and your household are prepared to handle them—perhaps with the assistance of home healthcare workers.

While in many cases, families merge households with an elder who has only limited needs for assistance, the direct opposite situation is also common: Caring for an elder in your home is often the last-stage choice for a terminally ill elder who does not wish to spend his or her final days in an institutional environment.

Keep in mind that, in cases of severe physical illness, your family will cope with more than just a major commitment to caregiving tasks—they are also going to have to deal with some very difficult emotional issues. But providing care for your elder through a medical crisis and seeing your elder through the final stages of a terminal illness can also be a profoundly moving and rewarding experience. This is an opportunity to express your love for your elderly parent in a singularly intimate way.

Be as honest as possible with yourself in assessing your limitations—both physically and emotionally. And be very aware of the impact that providing extreme levels of care may have on your spouse and especially your children. (If your children are very young, or very sensitive, they could be frightened by your elder's frail health and physical needs. If that's the case, you may want to have them spend more time with friends or neighbors while you care for your elder.)

Try to be sensitive to everyone's emotional needs, and be prepared to use outside sources of care, support, and therapy when necessary.

Can we handle our elder's mental and emotional problems?

Elders exhibiting dementia can be particularly difficult to fit into a family situation, even—or perhaps especially—when your elder is otherwise quite

Unofficially... Providing in-home care for a terminally ill elder can provide your whole family (including your elder) with a final opportunity to express your deep, abiding love for one another.

Bright Idea
If you realize that the burden of caregiving in your home has gone beyond your capabilities, do not be ashamed to say so. Ask for help from other siblings, and be sure to look into services within your community.

healthy. Family members can feel trapped by the full-time need to supervise an elder suffering from advanced Alzheimer's disease, but relaxing the supervision can lead to serious dangers for the elder and the household (see Chapter 2, "Who Needs Eldercare?" for a discussion of some of the issues involved in caring for an elder with dementia).

Because of the unique stresses of caring for an elder with severe memory disorders, it is critical for you and other family members to have access to support groups and perhaps even therapy. The slow degenerative effects of Alzheimer's disease are particularly heartbreaking to watch. Having adequate practical arrangements in place to provide the necessary care and supervision still won't spare your family the sorrow of having to stand by and watch as the disease runs its course.

Other problems related to deteriorating mental abilities may be much more difficult to address. Sadly, some elders in advanced stages of dementia become abusive, either verbally or physically. You need to carefully assess the ability of your household to cope with this possibility before moving your elder in. There is no shame in acknowledging that you cannot handle some aspects of eldercare on your own. In fact, it is far kinder to your elder if you spend your energies locating a care situation that can appropriately address these needs than to insist on assuming a caregiving burden that you really deep down know that you are unsuited to carry out.

We all need our space!

If you're like most of us, you weren't thinking about moving your parent into your home permanently when you chose your current house or apartment. But what now seems adequate—or even more than adequate—space may well become inadequate when you need to find full-time space for your parent. Take a close look at your home, its physical layout and facilities, and the degree to which you can change your current use patterns to see if you can offer your parent a place in your home.

Keep in mind that you need to consider more than just whether or not you have an extra bedroom available. If your elder has difficulty negotiating stairs and all the bedrooms are on an upper floor, you're looking at a problem from day one unless you have a ground-floor room that can be converted to a sleeping area. There should also be a bathroom located close by. In addition, look at problems of access, both inside your home and outside. Can your parent move safely and easily from one part of the house to another?

The problems presented by all these considerations are of three types:

- Financial, as you incur expenses necessary to refit your home to make it safe for your elder

- Aesthetic, as you make the changes needed to improve accessibility for your elder and any equipment or devices needed

- Personal, as each of your family members make sacrifices to make space for your elder and his or her needs

In Chapter 8, "When There's No Place Like Home," you read about ways to convert your parent's home to an elder-friendly environment. Most of those tips are appropriate for your home as well, now that you've decided to move your elder in with you. That may mean a significant change in your home's appearance and atmosphere. Those tasteful scatter rugs in the hallway must go if your parent is having trouble with balance or needs the support of a cane or a walker. And that charming sunken living room will look a little different once you've installed a ramp.

Will the little things drive you nuts?

The cosmetic changes to your home are only a part of the story—be prepared for some fairly major changes to your lifestyle as well. For example, mealtimes may become more complex if your elder has a restricted diet (for high blood pressure or a troubling cholesterol count). Either the rest of your family foregoes some of their favorite foods, or you're cooking separate meals.

Scheduling can also become a nightmare, especially if you have a highly active family. Can you accommodate your daughter's need for a ride to cheerleading practice at the same time that your elder needs to get to her senior center's bingo game? It's helpful to have more than one member of the family willing to enlist in the household taxi service, but you may also want to look into transportation services available in your community. Contact your local senior center—they can usually give you information on this and other locally available services.

Perhaps the most difficult adjustment to make when merging your elder into your own household is the constant minor abrasions that occur when your ways of doing things conflict with your elder's very different style. We all have our pet peeves, and we all have a tendency to believe that our way of doing things is the right way. And we all find it at least a little difficult to accommodate the habits of others when their way of doing things is not the same as our "right way." Complicating the issue is

Timesaver
For a busy family, coping with everyone's transportation needs can become logistically overwhelming. Press your teenager into service if he or she has a driver's permit, and look into locally available transportation services.

the fact that you have taken on the role of caregiver to your parent, a role your parent once had in regard to you. The role reversal implicit in this new arrangement may be hard for you both.

You, your spouse, your children, and your elder must work out a certain amount of give and take on a lot of little day-to-day points of friction. You will both need to develop a sense of humor when you discover for the umpteenth time that once, again, Mom has commandeered the TV in the family room and is forcing everyone to watch re-runs of her favorite shows from the '70s. Or, although you've asked time and again that you get to read the paper first at breakfast, Dad once again beat you to the door and made off with the Business section before you had a chance to read it. These may sound like small things, but like the slow drip, drip, drip of water torture, lots of these small conflicts can build up into major resentments over time, if you let them.

Watch Out!
Don't let frustrations or resentments build to overwhelming proportions. Deal with problems as they arise, and save yourself from the possibility that they might later blow up beyond all reasonable proportions.

Who knows where the time goes?

For the primary caregiver, perhaps the biggest burden to overcome when your elder moves in with you is finding the time to cope with all your responsibilities. One of the needs your decision was intended to address, most likely, was your parent's need for company, for companionship. In a busy household, your free time to provide that very commodity may be in very short supply. When your mom's need for quiet company coincides with your child's desire that you attend her dance recital, something obviously has to give. And each claimant on your time may feel less than willing to give way to the other(s)—sometimes it really does come down to an insistence that you must choose, with all the potential for hurt feelings and resentment that such a choice implies.

Be prepared to accept that sometimes you are simply going to be unable to please everyone, and accept that your limitations are perfectly normal. Many demands on your time would be felt even if your elder lived elsewhere than in your own home, but the temptation is strongest when you are living *right there* to assume that you must personally attend to all your elder's needs—after all, you're right there, aren't you?

One very simple and extremely important thing to keep in mind is that all the professional home care service providers are equally accessible for your elder whether he is living with you or living on his own. There is no reason not to use such services to take some of the time and work pressure off your shoulders. For example, having a healthcare worker come in a couple of times a week to handle your elder's bathing and grooming will free you to see your children and spouse off to work and school. If you're holding down a full- or part-time job but your elder needs some sort of structure and supervision during the day, consider hiring a daily companion or getting your elder involved in a senior center or adult daycare facility for the hours you must be absent from the home. The simple relief from worry that such a decision can bring is immeasurable.

Whom can you count on?

Be aware right from the start that caregiving to your elder in the context of your family home will require the cooperation and assistance of every family member to make it a smooth and comfortable adjustment. The person who may be least able to make that cooperative effort is, of course, your elder, especially if he or she is severely ill or emotionally impaired. But everyone else in the household will be to some degree or another involved in helping provide care, comfort, and companionship. The good news is that, if they're properly prepared for what to expect when your elder moves in with you, your children and spouse will most likely be very willing to volunteer their time and services to help in the care of Grandma or Grandpa. How can you accomplish that preparation? Here are some simple tips:

- Include every member of the family in the decision-making process before your elder moves in.

- Take care to solicit the opinions and suggestions of every family member, from the youngest to the oldest. Listen to them seriously, and respond as honestly as possible to their concerns.

- Keep communications open—make certain that your spouse and children know that they can talk to you if the eldercare situation is troubling or overwhelming them. Be willing to work with them to cope with these problems.

- Always make it clear that each person's contribution to your elder's care is noticed and appreciated—don't let them feel as if they are being taken for granted.

Acknowledging that this is a difficult choice

A 1995 study of caregivers revealed that the most-reported problems cited by care providers who moved their elders into the family home were all related to the impact that this responsibility had on

Moneysaver
If you can make the time to personally screen and hire health or home care aides, you can often save close to half the fee that the same worker would cost when hired through an agency.

their personal lives. Caregivers reported problems with maintaining adequate standards of health and complained of lack of sleep and loss of privacy. Even though you may be providing the lion's share of the caregiving in your household, keep in mind that to one degree or another all the other members— including, quite often, your elder—are sharing in these stresses. It is important that each one of you have opportunities to escape the stress every once in awhile.

The wonders of respite care

Even though your elder may be largely capable of caring for him- or herself, and even though you feel that you and your household should be able to handle everything, don't rule out getting at least the minimal relief offered by respite care. A simple four-hour break once a week when you and your family members are free to go off and do something just for you can work wonders in keeping everything on an even keel.

Senior and adult care centers

You, your spouse, and your children are not the only people likely to feel stressed when your elder moves into your home. He or she is also making a major adjustment at this time. Your elder has just faced moving out of a home of many years, and by moving in with you has had to acknowledge a loss of at least some degree of independence. The move may also have entailed leaving behind a community of friends and acquaintances and represents a profound disruption of his or her social circle. While your elder no doubt loves you and your family, you can't fulfill all his or her needs for companionship. The good news is that senior centers and adult care centers can be a welcome relief for all concerned.

Watch Out!
You aren't doing anyone— including your elder—any favors by running yourself ragged. Be good to yourself, and you'll have more energy and patience to handle your eldercare responsibilities.

In the terminology employed by the Administration on Aging, *senior centers* are community-run programs that cater to the needs of elders with minimal disabilities. They offer inexpensive hot meals, structured activities, exercise programs specifically geared to the abilities and limitations of the elderly, and, most of all, a social outlet where your elder can get to know others in the same age group. *Adult day centers* (also called elder day services), on the other hand, are programs that cater to elderly people with more pronounced disabilities. Some specialize in providing services to elders with particular problems, such as Alzheimer's disease. Most offer nursing services, and many offer rehabilitative services as well.

Making the right choice for everyone

First and foremost, recognize that over time, every family develops a dynamic of its own—a dynamic based upon the interaction of all the members' styles of relating, personal habits, preferred pastimes, and daily schedules. In the normal course of family life, this dynamic evolves gradually. Most of the time, changes are incremental so that everyone has ample opportunity to adjust as they are introduced. But when you and your previously independent elder merge households, there is little time for adjustment. This is true even in the closest of families.

It may be surprising to learn that the big issues and problems—a sudden medical emergency, for example—aren't what will cause the family stress. It's the day-to-day issues that will wear you and your family down. A crisis gives everyone something to focus on and has a foreseeable ending. The day-to-day, on the other hand, can seem like it will go on

forever. Your family also will be making daily sacrifices—of your time and attention, of their own preferences and choices—that may seem never ending.
Your teenage daughter will wonder why she can't
ever play her heavy metal tapes loudly. Your 10-year-
old will wonder why you keep shushing him near
Grandpa's bedroom. Your spouse will wish you
weren't always soooooo tired.

What about us?

As the primary eldercare provider with your par-
ent(s) living in your home, you may feel caught in a
net of competing sets of needs: your elder's, your
family's, and your own. This is an extraordinarily difficult position to be in. You want to be fair to everyone, and you're likely to try to do it by sacrificing
your own needs.

Whatever this may say about turn-of-the-century
American society, a few things remain true about
family structure:

1. Most eldercare primary caregivers are married
   daughters with families of their own.

2. Parents (aging or otherwise) expect their children to respect their wishes as well as their
   needs.

3. Husbands expect their wives to put a high pri-
   ority on their needs and wishes.

4. Children expect their mothers to see their lives,
   problems, and issues as the absolute center of
   the universe.

And if you, as primary caregiver, are a son rather
than a daughter, you're not exempt from the pressures implicit in these four points. The point is this:
By deciding to undertake caregiving for your elderly
parent(s) in your home, you will find yourself at the

center of competing demands on your time, patience, and understanding. It is not a decision properly made by the faint of heart.

Just the facts

- Families make the decision to move an elder into their homes for a variety of reasons, from a simple desire to provide companionship to offering their elder a chance to spend his or her last days in a family setting.

- Moving your elder into your household will entail sacrifices from all family members, but at the same time it can be the most rewarding eldercare choice you can make.

- Every member of your household should be consulted before actually merging your elder into your home. If all members are part of the decision, they will more likely be willing to be part of the process.

- Keeping communications open with all members of your household, from the youngest to your elder, will go a long way toward alleviating any adjustment problems you will face.

GET THE SCOOP ON...
Who chooses assisted living? ▪ Facilities ▪
Services ▪ Costs ▪ When you need to make
a change

Assisted-Living Facilities

Chapter 10

A ssisted living is relatively new in the range of eldercare options. Rarely available as recently as the 1980s, it is now one of the fastest-growing housing options for elders. Assisted-living facilities (ALFs) combine housing, supportive services (such as meals), and some access to onsite healthcare. They provide access to emergency call assistance and may also provide transportation. They also generally ensure numerous opportunities for residents to socialize with other residents in the building or complex.

ALFs are important because they promote continued independence for the elderly—while preventing inappropriate institutionalization—by meeting residents' needs for support and assistance in one or more activities of daily living. These facilities are known by many names: personal care homes, sheltered housing, catered living, board and care, and domiciliary care.

Who lives in ALFs

One impetus for the growth in popularity of ALFs is the surge of growth in the over-85 population. As you learned in Chapter 1, "The Growing Need for Eldercare," in 1990 this group numbered approximately 3 million. By 1996, that number had increased to 3.7 million, and it is expected to increase by as much as 32 percent between the years 2000 and 2010.

Unofficially
According to the July 1997 issue of *American Demographics*, assisted living has become a $12 billion to $15 billion industry—it's expected to increase to more than $20 billion by the year 2020.

Why ALFs have grown in popularity

As stated in Chapter 1, the burgeoning population of the very elderly is generally far healthier for far longer than in earlier decades. But the elderly are frequently no longer capable of handling completely independent living. In the past, the choices available to such people were to live with one of their adult children—usually a daughter who was at home full-time—or to move into a nursing home.

But these days, more of those adult daughters (or daughters-in-law) are working full-time. Today far fewer families can afford to do without a second paycheck, so fewer families have members available to take on eldercare in addition to their other responsibilities. At the same time that this change in American society has occurred, however, the costs of full-service nursing homes have increased. What's more, many elders who *could* afford to live in a nursing home are themselves resistant to the idea when their care needs are not yet extreme—they prefer to retain at least some degree of independence for as long as they can.

The promise of independence

Assisted-living facilities make that dream of continued independence possible for far longer than most other alternatives can. By combining private residential units with an in-house caregiving staff and other amenities, they grant elderly residents a greater degree of freedom than most other eldercare options can provide.

Enter the ALF

Assisted-living arrangements vary widely in size and in the services and amenities they offer. A resident might have a studio-like apartment or a full suite of rooms. Facilities range from high-rise residential complexes to smaller-scale buildings, such as a converted Victorian home or a renovated schoolhouse. No standard "one-size fits all" plan exists for these facilities.

Basic features of an ALF

Residents in this type of facility usually maintain a relatively high degree of independence and privacy. They generally have their own phones, many have at least minimal private cooking facilities, and residents are usually free to entertain guests and visitors just as they would in a private apartment situation.

The principal difference between ALFs and private apartments is that in an ALF, staff members regularly monitor the residents' status and provide assistance with basic living tasks and medical care. A special feature is the availability of emergency assistance on a 24-hour basis: An emergency button within each apartment summons assistance.

Some senior living complexes combine assisted-living facilities with *independent-living units*. This latter term generally is used to refer to any senior housing situation that provides no specialized service or staff intervention. People in independent-living facilities are assumed to be in no need of

Watch Out!
Because there are no established standards for ALFs, they can vary widely in quality and in services provided. Make certain that you carefully research any facility offering assisted-living services before you sign a lease or purchase a unit.

regular assistance, and to be capable of handling their daily tasks on their own. When independent-living facilities are combined with ALFs in a single complex, a resident who enters as an independent-living tenant may usually transfer over to an ALF unit should his or her abilities become limited. Thus, there is less disruption in the tenant's life, regardless of how his or her eldercare needs change.

Qualifications for life in an ALF

The Assisted Living Federation of America (ALFA), a trade association in Fairfax, Virginia, profiles the average assisted-living resident as follows:

- Early to mid-80s

- Female

- Divorced or widowed

- Suffering from some mildly disabling disorder (mental or physical), but still capable of performing many of the tasks of daily living on her own

People usually enter assisted-living facilities directly from their own homes or after living for a time in the home of one of their children, where they had maintained a largely independent lifestyle. Most ALFs require that an incoming tenant demonstrate some minimal level of independence when it comes to performing the tasks of daily living. At present, no formal standards are set for use by all ALFs when screening residents.

ALF life: pros and cons

For many families, assisted-living facilities provide a welcome alternative to the options of taking full responsibility for an elder in their own home or having their elder admitted to a nursing home. Elders

Bright Idea
Each state regulates and licenses assisted-living facilities according to its own standards—there are no federal licensing guidelines. Check with your state's Agency for the Aging to find out what the minimum standards are in your state before you go in to appraise a facility.

favor ALFs too: Most elders want to remain as independent and active as possible, for as long as possible. They do not relish the loss of personal autonomy that is implicit in nursing home care. Here's how eldercare's three major residential options compare to one another:

TABLE 10.1: COMPARISON OF RESIDENTIAL CARE SERVICES BY TYPE

Services Provided	Private Apartments/ Independent- Living Facilities	Assisted- Living Facilities	Nursing Homes
Meals	No	Yes	Yes
Panic button	No	Yes	Yes
Privacy	Yes	Yes	Limited
Planned activities	No	Yes	Usually yes
Pets	Yes	Some- times	Rarely
Transportation	No	Yes	Yes
Visitors at any time	Yes	Yes	No
Nurse available	No	Yes	Yes
Help with dressing and bathing	No	Yes	Yes

← Note! Data in this table reflects the services encountered in a *representative* sample of each residential type. Not all facilities in each category will conform exactly to this list of attributes.

The pros of an ALF

ALFs combine a number of positive features in a residential setting:

- Continued independence for the elder
- A safety net of onsite services
- Access to a social life
- Access to offsite opportunities and services

The ALF safety net. As Table 10.1 illustrates, the assisted-living option combines much of the autonomy of independent living with a staff-and-services safety net for the frail but still largely competent elderly. That is the ALF's strong suit.

Social life, ALF-style. In addition to offering an opportunity for continued independence, most assisted-living facilities help their residents avoid one of the more pernicious problems of the elderly: isolation. Older people frequently experiencing less mobility—failing eyesight may mean they can't drive the car anymore, and if they live in areas with limited public transportation options, they can find that their social lives become constrained against their will. Most ALFs have a regular program of lectures, classes, and other events that give residents a reason to get out of their rooms and socialize. These facilities also provide dining facilities—in either a cafeteria or restaurant-style setting—that brings the residents together at mealtimes.

Offsite access. Among the many services offered by assisted-living facilities, one key element is access to transportation offsite—to doctor's appointments, for shopping trips, and even to local events of interest. Many ALFs provide transportation through their own staff (if so, be sure to check the qualifications required of their drivers), while many others contract with a transportation service to provide vans or buses on a regular schedule.

From the family's viewpoint, ALFs can contribute wonderfully to peace of mind. If you've been careful in your evaluation of the facilities available, you will know that the services and staff that your elder needs are there. You will know that your elder has the opportunity to meet and interact with others on a regular basis. And you will know that your elder

Unofficially...
The Eldercare Locator Service (800-677-1116) can provide you with free information on the Agency on Aging nearest you. The agency can then give you information on the ALFs in your area.

has not had to trade in autonomy for safety, whereas before such a trade-off was absolutely necessary.

The cons of an ALF

If your elder is capable of some degree of independence, ALFs are, in theory, one of the best options available. But there are some negatives to consider as well.

First, no broad protections are in place to guarantee you a minimal level of service. You can get promises, promises, promises—but will the facility actually deliver? Each state approaches the licensing of these facilities differently: Some don't require licensing at all, and most that *do* require certification or licensing lack sufficient investigative personnel on staff to ensure that state regulations are followed.

A second negative to ALFs is their cost—and this concern has two aspects. First, assisted-living facilities can be very expensive, but the price is generally not a foolproof indicator of the quality of service that will be provided. This means that you have to research the ALFs in your area carefully and spend time examining their various fee schedules. Later in this chapter, you'll learn how to evaluate an ALF in detail—right now, just be aware that the best protection for yourself and your elder is to take time to compare available ALFs carefully before committing to any fees.

The second aspect of the cost-related drawback to ALFs is that, in the majority of states, Medicaid and other insurance carriers do not cover the cost. Before you sign your elder up for admittance to an ALF, look carefully at the fees and how you plan to pay them. (Later in this chapter, we'll take up the issue of fees and how much services typically cost.)

Bright Idea
As you begin your research into eldercare facilities in your area, keep a log of every site you investigate. Make standard columns covering the services you need and the fee (or fees) required. In this way you'll be able to make a clear comparison among the facilities you visit so that your final decision will be that much easier to make.

Finally, keep in mind that ALFs are often *not* the final stage in your eldercare decision-making concerns. If your elder becomes incapable of even minimally maintaining independent living, he or she may cease to qualify for residence in the facility. At that point, you'll be looking into other forms of eldercare that provide greater services at perhaps significantly greater cost. At that point, you may find that your resources—and those of your elder—are stretched to the breaking point.

Carefully screen every ALF you're considering. It's important to choose a good facility with experienced management and staff, with fees that are well in line with the services offered—and that are also well within your budget.

Some relief on the way

The good news is that some insurers are beginning to provide at least limited coverage for ALFs. Some states also allow for Medicaid *waivers*—permission from the federal government to use some Medicaid funds for ALFs in certain low-income situations. As of this writing, 31 states offer (or have applied to the federal government for permission to offer) some form of Medicaid coverage for ALFs. The states that do not yet participate in such a program are listed here:

- Alabama
- Arkansas
- California
- Connecticut
- Kentucky
- Idaho
- Indiana

- Michigan
- Mississippi
- Nebraska
- New Hampshire
- Ohio
- Oklahoma

- Pennsylvania
- South Carolina
- Tennessee
- Utah
- West Virginia
- Wyoming

The first steps in choosing an ALF

Once you and your elder have determined that assisted living is the appropriate choice (at least in theory), it's time to start looking at the actual facilities in your area. This crucial research involves determining the specific services and amenities your elder requires, developing a list of the ALFs to examine, comparing the facilities in terms of ser vices offered and general facility quality, and comparing fees. Let's take these points one at a time.

Determine the services and amenities you need

Mom has always had a cat, and she can't imagine life without one. Dad's starting to have trouble managing his shaver on his own. Maybe your elder has some food allergies that need to be accommodated. Then there's the elder who has always been socially outgoing, but who recently has become isolated as his or her mobility has been reduced. All these, and more, are issues you need to consider when you're looking for the right ALF for your elder. Certainly, there are other concerns —issues of cost and safety, just to name two very important ones. But at this preliminary stage, when your elder may be facing the major life-upheaval that moving into a new home represents, it's good to take time out to get a sense of what he or she personally wants in a residential setting.

You'll notice that some of the issues listed here are practical: Can the facility accommodate special meal plans, if required? Does it offer daily assistance in simple tasks that might now be beyond your elder's abilities? Some issues can be termed "quality of life" issues—those that relate to maintaining practices or property that provide comfort or pleasure to your elder, such as keeping a pet or having

Bright Idea
It's hard for people to leave home and a way of life they've enjoyed for many years. By identifying the things that would make your elder more comfortable with the idea of moving, you will ease his or her fears and make the whole process easier on both of you.

access to a broad social circle. But *all* have to do with the personal experience your elder will enjoy in his or her new living situation.

Keep in mind that ALFs vary across the board in the degree to which they can accommodate personal preferences and requirements of their residents. Before you start making your list of ALFs to visit, sit down with your elder and list the items you consider minimally necessary in any ALF you choose. Here are a few questions to get that discussion off the ground:

1. Does your elder wish to keep a pet?

2. Does your elder wish to keep some of his or her personal furnishings?

3. How important to your elder is the opportunity to attend social or educational events?

4. Does your elder have specific meal requirements? What about food allergies to be accommodated, or personal or religious dietary requirements that must be met?

5. Are there activities of daily living (ADLs and IADLs) with which your elder needs help? (See Chapter 2, "Who Needs Eldercare?," for a discussion of activities of daily living and the assistance that elders often require for them).

The answers to all of these questions—and any others that might arise during discussion with your elder—should be brought out into the open *before* you begin the full-scale search for ALFs in your area; they'll give you your basic list of requirements that the facility you choose must meet. After all, your elder's happiness and comfort in his or her new home are issues that are as important as safety.

Consider the costs

As mentioned earlier, ALFs can be expensive—depending on the state in which you live, Medicaid also may not cover any of your costs. The majority of fees paid to assisted-living facilities come from private sources; some estimates put the figure at 90 percent. The remainder is usually covered by the elder's retirement checks and by Social Security.

Before you can choose a good facility for your elder, you need to work out a clear, realistic budget. Chapter 6, "Organizing Your Elder's Finances," takes you through the steps you need to follow to organize your elder's financial information so that you can get a clear picture of the resources available for covering these costs. Now you need to have an idea of just where that money will be expended if you select the ALF option.

Unofficially... Some states provide rent or service subsidies, but reimbursement rates are often too low to assist elders who have relatively high service needs. Contact your Social Security and Medicaid offices to find out if they can help.

Check out the entrance and rental fees

The monthly rental fee you may initially be quoted might tell only a small part of the financial story. Many ALFs require a substantial up-front payment—often called an *entrance fee*—which is usually nonrefundable. One southwest Florida facility, for example, charges a whopping $78,000 nonrefundable entrance fee to secure a standard one-bedroom unit—the deluxe one-bedroom calls for $110,000 up-front. In addition, this facility imposes a monthly service fee of $1,500 on all residents.

That up-front fee can be a major issue for you and your elder, particularly if there is a possibility that a further move may be needed in the future. If the facility you're currently considering has no means of accommodating a decline in your elder's ability to manage at normal levels of ALF care, you may be looking at another move further down the

Bright Idea
Many facilities offer financing for the entrance fee. Check into this possibility at every site you investigate— such options vary radically from site to site. A good financing agreement with a reasonable interest rate may be the deciding factor in your choice of ALF.

line. Entrance fees are rarely refundable, but they buy you no equity in the ALF unit, so any fees or charges imposed by a second facility may impose severe financial hardship on you and your family.

At your service—for a price

In addition to rent and those up-front or entrance fees, many ALFs impose monthly charges sometimes referred to as fees for services. These fees can vary widely depending upon where you live and even across individual facilities in a single community. Other facilities may impose charges for services only on a per-use basis. Look closely at any fee schedule provided by the ALF: Compare fees you're quoted with the services covered by the charge. Two similar-looking residential complexes may have widely different fee structures.

Making a list and checking it twice

Now that you've discussed general questions and issues that your elder wants —and once you have calculated the budget—it's time to do your research: Generate a list of the ALFs in your area.

A good place to start developing your list of ALFs is to contact the Eldercare Locator, published by the Administration on Aging and available free. To order a copy, call 800-677-1116. The Locator will provide you with the contact information for the Agency on Aging in your state. The next step is to check with your state and city offices for the aging (see Appendix B) and the agency responsible for licensing ALFs in your state.

Beyond the governmental resources, you might consider contacting the Assisted Living Federation of America, which publishes information on all aspects of the ALF industry, and the American

Association of Retired Persons (AARP). Both of these have informational Web sites that you might visit as well. (Appendix B lists contact information on these and other sources of information on ALFs and other eldercare options.)

Record your research

Once you've pulled together a basic list of ALFs to consider, you can begin trimming it down. Organize a log or other recording form so that you can keep track of the results of your investigation. Whether you're more comfortable using a notebook or a spreadsheet-style program on your computer, be sure to establish standard questions that are answered at every site you consider. Such questions should include these:

- All the issues that you settled upon in your discussion with your elder about his or her personal preferences (such as policies on keeping pets, the possibility of bringing personal property, and so on)

- General characteristics of the facility itself:

  Does the residence have a home-like atmosphere?

  Does it offer personalized healthcare services?

  Does the staff encourage independence among residents while remaining available to provide service as needed?

  Is the location convenient enough to family and friends to allow for frequent visits?

  Is there an emergency call system installed?

  Is there any arrangement to accommodate your elder when independent living is no longer an option?

Unofficially...
As of the mid-1990s, an estimated 1 million Americans lived in the approximately 30,000 assisted-living communities nationwide.

- Specific fees charged by the facility:

  Entrance fee

  Monthly rent

  Monthly service charge (if not included in rent)

  Additional fees (enumerate the individual fees, which may include meals, daily dressing and grooming assistance, regular status checks, supervision of medication, laundry service, and transportation offsite, among others)

- Specific services provided by the facility

Check carefully and do plenty of comparison shopping. Be careful not to compare apples to oranges, either. One facility may charge a high initial fee or monthly rent but might provide within that charge three meals a day, while a less expensive facility may offer fewer meals or charge for them individually. Find out exactly what is included in the price.

Take a closer look

With your list of queries, you're ready to start calling around to get general answers to your questions about the facilities in your region. Once you've seen what's available, whittle your list down to a manageable number—manageable, that is, for you to start planning personal visits to the sites you're considering. Of course, you may make an appointment to view the facility, but also ask if you can drop by. A facility that bristles at the suggestion may have problems they're anxious to hide.

Similarly, when you take a scheduled tour, ask to see rooms that are not part of the regular tour route. For example, most facilities will happily show off their dining area but may not volunteer to let you go backstage to the kitchen. Many have model rooms or apartments to show prospective residents—ask if you can see one that's currently occupied.

The Assisted Living Federation of America recommends that you check the following specific items when investigating any ALF:

▪ Is the floor plan easy to follow?

▪ Can doorways, hallways, and rooms accommodate wheelchairs and walkers?

▪ Are elevators and ramps available for residents who can't manage stairs?

▪ Are the cupboards and shelves in each unit easy to reach?

▪ Are the floors non-skid and the carpets firmly tacked down?

▪ Does the residence have good natural and artificial lighting?

▪ Is the residence clean and free of odors?

▪ Is the facility (and individual units) appropriately heated in winter and cooled in summer?

▪ Are there handrails installed along the hallways and grab bars installed in the bathrooms of the individual units?

▪ Are there clear plans in place in case of fire or other emergency? Are exits clearly marked, and will residents be escorted to safety?

In addition to these concerns, make a point of checking into the facility's financial condition. Some less than reputable individuals have entered the market hoping to benefit from the huge growth in demand for eldercare services, only to go bankrupt shortly thereafter—taking their residents' life

Bright Idea
When visiting an ALF, take a moment to talk to some of the staff, and observe how they interact with current residents. You may be able to get a sense of the level of compassion and commitment that these people who will be with your elder daily have toward their charges.

savings with them. Try to find out what earlier residents paid to determine if there's a great disparity between charges then and charges today. According to a 1997 article in *Accounting Today*, it's important to be "wary of [ALFs] that undercharged early residents and must make up the difference from their most recent residents."

Check out the contract

Make sure you understand all the terms of the contract before you sign on the dotted line. Here, too, the Assisted Living Federation has some useful suggestions:

- Is there a written plan for the care of the resident?

- Does the residence have a process for assessing the resident's need for services, and are those needs periodically reevaluated?

- Is the residence prepared to work with the family and the physician of the resident to best meet the resident's needs?

- When may a contract be terminated? For what reasons? At termination, what is the refund policy?

- Are government, private, or corporate programs available to help cover the costs of services?

- Is staff available to meet scheduled and unscheduled needs?

Further research resources

Several public and private agencies make informational brochures available to the public. Here's a partial list of such agencies and the titles of some of their ALF-related publications:

American Association of Retired Persons
attn: Fulfillment Department
601 E. Street NW
Washington, D.C. 20049

    A Home Away From Home (Free)

American Association of Homes and Services for the Aging
901 E. Street NW, Suite 500
Washington, D.C. 20004-2037

    Assisted Living: Offering Supportive Care for the Older Adult (First copy free, $15 for 100 copies)

    Non-Profit Housing and Care Options for Older People (First copy free, $15 for 100 copies)

Assisted Living Facilities Association of America
9401 Lee Highway, Suite 402
Fairfax, VA 22031

    Consumer Guide and *National Directory of Assisted Living Residences* (Write for price)

The Assisted Living Facilities Association listed here is a for-profit trade organization and is therefore likely to boost its appraisal of the industry, as is evident in their video. However, the directory this organization publishes is extremely useful and frequently updated.

Just the facts

- ALFs are a fast-growing branch of the eldercare industry designed to bridge the needs gap between complete independent living and full-service institutionalized care.

- As yet, no consistent government standards regulate ALFs or the menu of services that they should provide.

Watch Out!
While many ALFs are well-run, others may fail to provide appropriate levels of service for residents. Proponents for the industry are currently resisting regulation of the industry, claiming that more rules would limit the independence they can offer residents. Critics want standards set for staff training and security.

- ALFs are important for the role they play in promoting independence among the elderly by meeting their residents' support needs.

- ALF care is expensive, and fees vary widely across the industry.

- Some ALFs offer care with an eye to the longer term and have procedures in place by which a resident who can no longer live alone may move to more intensive full-service care.

GET THE SCOOP ON...
Full-care facilities ▪ Services and staff ▪
Costs and contracts ▪ Emotional issues

Chapter 11

When Long-Term Care Is Needed

Many compelling reasons exist for choosing a long-term care facility—popularly called a nursing home—for your elder. It is difficult for most of us, however, to face the prospect of turning our parent's care over to "strangers." The choice is made even more difficult because of the reputation that nursing homes have had in the past—as unpleasant, dingy places with an inattentive staff, at best. While some facilities out there still are more interested in making money than in providing care, many nursing homes provide good to excellent care. In this chapter, we'll explore the reasons for choosing nursing home care, the services that they provide, and the current state of the industry.

The nursing home option

With increasing age, many elders who initially choose to age in place—to remain in their lifelong home and bring in part-time or even live-in help—eventually come to recognize that this is no longer a

Unofficially...
The likelihood of needing nursing home care increases dramatically with age: Only 1 percent of all elders between ages 65 and 74 needed full-service care, compared to 5 percent for elders between ages 75 and 84, and 15 percent for all elders age 85 and older.

viable option. If the elder is still to some degree self-sufficient, an ALF may be the next choice (see Chapter 10, "Assisted-Living Facilities"). But if the care-related problems escalate to the point that full custodial care is required, a much more intensive—although intrusive—eldercare arrangement may be necessary. In this situation, unless there is a member of the family with the expertise and the available time to make eldercare his or her full-time job, the nursing home becomes a probable best option.

When to make the move

At one time, nursing home care was the only option available for an elder who needed daily assistance or nursing care that family members could not provide. With the development of ALFs and the expansion of home-based care services, however, nursing homes have become the choice of last resort. Today they are considered appropriate only for elders who need intense daily therapy or 24-hour nursing care, who present severe behavioral or mental problems, or who have advanced Alzheimer's disease.

When your elder's need for care has become intense, your first impulse may be to move him or her into your home. Many elders strongly resist the concept of entering a nursing home, and many adult children swear that they will do all they can to avoid that option. But the time may come when a nursing home is your only viable option, however much you wish to avoid it. Once your elder's condition has significantly deteriorated to the point that intense care is required, how do you know that a nursing home is the appropriate choice? A lot of the decision must be based on your own household's ability to cope with your elder's escalating needs.

Here are some indicators that you may need to consider a nursing home for your parent:

▪ Your own health is deteriorating, to the point that much of your current load of caregiving duties now falls beyond your abilities.

▪ Your ability to handle the stress and emotional burdens of caregiving has diminished, so you find yourself losing your patience and your temper when dealing with your parent.

▪ You can no longer afford the many expenses associated with caring for your parent at home.

▪ Your current caregiving arrangement is placing the safety of your household in jeopardy because your elder's abilities have deteriorated too far for you to cope with them safely.

▪ Your elder's needs have become so time-consuming that you can no longer meet them and also fulfill your other obligations to work and family.

When your own health is compromised

Some primary caregivers are themselves technically classifiable as elderly—the caretaking children of elders over the age of 85 may be well into their 60s and may be coping with declining health themselves. But you don't need to be aging to find yourself facing significant health problems. If up to now you have been the primary caretaker for an increasingly fragile or ailing elder, the stress of your caregiving role may *itself* contribute to a decline in your health.

Your health is important, and one factor that may compromise it is the ongoing stress of caring for your elder. Some signs that your caregiving

Watch Out!
Don't make
promises you
can't be sure you
can keep—that's
a sure-fire recipe
for unnecessary
guilt. Don't
promise your
elder that you'll
"never" consider
a nursing home.
There is no guar-
antee that cir-
cumstances
beyond your con-
trol won't make
you have to
break your word.

burden is seriously impacting your own health and well-being include these:

- Insomnia or other sleep disorders that persist for a month or more

- Unintended weight loss of more than 20 pounds

- An unaccustomed problem with significant weight gain, and an inability to regain normal control of your weight

- The sudden onset or intensification of chronic physical complaints, such as back pain

- An aggravation of existing physical conditions, such as arthritis

All these are indicators that your caregiving burden may now exceed your ability to carry out your responsibilities. On their own, these problems may not be enough to make the nursing home option necessary—availing yourself of home-care services may lighten your load enough to carry on. But if you find your own health continues to deteriorate even with outside assistance, a nursing home may be the next step for you to take.

When the emotional stress is more than you can handle

The responsibility of providing eldercare can place extraordinary stress on your own emotional stability. Watch out for signs of depression—it can manifest itself in a variety of ways. If you find yourself resuming a long-conquered smoking habit or relying too much on alcohol to unwind, you may be in over your head. In addition, if you find yourself unable to work up an interest in previously pleasurable activities, or are withdrawing from your normal network of friends and relatives, watch out. These also can be strong indictors of depression.

But depression isn't the only emotional problem that caregivers may face when the task of eldercare has exceeded their abilities. You may find that the constant stress of caretaking manifests itself in mood swings, episodes of uncontrollable temper, and other destructive behaviors. In Chapter 5, "Strategies for Coping," you'll find a discussion of resources and techniques to help you cope, but sometimes the stress can become unmanageable. Again, if your elder's condition requires full-time care and observation, a nursing home might be your only option.

When you can't afford to continue home-based caregiving

People often think that caring for an elder at home is certain to be less expensive than high-priced nursing home care. True, the average cost for a year's stay in a nursing home runs high—$45,000 per year in 1997—but home care can be very expensive as well. Here's just a partial list of the expenses you may be adding to your normal family budget when you assume the care of an elder with significant medical and emotional problems:

▪ Adult diapers

▪ Medications (both prescribed and over-the-counter)

▪ Increased laundry and dry-cleaning costs

▪ Special foods to accommodate your elder's dietary needs

▪ Costs of "elderizing" the home (though some of these may be covered by Medicare and Medicaid)

▪ Costs of professional services (visiting nurses, home health aids, household help)

Unofficially...
Nursing home contracts may request you to sign as the responsible party for your elder, implying that you assume liability for your elder's bills. This is unenforceable—no nursing home can require that a resident's family or friends take on the obligation to pay the bills. It is against the law.

When your own out-of-pocket costs exceed your ability to pay, a nursing home may indeed become your only option. It may be easier to find third-party support for nursing home costs through federal, state, or local programs than it would be to find coverage for providing the same level of care at home.

When your elder presents a danger to the rest of the household

Dementia and Alzheimer's disease are two very serious conditions that afflict the aging, and each carries a potential for danger for the elder and other family members. In the case of dementia, on rare occasions an elder can become violent and physically abusive. Medication can sometimes help, but if the situation continues, you or other members of your household may be at risk for injury.

In addition, individuals suffering from dementia or Alzheimer's disease may be forgetful or so out of touch with reality that your family runs a significant risk of dangerous accidents—kitchen fires, for example. Of course, there is also the danger that they may present to their *own* safety and well-being, if you and your family can't watch over them. However difficult it may be to accept, situations such as these are beyond most families' capacity to cope.

When your parent's needs require more time and care than your family can provide

When your elder's health deteriorates to the point of needing constant, round-the-clock care, you and your family may no longer be able to handle the situation on your own. Unless you have someone able to act as full-time caregiver (a circumstance many families cannot afford), or if you have a very efficiently organized schedule and several family members share caregiving responsibilities, your elder may need to be admitted to a full-service facility.

Steps in selecting a facility

But even when all other alternatives are clearly not workable, choosing the nursing home option is difficult for many elderly and their children. The image of the sterile, uncaring institution of past decades dies hard, sometimes with good reason. A 1997 report in *Time* magazine, for example, cited several nursing homes as being so inadequate that several patients died of neglect. Too many institutions still are in the business solely to make money and keep their profits safe by cutting back on services and medical attention.

On the other hand, the number of *good* nursing homes has increased, and the oversight of nursing home operations has improved dramatically since the mid-1980s. You aren't condemning your parent to a Dickensian horror when you choose a nursing home—unless you choose a bad one. That means doing your homework and personally inspecting the facility before you even think about signing in your elder.

Getting started

Finding an appropriate nursing home is not easy. In 1945, fewer than 200,000 elderly Americans lived in nursing homes. By 1970, that number had increased to about a million. Today, that figure has risen to approximately 1.5 million. The dramatic increase in the need for nursing home beds has not been met with a similar rise in the number of nursing home facilities—in 1985, there were 19,100 nursing homes nationwide. This number fell to 16,700 by 1995.

Unofficially...
Nursing homes often change hands and what was once a well managed facility can go downhill. You need to visit often and note if the quality starts to decline. If your elder is not getting the quality of care she once received, you may want to move her to a different nursing home.

Bright Idea
Ask around for word-of-mouth recommendations of facilities in your area. The personal experience of real residents and their families may provide much useful information that you'll never get from an official report.

When looking for a nursing home, it's best to start with the basics. Put together a list of local facilities, drawing on the listings in your Yellow Pages, the advice of your doctor and local hospitals, and by contacting the Area Agency for Aging (AAA) nearest you. The AAA is a federally run agency charged with providing all sorts of information, including the names and locations of certified nursing homes. You can track down your AAA by calling the Eldercare Locator (800-677-1116), an organization affiliated with the federal Administration on Aging.

Refining the research

Once you've made your list of possible facilities, gather some preliminary information to whittle it down to manageable size before you start scheduling visits. One good way to do so is to contact your state ombudsman (see Appendix B for the Ombudsman's Office phone numbers by state). This office will be able to give you the latest information on nursing homes in the state. You don't want to overlook any complaints or violations charged against a facility.

Next, call ahead. While the numbers of people in nursing homes have increased dramatically, the number of available facilities have decreased. There are long waiting lists for beds in many homes, so you're wise to make your inquiries well before your elder actually needs to be admitted. When you make initial calls, ask for brochures and other materials that you can review prior to making an actual visit. In that preliminary information packet, request that a sample menu or two be included.

How to evaluate the facility

Positive official evaluations and doctors' recommendations can tell you only part of the story when it comes to deciding on a nursing home. After all, you're not admitting your elder for a short-term medical treatment here—this may well be where she lives out the remainder of her life. It is essential that you physically inspect any nursing home on your list. Check out the staff, the residents, and the overall feel of the place.

Sizing up the staff

Most people are easily impressed by the overall appearance of a nursing home facility—beautiful furnishings, landscaped grounds, handsome physical appointments can be very impressive. But in the end, the single most important factor by which you should judge a nursing home is its staff.

The healthcare professionals and support service workers are the people who will be interacting with your elder on a daily basis. Therefore, it is extremely important that you meet with as many of them as possible during your first visits to the facility prior to applying for admittance. It is not enough to schedule a formal interview in the administrator's office—you should see how the staff interacts with current residents. Arrange a drop-in visit, during which you can observe the following:

▪ Does the medical personnel appear to respond quickly and compassionately to residents' needs?

▪ Are there aides available, on call, for such basic services as wheeling a chair-bound resident to the bathroom or to a recreational area on request?

▪ Are the residents afforded some degree of privacy? Nursing homes generally care for elderly with significant health problems, so the degree of privacy available will be less than in a more

Watch Out!
Listen to how staff members refer to residents. If it's "Bed 3" instead of "Mr. Jones," it's likely that the staff doesn't take a personal interest in patient care. That may be efficient, but it makes for an unpleasant living experience for any resident of the facility.

independent living situation, if for no other reason than that the medical staff may need to
observe their patients. But screens should be
available, and residents should be allowed the
basics of personal privacy—the right to wear
robes when in public spaces or hallways.

■ Do most of the residents appear alert? Some
  facilities use medications to control their
  patients even when no medical condition exists
  to justify the use of drugs.

■ Do staff members speak calmly and respectfully
  to the residents? Do they call them by name?

Make a point of speaking with the director of
nursing—this is the person who establishes the tone
and morale of the rest of the staff. An effective director of nursing can retain employees—high
employee turnover plagues many nursing home
facilities and is one major cause of poor or inattentive care for the residents. If every staff member you
speak to is relatively new on the job (worked there
for a year or less), you should be concerned.

Using your common sense(s)

Next in importance after the staff, but directly
related to staff quality, is the overall fitness of the
nursing home's physical plant. You don't need to do
a microscopic examination of the place to get a
good idea of its level of physical upkeep and safety—
you can do some simple sensory observations to get
a sense of how well the place is cared for. Here's
what to watch out for:

■ **The smell test**. When you walk through the
  door, are you assaulted by an overpowering
  odor of urine? Because many of the elderly have
  problems with incontinence, this is a common

housekeeping problem for nursing homes. A good one has adequate staff to handle the necessarily high volume of laundry and clean-up to keep this problem at bay. An overpowering odor of disinfectant, however, is not a good sign—it may mean that actual cleaning is being neglected and that the disinfectant is being used to mask, not clean, the problem.

▪ **The visual test.** Appearance counts. Institutional colors and a lack of even minimal decoration can make for a depressing living situation. Look for good lighting, bright curtains, and at least minimal attention to decor. Keep an eye out for evidence of efficient housekeeping—is the furniture kept in good repair and dust-free?

▪ **The listen test.** Residents—your parent included—have a right to quiet and calm surroundings. There should be a visitors' lounge where residents can entertain family, as well as a recreational area away from the patients' rooms where television, radio, and other noisier activities can be enjoyed without disturbing other residents.

▪ **Dietary concerns.** When you drop in for your visit, aim for a meal time—preferably dinner—and inspect a meal tray or two. Look at food quality, portion size, and whether or not specific dietary instructions are being followed. Observe the staff who are feeding patients who need assistance—are they rushed or impersonal? Neither behavior is appropriate. Drop into the kitchen to check it for cleanliness.

▪ **Safety check.** Look for obvious—and not so obvious—safety problems. Are there exposed wires or pipes? Are carpets in good repair and well-anchored? Are there ramps for the residents who use walkers or wheelchairs? Are the bathrooms fitted with safety rails or seats?

Examining state inspection reports

Nursing homes must undergo state inspection about every 18 months, and the facility is required by law to have a copy of the report available for your viewing. If the nursing home balks at letting you see the report, expect that the results of the last inspection were unacceptable. But a good report doesn't guarantee you a good facility. Why not?

- Most states lack adequate personnel to do detailed inspections of every facility in the state.

- Inspectors are often appointed, not hired for any particular expertise they may possess.

- "Surprise" inspections are rarely that—most nursing homes have adequate advance notice to prepare for the inspection.

- Follow-up is rare, again usually because the state generally lacks adequate personnel.

Nevertheless, it's worthwhile to request and read the two or three most recent inspection reports of every facility on your list. If nothing else, they may help you eliminate the worst of the bunch.

Using the evaluation checklist

When you choose a nursing home, you are quite possibly choosing your parent's final home. Therefore, you want to be as thorough as possible in your evaluation of your options, so check several facilities—not just the one nearest you. To ease your comparison among nursing homes, here's a standardized checklist you'll find useful. This checklist

Timesaver
Organize your family visits to your elder. Once you've worked out a schedule, you can share carpooling duties on visiting days.

was reproduced with permission from the MetLife Consumer Education Center. (See Appendix D for a copy you can detach and reproduce for use at each of the facilities you visit.)

Quality of life issues

The best of today's nursing homes are a far cry from the dreary institutions of yesteryear. One of the biggest improvements in nursing home care has been the increased attention paid to quality of life issues. Most modern facilities take pride in providing opportunities for physical and intellectual exercise. This development has occurred in recognition of the fact that even the most frail among us can benefit from some degree of physical activity, and intellectual engagement provides meaning and value to life even for patients suffering from dementia.

Getting physical

If you've worked through your checklist, you've already checked to see that the facility provides exercise and physical therapy. Look for a range of alternatives, from low-impact aerobics, swimming, Tai Chi, and weight training, to supervised walks or even simple massage. The Washington Manor Nursing and Rehabilitation Center in Hollywood, Florida, has instituted a weight-training program open to all its residents. Participants include patients as old as 98 and can even accommodate residents with dementia.

Fitness programs such as the one at Washington Manor have been successful in improving overall health and in decreasing the number of falls suffered by residents. But the benefits don't stop there. The group format provides residents with an

Bright Idea
If your elder is going to participate in any physical exercise programs, make sure that it is supervised by a trained therapist experienced in working with the elderly.

NURSING HOME EVALUATION CHECKLIST

☐ Does the nursing home have a current state license on display?

☐ Does the administrator have an up-to-date state license?

☐ Does the facility have a history of serious violations? (Check with your state ombudsman or ask the home for a copy of its latest survey report.)

☐ Is the nursing home certified for Medicare or Medicaid? (Even if these problems are not important to you now, they may be in the future.)

☐ Do the residents seem happy?

☐ Is the location convenient to family and friends?

☐ Is the location convenient to the patient's physician?

☐ Is the facility near a hospital?

☐ Is a Patients' Bill of Rights posted in plain sight?

☐ Are there handrails in the hallways, grab bars in the bathrooms, and other features aimed at accident prevention? Are toilet facilities raised and doors designed to accommodate residents in wheelchairs? Are wheelchair ramps provided indoors as well as outdoors?

☐ Are the hallways wide enough to permit two wheelchairs to pass with ease?

☐ Are there clearly marked exits and unobstructed paths to these exits?

☐ Are there fire extinguishers, automatic sprinklers, and smoke detectors throughout? Are they checked annually? Have they recently been checked?

☐ Is there emergency lighting in rooms and halls?

☐ Is the furniture sturdy?

☐ Is a physician available at all times for emergencies?

☐ Is there security personnel to prevent confused residents from wandering away from the building?

☐ Is the facility clean, well-maintained, and odor-free?

☐ Is a licensed dietitian on the premises often enough to provide adequate supervision of planning and preparation of meals? (Ask to see the kitchen area in order to observe cleanliness.)

☐ Is a weekly menu plan available? Are the meals nutritious and tasty?

☐ Does the staff assist residents who have difficulty feeding themselves?

☐ Is the staff friendly, available, caring, and accommodating to residents and visitors?

☐ Is there an activity room where residents can read, do crafts, play games, or socialize?

☐ Are physical therapy and rehabilitative services available?

☐ Is a list of references available?

☐ Would this nursing home provide the best possible care for your loved one?

Source: MetLife.

opportunity for socializing as well, and this in turn helps patients remain alert and engaged with the world around them.

Sparking those synapses

Aging does not need to mean loss of alertness or intellectual ability. But everyone—not just the elderly—needs to have regular access to food for thought. A television in the nursing home's dayroom or even in the patient's own room is not enough. Your parent needs more than entertainment—he or she needs opportunities for social interaction and intellectual challenge as well.

For this reason, some of the best nursing homes have regularly scheduled games and craft activities. Some bring in local musicians—often music students at local schools—for periodic concerts. Many have programs in which volunteers from the community read to residents whose eyesight has degenerated too far for them to manage it on their own. Some even offer regularly scheduled lectures or classes for interested residents.

Watch Out!
If your elder is distressed at the idea of moving to a nursing home, he or she can become seriously depressed. Talk to the facility about the availability of counseling services to help your elder adjust to the move.

Finding a little furry TLC

Dr. William Thomas, the director of a nursing home in New York, found the traditional concept of the nursing home too impersonal. He set out to design a new approach to full-service eldercare, which he called the "Eden Alternative." His goal: to decrease the levels of helplessness, boredom, and loneliness that he observed among his patients. His method: He opened the doors to pets—parakeets, dogs, and cats—and to regular visits from small children.

The program has been a resounding success. Four years after "Edenizing" his facility, death rates there dropped by 15 percent. Medication use also decreased as well. Some facilities even offer visits from beauticians, podiatrists, and other specialists who can help the patients look and feel their best. And the benefits have not only been enjoyed by his patients: Employee turnover rates dropped dramatically as well. Today there are about 100 "Edenized" nursing homes across the country, with many more being planned.

Ways to include your elder in the final choice

So far, we haven't said much about your elder's participation in choosing a nursing home. In some cases, the final decision falls exclusively to the family of the elder. This is the case when the elderly person is unable to participate in the discussion of his or her care options due to problems with dementia. But as with any eldercare choice, you should consider your elder's needs and concerns right from the start, and involve him or her as much as possible in the final choice.

Many elderly people are strongly resistant to the idea of going into a nursing home. Some of this resistance is understandable—nursing homes have long had a bad reputation, and many older facilities have earned that negative image. No one would voluntarily enter a place they thought was depressing, neglectful, and insensitive to their needs.

If you've been careful in your research, evaluation, and selection of a nursing home, however, you will have eliminated any facilities that would cause concern. Now is the time to bring your elder into the decision-making process so that the move need not be traumatic.

Addressing common fears

Elders have specific, easily articulated fears of what "entering the home" will mean for them. If you take time to familiarize yourself with these fears, you can address them and help your parent overcome them. The most prevalent fears elders report about nursing home care are listed here:

- Nursing home care means heavy sedation.
- Nursing home care means loneliness—the family will forget them.
- Nursing home care means neglectful or abusive treatment.
- Nursing home care means death is coming soon.

Bright Idea
Get involved in eldercare issues in your area, particularly those to do with regulating nursing home care. Supporting general legislation geared to protecting the rights and safety of all the elderly will result in improvements in your own elder's care as well.

All these fears derive from some aspect of the old, Dickensian view of nursing homes—a stereotype that the best of today's nursing homes have taken great pains to explode. Let's take them one by one.

Medication as caregiving. There was a time in the not so distant past when sedative or psychiatric medication was routinely used to make it easier for nursing home staff to cope with their residents. Following exposés in the 1960s, 1970s, and 1980s, state regulatory agencies have cracked down on such operations, as have federal programs such as the Social Security Administration and the Department of Health and Human Services. Your research and onsite visits can alleviate this fear.

The loneliness issue. Nursing homes are often perceived by the elderly as a warehouse where they're sent so they won't be in anybody's way. This is one issue that can be only partially addressed through your research of potential nursing homes. As long as you select a facility located near you that has liberal visiting hours, your only real means to relieve this concern is to establish a strong relationship of trust with your elder. Make realistic arrangements for regular visits—and *keep to them.*

But do keep in mind that a part of the fear of loneliness is not strictly related to a fear that *you* won't visit. Moving to a nursing home often means leaving behind a whole community of friends and acquaintances. If the places you're looking at don't provide ample activities and opportunities for socialization, your elder will justifiably feel exiled, and will be that much more dependent upon your visits for stimulation and attention. It is imperative, then, that you carefully consider the programs and activities that the nursing home provides for its residents, and that you find some that coincide with your parent's own interests.

Fears of neglect and abuse. Your inspection of nursing homes in your area must include at least one unscheduled visit so that you can see how staff and patients interact. It is sad but true that some facilities still are more interested in collecting checks than providing care, but such places are coming under increasing scrutiny from state and federal watchdog agencies.

Your state's Long-Term Care Ombudsman, the agency that collects—and seeks to resolve—complaints about nursing home abuses, can provide you with the information you need to avoid improperly run facilities. But don't stop there. Once your elder has been admitted to a facility, make a point of making periodic, unscheduled visits. This way you can spot any slippage in the quality of care provided.

Intimations of death. A parent's fears that going into a nursing home means preparing for death is easy to understand if you make an effort to look at the issue from your elder's point of view. It is rarely a literal fear that the nursing home itself will cause their death. It is more likely an honest recognition that this is usually the last-resort eldercare choice short of hospitalization for a fatal illness. Accepting the need for nursing home care means accepting the fact that he or she probably will not resume an independent life again. This is very difficult to accept.

There is no simple way to alleviate this concern. However, you can be willing to talk with your parent about these feelings. If counseling is appropriate, you might consider finding professional help for your parent as well. (If your elder chooses a nursing home with religious affiliations, he may find comfort from the religious services or counseling offered.)

Preparing your family for the change

More than any other eldercare choice, the decision to admit your parent to a nursing home is fraught with guilt and pain. It will probably be hard enough for you to accept the need for this change—it may become even more difficult if other family members are not supportive of the decision. If you have been the primary caregiver all along, however, only you can judge your ability to continue in that capacity. Obviously, if a sibling or other relative can take over some or all of the task that has become more than you can handle, you may be able to avoid the nursing home choice entirely. Just be sure that any new arrangements will, in fact, effectively lighten the burden you've been carrying.

Once the decision has been made

If you've done your homework, you've found a good facility and can feel comfortable about your elder's continuing care. But, of course, you will want to follow up by monitoring your elder's care over time.

You will probably never be completely satisfied with the care your parent receives in a nursing home—after all, no institution can provide every resident (and resident's family) all the individualized services and amenities they might want. But the good nursing homes do make an effort to meet your needs. The trick is to establish good communications with the staff.

Keep in mind that the staff—particularly the nursing assistants—tend to be overworked. There simply aren't enough to go around, even in the best of facilities. It helps if you can manage to personalize your elder's care for the staff—make the effort to know the names of people who care for your elder and to introduce yourself to them. When you visit your elder, take the time to chat a moment with the staff. If you go to the trouble to create a working relationship with the nursing assistants and other facility workers, you're much more likely to receive their cooperation when you need a problem resolved or special needs tended to.

Just the facts

- A nursing home is the appropriate option when your elder's care needs can no longer be met by other, less intensive alternatives.

- There are good nursing facilities and bad ones—careful research of the homes in your vicinity will help you make the best choice for your elder.

- The single most important element to nursing home care is the quality of the staff.

- Establishing a personalized relationship with staff workers at the nursing home will go a long way toward securing quality care for your elder.

PART V

The Financial, Legal, and Social
Realities of Eldercare

Managing Eldercare Costs

Chapter 12

C hapter 1, "The Growing Need for Eldercare," introduced you to a few financial facts of life in America today. You learned that many claim Social Security as a primary source of income. You also learned that many others claim income from assets, pensions, wages, and public assistance, and that about 12 percent of them were either employed or actively seeking employment. Most importantly, you also learned that a significant proportion of the elderly (37 percent) live on incomes at or below the near poverty level.

Clearly, for many elderly, regular income is not enough to cover the often extremely high costs associated with eldercare. Medicare, Medicaid, and other sources of financial insurance or support are important resources that can enable the elderly to secure adequate eldercare.

But negotiating the financial side of eldercare can be confusing. This chapter introduces you to some sources for which your elder may qualify when

215

seeking to cover the costs of necessary care. We begin with the two biggest names in the field: Medicare and Medicaid.

Medicare: healthcare's basic version

We hear about both Medicare and Medicaid, but we generally don't take the time to look into either until we need them. Most people assume that because they sound so much alike, they must be similar programs. But nothing could be further from the truth. Both are resources that your elder can use to cover eldercare costs, but they differ significantly from one another.

Of the two, Medicare is the program specifically designed for the elderly: It's the health insurance section of Title XVIII of the Social Security Act that was passed into law in 1966. It's a federally administered program for anyone who qualifies for old age or disability benefits.

Determining eligibility for Medicare

Every year that you've worked, you've accrued Medicare benefits, computed as "quarters" of years by the Social Security Administration. If your elder has worked long enough to qualify for Social Security benefits, he or she is automatically eligible for Medicare. That's true for most Americans over the age of 65.

Some few people, however, may not have earned enough over the course of their lifetimes to qualify for full benefits. These individuals must pay extra premiums for part of their coverage (called Part A, which we'll discuss in greater depth in a moment).

Understanding Medicare basics

You and your elder need to know several things about Medicare before you can make the most of your coverage:

- How to apply for benefits
- What the two parts of Medicare coverage (Parts A and B) are all about
- What is and is not covered under Medicare
- How Medicare payments are processed

Applying for benefits. If your parent is over age 65 and has not yet applied for Social Security and Medicare benefits, it's wise to correct this oversight immediately. In fact, it's best if your elder begins the application process three months prior to his or her 65th birthday. Your elder will need to go to the local Social Security office to file application forms.

The A's and B's of Medicare. Medicare, Part A provides coverage for hospitalization and some limited nursing home care. Private insurers such as Blue Cross and Blue Shield contract with the federal government to pay benefits to the hospital or other institution.

Part B is the aspect of Medicare that covers doctor visits and treatments. It also covers the cost of "durable medical equipment," such as wheelchairs and walkers. Part B payments are handled by private insurers in much the same way that Part A payments are made.

In either part of the Medicare program, you can almost invariably expect to pay a co-payment. In other words, your parent will need to pay part of any bill that is filed under Medicare unless he has additional private insurance (commonly known as Medigap coverage).

Falling into the Medigap. If your parent has private health insurance through a pension, as many elders do, usually the private insurance will pay first on all bills, with Medicare covering the balance. If your parent does not already have such insurance, he or

Timesaver
Before your elder heads off to the Social Security office, call ahead to ascertain just what types of documentation must be presented at the time of application. Have all this organized beforehand.

she should purchase coverage privately to avoid the need for paying out of pocket when Medicare fails to cover the total cost of treatment or hospitalization. This extra coverage is popularly known as Medigap.

Medigap arose to address the need experienced by most elders to be insured for the portion of treatment costs that Medicare does not pay. In addition, Medigap covers services and treatments that Medicare specifically excludes. A partial list of such excluded expenses follows:

- Nursing home services for chronic health problems (Medicare *will* cover short-term nursing home stays if the patient is sent to the facility to recover from hospitalization)

- Glasses and hearing aids

- Dental work

- Regular checkups

- Medications

- Private nurses

- Chiropractic services

For insurance for these expenses, Medigap coverage is reqired. However, the list of services and treatments covered by Medicare does change periodically. On January 1, 1998, Medicare extended coverage in several key areas that had previously been deemed ineligible:

- Annual mammograms to screen for breast cancer.

- Screening for cervical and vaginal cancer. The screening schedule is two-tiered: One exam every three years is covered for women with average risk factors; an annual exam is covered for women who are at high risk.

■ Annual screening for colorectal cancer.

■ Annual screening for prostate cancer.

Therefore, don't assume that a condition or treatment that was ineligible for coverage in the past is still ineligible today. Always check with your Social Security office.

Medicare calls the shots. Medicare calculates payments for treatment and services according to its own schedule of fees. In other words, Medicare—not your doctor—determines what you will be charged. You and your doctor must accept Medicare's judgment on charges: You may not, for example, arrange to pay your doctor any amount above and beyond what Medicare deems to be an appropriate fee for a particular service. In addition to calling the shots on what charges can be imposed for a particular treatment, Medicare also reserves the right to determine whether a normally covered expense will be reimbursed in a particular instance. For example, although home health services are covered to some extent, your elder must meet certain minimum criteria before these services are certified for payment. Make certain that you've gotten approval before hiring a care worker, if you're counting on Medicare to pick up the tab.

Medicare and hospitalization. Medicare benefits cover your elder's hospital costs, but here again, coverage is limited. Medicare will pick up the cost of the first 60 days, minus a relatively small deductible. After 60 days, Medicare's portion of the expense drops dramatically, and your elder must cover the remainder of the cost. After 90 days, it is expected that your elder will be well enough to be discharged—but this is subject to emergency appeal, during which time your elder must be allowed to remain in the hospital.

Watch Out!
Many doctors feel that the Medicare fee schedule is set unrealistically low and that they can't break even if they are bound by it. For this reason, some doctors try to avoid maintaining a practice consisting mostly of Medicare patients, and they may refuse to see a Medicare beneficiary as frequently as the patient might wish.

The pros and cons of Medicare. The biggest plus of Medicare is its broad availability. Although it doesn't cover every cost your parent may face, it provides a solid insurance foundation for nearly all people over age 65. In addition, it is so widespread that it's easy for most doctors and hospitals to handle filing claims. If your elder moves from one state to another, the coverage follows.

On the downside, many doctors don't look all that favorably on Medicare because they find the fee schedule set too low. As a result, some doctors refuse to treat Medicare patients at all. In addition, Medicare's insistence on prior approval of some tests and procedures means that often a delay may occur before these can be scheduled. Also troubling to many is the need to co-insure (Medigap) to cover procedures disallowed by Medicare. Perhaps the biggest complaint of all is that Medicare does not cover medications.

Medicare-related issues

Elderly patients who rely on Medicare benefits—and that's just about everybody, to one extent or another—find that they must address a number of questions directly related to their Medicare coverage:

- Choosing a good Medigap provider
- Considering the merits of a managed care plan as opposed to a fee-for-service provider
- Understanding—and complying with—Medicare's complex rules and requirements

Each of these issues is addressed in the following sections.

Unofficially...
Each year, the government sets the annual premium rates for Medicare, Parts A and B. The Part A premium, which is paid by relatively few, was set at $764 in 1998. Part B's premium, paid by all, was set at $43.80 for the year.

Buy me! No, buy *me!*

Choosing a Medigap carrier is no simple task—literally hundreds of companies are in the business of offering this type of coverage. You'll have your homework cut out for you as you search for an appropriate insurer. Fortunately, your state insurance office can provide you with some useful tips and guidance.

Managed care's entry into the Medicare arena

Managed care, one form of which is HMOs, places the control of medical care decision-making in the hands of a single facility. The managed care patient must choose his or her physician from a list of doctors approved by the plan, and all visits to specialists must be preapproved by the plan doctor. Managed care plans require that patients sign an assignment of benefits form, which stipulates that the service provider will receive payment directly from the insurer.

Medicare was once totally geared to fee-for-service medical care, but increasingly managed care is becoming more prevalent. Because the purpose of managed care plans is to keep medical costs down, HMOs and other managed care plans may be less reluctant than private physicians to accept the Medicare fee structure. But keeping costs down means giving up certain freedoms that a person accustomed to fee-for-service care may take for granted. In managed care, the patient is restricted in the choice of doctors; as noted previously, the patient cannot seek specialist treatment without prior approval by her plan physician.

In an effort to attract more Medicare business, many managed care plans have begun sweetening the deal for the elderly by offering coverage for

Bright Idea
If you need legal assistance on Medicare or other Social Security issues, contact the National Organization of Social Security Claimants Representatives (6 Prospect Street, Midland Park NJ, 07432. Tel: 201-444-1415). This organization can recommend an attorney in your area and will send you informational pamphlets on Social Security law.

medication and other items that Medicare doesn't cover. This may represent a significant savings for your elderly, but it comes at the price of reduced choice and flexibility in choosing physicians. Only your parent can decide whether managed care or fee-for-service is best.

Medicaid: help for the low-income elderly

Medicaid, formally known as Title XIX of the Social Security Act, is a state-administered, federally mandated program that is financed by a combination of state and federal funds. Because it straddles the two jurisdictions (state and federal), the Medicaid program varies from state to state in terms of coverage offered.

Medicaid is targeted to low-income people who would otherwise be denied access to healthcare. Some who qualify for Medicaid also participate in the federal government's Supplemental Security Insurance program (SSI), which benefits the elderly and disabled who are ineligible for coverage under the Social Security employee benefits program. If your elder never held a paying job or was not in the workforce long enough to qualify for regular Social Security benefits, SSI may cover his or her essential needs. When a person is accepted into SSI, he or she is automatically entitled to Medicaid as well. In most states, enrollment is automatic.

Income levels and Medicaid eligibility

How much your parent earns and the value of the assets he owns count toward his eligibiliy for Medicaid. The key criterion is the value of "countable assets," a concept that excludes certain items from consideration of eligibility. The excluded assets are listed here:

- Your elder's home
- Your elder's car
- Your elder's personal belongings and household furnishings
- Life insurance policies with a cash value of $5,000 or less

Once your parent's income and the value of all included assets (which would include investments, investment properties, and the holdings in a savings account or safety deposit box, among other things), the resultant income and assets are evaluated to determine whether he or she qualifies as "low-income," as defined by federal and individual state guidelines.

Many elderly who, by virtue of too-high incomes, don't initially qualify for Medicaid will "spend down" to Medicaid eligibility. This is commonly done when long-term care is needed. Long-term or nursing home care is not covered by Medicare, as you'll recall, so the only way to guarantee coverage for the expense is for your elder to deplete his or her assets to the point where Medicaid assistance will kick in. It is not enough for your elder to simply sign over his or her assets to you or another family member—the law requires that such transferrals of assets must take place three years or more before the elderly person may qualify for Medicaid coverage.

Medicaid's pros and cons

Medicaid is primarily intended as the last-resort insurer for the elderly or disabled person who could not otherwise afford necessary care. Therefore, it is distinctly no-frills in scope and intent. It does cover more services and treatments than Medicare, but your convenience is not a prime consideration:

Simple access to care is the point of the program. On the plus side of the Medicaid column are the following considerations:

- Hospitals *must* accept Medicaid.

- Unlike Medicare, Medicaid covers medications (although you may be required to buy generic rather than named brands).

- Generally no co-payment is required; where one applies, it is usually a token sum.

Because this program is intended solely to provide the low-income elderly and disabled with access to medical care, you won't find the same level of convenience that characterizes Medicare—and you will certainly find it less convenient than you would expect with fee-for-service providers. Among the negatives associated with Medicaid are these:

- Difficulty in finding a physician who will accept Medicaid patients. Many doctors find the rules and paperwork prohibitively restrictive and time-consuming, and many complain that payments come far too slowly.

- You may have to travel farther than you'd like to find a doctor who will accept Medicaid payments.

- Medicaid clinics are notorious for making patients wait a long time to be seen by a doctor.

- Most nursing homes set aside only a limited number of beds for Medicaid patients, which means it may be tough to find a place that will take your elder without requiring a very long wait.

- The peculiar split of authority between state and federal jurisdictions means that the rules can be hard to follow and quick to change. Keeping up with all the regulations can easily become a full-time job.

■ As with Medicare, Medicaid reserves the right to disapprove a treatment, even if your doctor recommends it. (As with Medicare, however, such a refusal of coverage can be appealed.)

But Medicaid's biggest drawback by far is the procedure by which your elder must qualify. This can be very time-consuming—it may take several months and a great deal of back-and-forthing with your physician to provide the necessary documentation for eligibility.

Managed care and Medicaid

Nearly every state has instituted some form of managed care program for Medicaid recipients, although this trend has neither become universal nor required. At present, managed care plans are newcomers to the Medicaid universe, and the precise effect of their participation has yet to be fully studied.

A comparison of two programs

Medicare and Medicaid differ from one another in very significant ways. Table 13.1 provides a side-by-side comparison of some of the more important features of each program.

Other insurance alternatives

As the field of eldercare grows seemingly exponentially, all sorts of new options designed to meet elders' needs have sprung up in the last decade or so. In addition, there are alternatives that provide many people with welcome assistance in facing the high costs of eldercare. We'll take these alternative approaches to covering eldercare expenses one by one.

Note! ➡
Remember:
Medicaid was and
is intended as a
last-resort
resource for indi-
viduals who had
no other access
to costly medical
care. It should
not be treated as
a clever way to
"outwit" the
system and get
low-cost care
when your elder
has other
options
available.

TABLE 13.1: MEDICARE AND MEDICAID: A COMPARISON

Feature	Medicare	Medicaid
Eligibility	Past earnings.	Disability, low income.
Does current income matter for continued eligibility?	No.	Yes.
Are there limits on the assets you can have to stay eligible?	No.	Yes.
Is a premium charged?	For Part A, a premium of several hundred dollars is assessed only on those who don't have a adequate work history to have earned full coverage; Part B requires a nominal annual premium.	No premium required.
Are co-payments required?	Yes.	No, or minimal fee (varies by state).
Are medications covered?	No.	Yes, but patient may be limited to generic drugs.
Is nursing home care covered?	Only for short-term stays.	Yes, but available beds are limited.
Is home health covered?	Yes, with program approval.	Yes, with program approval.
Are doctor visits covered?	Sometimes (not regular checkups).	Yes.
Is hospitalization covered?	Yes.	Yes.

Long-term care insurance

A newcomer to the insurance field is something called *long-term care insurance*. This insurance is sold to people in their middle or early senior years with the promise that in later years the policy will pick up the tab for home healthcare or care in a nursing home. Some carriers go a step further and offer coverage for all eldercare services, including those not strictly health-related. Thus, you might find that the terms of a policy would provide payment for the twice-a-week chore worker who assists your elder with the heavier housecleaning tasks as well as covering a visiting nurse's care.

Right now, the experts are still debating the need for long-term care insurance. It has not caught on among consumers, but some financial planners see merit in the concept if your elder has assets he or she wishes to protect from being consumed by the high cost of nursing home care or other eldercare expenses. Contact your state insurance office for information on carriers who offer this coverage, and make certain that you understand all the provisions of the contract before committing to purchasing this type of policy.

Reverse mortgages

According to the latest U.S. Census, a great many of America's elderly own their own homes—and a large percentage own the home outright. This fact, coupled with the acknowledged high costs of eldercare, has given rise to a relatively new mortgage instrument known as the *reverse mortgage.*

The reverse mortgage is just what its name implies: Your elder enters into an agreement with the bank, according to which the bank makes regular monthly payments to gradually acquire equity in the home. It is almost exactly the reverse of the agreement by which your elder bought the home in the first place. The only real difference is that during the time that the bank is making payments, your elder retains his or her right to live in the house.

Watch Out!
Make sure that any long-term care insurance includes cognitive impairment along with physical ailments as conditions that justify coverage. If it doesn't—and if your elder is stricken with Alzheimer's disease or other cognitive impairments but remains physically healthy—the carrier may refuse to pay for her care.

For some elderly—particularly those who choose to enter an assisted-living facility and therefore have taken on a fairly substantial monthly expense—this may be a good way to guarantee a substantial, regular source of income. It is also a potentially good choice for elders who choose to age in place but who need to cover the expense of home care services or household "elderizing." In addition, the reverse mortgage allows your elder to realize—over time, of course—the value of the house without having to go through the trauma of listing, showing, and ultimately selling it for a lump sum.

While the reverse mortgage looks pretty good in theory, explore this option carefully before committing to it. After all, it involves deciding to turn over the title to the bank—if your parent or your siblings feel strongly about keeping the old homestead in the family, this option is not for you. The payments may be spread over time, and your parent may have rights of occupancy until he or she dies, but make no mistake about it: The house ultimately belongs to the bank. There are other considerations to take into account as well: For example, will your elder have to relinquish a substantial portion of the actual value of the house in return for the convenience of regular payments?

In the end, you and your elder need to do what any smart consumers would do with a financial decision of this magnitude: Check out the option carefully, consult with knowledgeable legal and financial advisors, and make sure that everybody knows precisely what they're getting into before signing on the dotted line.

An annuity for the elder years

If your elder is ready to give up the house in exchange for the convenience of assisted living, or perhaps because you've decided together that he or she should come to live with you in your home, another alternative would be to sell the property and establish an annuity with the proceeds. Of course, your elder needn't sell the house to go this route—if there are investments, she can use one or more of those to establish the annuity account. The basic concept of an annuity is simple: An interest- or income-earning account is established in your elder's name, and from this account a regular monthly sum is to paid out to cover expenses.

But while the general concept is the same across all annuities, you should look closely at the terms of any specific one you are offered. Annuities can be a good choice if your goal is to guarantee your elder a regular source of income, but unless you or your parent are very comfortable in the world of finance, this is one option for which you should seek— and heed—the advice of an experienced financial planner.

The venerable VA

No discussion of eldercare financial options would be complete without making reference to the Veterans' Administration (VA). Not everybody qualifies for assistance through the VA, but if your elder is over age 65 and is an honorably discharged veteran of military service, the VA stands ready to help. This is especially true if your elder incurred a disability while in the military.

The VA operates hospitals and clinics throughout the United States. In addition, it may provide assistance in covering the costs of home health services, home care and adult day services, and even the cost of nursing home care. For more information on VA benefits and eligibility requirements, contact your local VA office.

Bright Idea
For a download-able Federal Benefits Manual for Veterans and Dependents, see the Department of Veterans Affairs site at http://www.va.gov/benefits.htm

Just the facts

- Medicare is a federally mandated and federally funded program that seeks to address many of the health insurance needs of all Americans who have spent time in the workforce.

- Medigap insurance evolved to pay for expenses that Medicare will not cover.

- Medicaid was developed as a last-resort plan to extend healthcare coverage to the aged and the disabled who could otherwise not afford to pay for necessary medical care.

- Long-term care insurance allows your elder to plan ahead for the expenses associated with aging.

- Reverse mortgages and annuities are two mechanisms that your parent can establish to guarantee a regular monthly income during his or her later years.

- The Veterans Administration has long provided medical services and access to health and home care for the men and women who served in the armed forces.

GET THE SCOOP ON...
Powers of attorney ▪ Guardianships ▪
Living wills ▪ Healthcare proxies ▪ Last will
and testaments

Protecting Your Elder's Legal Rights

W hen your elder can no longer handle financial, legal, or medical decisions, you or someone else in the family must step in to make those choices on his or her behalf. Ideally, you will have discussed these issues with your elder before a crisis, and you'll have a firm understanding of your elder's hopes and preferences. Far too often, however, these delicate issues are avoided—no one feels comfortable bringing them up, so they are left unresolved until sudden action must be taken.

This chapter takes you step by step through some of the more important legal issues you'll need to address with your elder to protect his interests if he becomes incapacitated. You'll learn how to make certain that his preferences in the financial, medical, and legal spheres will be respected, even if he can no longer speak on his own behalf.

When legal action is required

Whether you've managed to plan ahead or whether you're responding to a crisis, certain circumstances definitely call for legal action. At the very least, you'll need to become involved in your parent's legal affairs in the following two situations:

- When your parent is very ill or is slated for surgery

- When your parent is no longer mentally competent to handle his or her own affairs

The powers of attorney

In the first instance, you are anticipating problems—if the surgery does not go well, or if the illness threatens to incapacitate your elder, you will need to be able to legally act on his or her behalf. For this you will need a power of attorney or a durable power of attorney.

> **Power of attorney:** The granting of certain rights to another individual to act in the name of another. This document is subject to a specific end date, at which time the power of attorney lapses.

> **Durable power of attorney:** This is similar to the power of attorney, but with no specified end date.

> **Springing power of attorney:** Some states permit a power of attorney drafted to go into effect at a future point in time. The trigger that puts it into effect may be a calendar date or a specific event (such as the hospitalization of your elder).

In whatever form you choose, power of attorney enables you to make key decisions for your parent if he or she becomes incapable of making them. This originated in law as a tool by which a representative was empowered to transact business on behalf of an absent third party.

This original form of the power of attorney was limited in some important ways: It was subject to restrictions specified by the principal, it had a specified time limit, it could be revoked at the principal's discretion, and it did not survive the death or disability of the principal. Clearly, these limitations make the regular power of attorney inadequate to your needs when you are trying to plan for your elder's future. For that, you need the durable form.

The sample durable power of attorney reproduced in this chapter courtesy of AdultCare, Inc., a Fortis company.

The durable power of attorney enables you to make key decisions for your parent if he or she becomes incapable of making them. Presumably, you will be acting according to your elder's wishes— or your best guess as to what those wishes would be. The durable power of attorney grants you rights in legal and financial matters—and sometimes even decision-making power with regard to medical care as well.

If you want to explore the power of attorney further, contact your (or your elder's) attorney for more information and guidance.

Guardianships

If a parent becomes incompetent to handle his or her affairs, and if no previously drawn power of attorney confers on you the legal right to act in his or her behalf, you may need to ask the court to order a *guardianship* (sometimes called a *conservatorship*). This decree places all decision-making power into the hands of the appointed guardian or conservator. Again, the terms of this power vary from state to state. Some states allow for limited guardianships, which specifically stipulate the areas

SAMPLE DURABLE POWER OF ATTORNEY

Be it known that _____, the undersigned Grantor, does hereby grant a durable
power of attorney to _____ as my
attorney-in-fact.

My attorney-in-fact shall have full powers and
authority to do and undertake all acts on my
behalf that I could do personally, including but
not limited to the right to sell, deed, buy, trade,
lease, mortgage, assign, rent, or dispose of any
real or personal property; the right to execute,
accept, undertake, and perform all contracts in
my name; the right to deposit, endorse, or withdraw funds to or from any of my bank accounts
or safe deposit box; the right to borrow, collect,
lend, invest, or reinvest funds; the right to initiate, defend, commence, or settle legal actions
on my behalf; the right to vote (in person or by
proxy) any shares or beneficial interest in any
entity; and the right to retain any accountant,
attorney, or other advisor deemed necessary to
protect my interests relative to any foregoing
unlimited power. My attorney-in-fact shall have
full power to execute, deliver, and accept all
documents and undertake all acts consistent
with the foregoing.

This power of attorney shall become effective
upon and remain in effect only during such
periods as I may be mentally or physically incapacitated and unable to care for my own needs
or make competent decisions as are necessary
to protect my interests or conduct my affairs.

My attorney-in-fact hereby accepts this appointment subject to its terms and agrees to act and perform in said fiduciary capacity consistent with my best interests as my attorney-in-fact as his/her best discretion deems advisable, and I affirm and ratify all acts so undertaken.

This power of attorney may be revoked by me at any time and shall automatically be revoked upon my death, provided any person relying on this power of attorney shall have full rights to accept the authority of my attorney-in-fact until in receipt of actual notice of revocation.

Signed under seal this _____ day of _____ 20_____

STATE OF _____

COUNTY OF _____

on _____ before me, _____,

personally appeared _____, personally known to me (or proved to me on the basis of satisfactory evidence) to be the person(s) whose name(s) is/are subscribed to the within instrument and acknowledged to me that he/she/they executed the same in his/her/their authorized capacity(ies), and that by his/her/their signature(s) on the instrument the person(s), or the entity upon behalf of which the person(s) acted, executed the instrument.

WITNESS my hand and official seal,

Signature _____

Affiant _____ Known

_____ Unknown

ID Produced _____

in which the guardian is permitted to act. For example, the guardian may handle all financial matters but be prohibited from making medical decisions.

If your elder suffers from Alzheimer's disease or another form of dementia, or she has an illness that has rendered her incompetent or physically unable to communicate her wishes, a guardianship may be in order. Because this is a status conveyed upon you (or some other responsible party) by the court, you will need legal assistance to draft the petition for relief. The law pertaining to guardianship varies from state to state, so a detailed, step-by-step explanation of the petitioning process cannot be given here. Consult an experienced attorney in your state: Your best bet is to look for a law firm or attorney who specializes in estate planning or elder law.

Upon reviewing your petition for guardianship, the court must determine whether your elder is truly incompetent, and whether the petitioner (that's you) is appropriate. Some states require guardians to file professional evaluations of the medical, psychological, and financial condition of the person to be placed in guardianship, so you'll have to make arrangements to secure these documents.

Petitioning for guardianship of your elder may sound drastic, but it may be essential to protect his interests. Here are just a few circumstances where guardianship would be imperative:

- Your elder owns major assets, such as a home, which could be lost if payments or taxes are not kept up.

- Ongoing medical care decisions need to be made, but your elder is incapacitated and cannot communicate her choices.

Watch Out!
Just because your parent is making what you consider to be silly decisions, that doesn't mean he is incompetent. The court defines the term strictly and will not willingly abridge your elder's freedom just because you don't like some of the choices he has been making lately.

- Your elder is no longer able to manage his or her money, but receives a pension or other funds that need to be handled.

For more information about guardianship, see the Internet Guide to Guardianship, offered by Usalaw, at http://guardianship.usalaw.com/. You should also see your own attorney for more specific guidance and information.

Legal issues in medical decision-making

One of the most important legal concerns facing you as caregiver is the issue of medical care decision-making. In the best of all possible worlds, long before your parent falls ill you will have had time to discuss who she wants to take charge of her medical care if she becomes incapacitated. During that conversation, you would have delved into her preferences regarding the level of care and the degree of intervention she is willing to accept.

Unfortunately, most of us don't want to think about a beloved elder becoming seriously ill, and we often put off this conversation until we are suddenly faced with just the sort of emergency that it would have addressed.

Choices in medical care

One reason we all tend to avoid talking about medical concerns with our elders is that the discussion inevitably turns to end-of-life issues. Of special importance and equally special delicacy, is determining how aggressively your elder wishes to be treated when incapacitated by a terminal illness. While your elder is still quite healthy, the question seems almost ghoulish—but leaving the question unanswered until illness actually strikes may well be

Bright Idea
Ease your elder into the subject of a living will. Try introducing the subject by bringing up the experiences of some safely distant other person who found themselves in a situation that a living will would have helped. Then gently swing the conversation to your elder's own thoughts on the subject. Sometimes the oblique approach is best.

leaving it until too late. It would be far better to talk these things through before disaster strikes, as recommended in Chapter 5, "Strategies for Coping."

When you give yourself enough lead time to truly work through these issues with your elder, you have time to assess a number of options. Two important alternative choices for organizing medical care on behalf of your elder are discussed here:

1. **The living will.** This is a legal document in which your elder indicates specifically the kind of intervention desired—and rejected—well in advance of actual incapacitation. For instance, your elder may specify that no life-prolonging treatment is desired if he or she becomes terminally ill. Conversely, your elder may specify that every attempt be made to continue to sustain life.

2. **The healthcare proxy.** This document designates someone other than the elder as the legal decision-maker once the elder can no longer make choices for himself.

Because both of these documents must be executed in advance of their actual use, they are sometimes called *advance directives.*

A comparison of the options

The living will has one paramount advantage over the healthcare proxy because its terms are specified by your elder on his or her own behalf well in advance of any actual illness. In other words, your elder retains the right of decision-making—your role is simply to make certain that the preferences and stipulations it sets forth are carried out when the time comes. A healthcare proxy, on the other hand, places the decision-making responsibility squarely on your shoulders. Whether or not your parent has confided to you his preferences, you have the final say.

While it may seem that the living will would be preferable—because your elder gets to make the decisions about the care he is willing to accept—in some circumstances the proxy would be the better option. Because the living will is executed well in advance of its actual use, it cannot anticipate every contingency that might arise. And with the rapid pace of technological and pharmaceutical advances, it is possible to find yourself wishing to make choices that the living will does not allow. The proxy permits you more leeway.

On the other hand, some states make it very difficult to assert your rights under a healthcare proxy. You may be required to provide proof that your parent made his or her specific treatment choices clear to you prior to his illness. Because the requisite language of the living will and the healthcare proxy differs from one state to the next, and because healthcare providers are very cautious about incurring legal liability, you need to be very careful that the form in which your advance directive—whichever one you use—is executed. You are best advised to consult legal advice rather than trying to do it yourself.

Your elder's legacy

Another area of anxiety—and sometimes contention—in many families is the parent's will. Many of us put off dealing with this very important legal document for as long as possible because it is such a strong reminder of our own mortality. Your elder may therefore resist any attempts to bring up the subject—or you may yourself feel uncomfortable,

Watch Out!
Do not go to all the trouble of drawing up a healthcare proxy or living will only to discover that your document runs afoul of the laws in your particular state. Even if you're committed to trying to do it yourself, at least have an attorney look over the final draft to make certain that what you've come up with is enforceable.

for fear that you will come across as grasping or morbid. But the formulation of a proper, orderly distribution of the estate is extremely important, and you must try to overcome your discomfort with the subject to help your elder complete this task while he or she is still able to do so.

What a will entails

Making a will involves two separate decisions:

- Appointing an executor
- Specifying how the estate will be divided

Many traditionally minded elders will be most comfortable naming the eldest son in the family as executor. But if big brother Joe is pretty scatterbrained when it comes to handling finances and baby sister Sue is a whiz of an accountant, Sue will be the better choice. The executor is charged with handling all the estate's business from the time of your elder's death to the final dispensation of all estate assets. That means Sue's accounting acumen will be put to good use when calculating taxes to be paid and the piecemeal dissolution of the property covered in the will.

But maybe Sue is a financial wizard but not particularly adept at handling delicate family politics, while middle-child Mary is the better peacemaker. In this case, your elder may prefer to set up a joint executorship setting Sue in charge of the dollars and cents, and Mary in charge of communicating the estate's business to the rest of the family. The goal is to select those individuals best suited to handle the task efficiently, effectively, and with minimal risk of triggering contention among the rest of the siblings and other interested parties.

As for the business of dividing up the estate among the family, this is truly something that should be done with the benefit of professional advice. The legalese of a will may seem impenetrable to non-lawyers, but it does have the saving grace of being eminently clear to the court—which means that there is less likelihood of someone successfully challenging and perhaps overturning your elder's specific intentions. In addition, a lawyer experienced in estate law will be able to advise your family on how to handle any odd situations that may come up.

For example, when one family was recently closing out their dad's estate, they were faced with what they came to call the "toy car conundrum." Their dad had fallen into picking up match-box cars years ago. It came to be something of a family joke: On every birthday and at Christmas, one of the kids would pick up another of the tiny cars as an inexpensive present. When the time came to draw up a will, dad was thinking "Who gets the house?" "Who should get the car?" He's certainly not thinking of an item-by-item inventory of all the little household knickknacks—like those cars.

But as the household items were being packed up in anticipation of the sale of the property, the executor discovered that match-box cars were now considered highly desirable collectibles—they may have cost only a couple of dollars apiece when they were first purchased, but they sold for nearly $100 apiece today! And dad had accumulated nearly 200 of the little toys. The estate's lawyer was able to put the family in touch with a dealer in this specialized branch of the collectibles market, and each of the three siblings realized a tidy extra dividend from the estate that the will didn't specifically address.

Timesaver
When your elder is ready to head to the lawyer's office to draw up a will, have prepared ahead of time a descriptive list of the major assets—particularly investments—that will need to be specifically included.

Watch Out!
When an individual dies intestate—without a legal will—the state assumes complete discretion as to the disposition of the property left behind. This may result in a settlement that directly contradicts your elder's wishes.

Bringing up the subject

The need for your parent to have a will drawn up is obvious, especially when you recognize that if your parent dies without one, the state makes the final choice as to how the property should be dispensed.

However understandable your parent's (or your) reluctance to talk about making a will, it is important that you do so well before incapacity strikes. It is generally easiest to discuss the subject if you take the focus off death and place it squarely in terms of protecting your elder's assets. After all, your elder has spent a lifetime of hard work to build whatever estate he or she now enjoys. That work can easily be lost if steps aren't taken ahead of time to make certain that its disposition is efficiently handled according to your elder's own preferences—by drawing up a will and appointing an executor.

If the urge to protect the estate is not enough to motivate your elder to draw up a will, a concern with maintaining family harmony just might do the trick. Families have foundered in bitter acrimony when children squabble over Mom or Dad's estate in the absence of a will. With a will in place, such bickering can be kept to a minimum. It's best, of course, when all interested parties are kept informed about at least the general terms of the will—where there are no secrets, there's less likelihood of later resentments.

Working it out as a family

If at all possible with your family dynamic, and if your elder consents, the best course to take would be for your elder to preside over a general family meeting in which this—and perhaps the issue of medical care decision-making—is discussed. By doing so, there's a greater chance that the process will be conducted in a civil manner because each sibling will have the chance to air his or her expectations and concerns. At the same time, your elder retains the right of final say as to how the estate—which, after all, is the result of his or her own life's work—will be distributed.

Of course, some families do not have the option of meeting in a group for this purpose. In some cases, the siblings have moved to distant locations; in others, the family lacks the necessary level of cooperation and mutual respect. If either case is true in your family, it is still important that your elder selects an executor and, together with that person, consults a lawyer and draws up a will. No matter what your family dynamic, at least one person other than your elder himself should be fully informed about your parent's final wishes for the disposal of his or her property.

Remembering that your elder has the final say

In many cases, the siblings who stand to inherit an elder's estate have expectations—acknowledged or otherwise—about what should come to them when the estate is settled. If sister Mary handled much more of the eldercare responsibilities than all the other siblings, she may feel that she is entitled to a larger share of the inheritance. Or brother Joe, the eldest son, may be convinced that he—and he alone—is the proper choice as your elder's executor. But once your elder has made his or her choices, all discussion and dissension should cease. This is your parent's property, and your parent ultimately has the final say in how it should be distributed.

Bright Idea
When you meet with your elder as a family to discuss a will, keep the attendees down to immediate family. In other words, for this first meeting at least, spouses should not be included. You want to avoid anything that might set off resentments, and some siblings may take offense at including "outsiders" in so personal a discussion.

Good legal advice for your parent

If you've overcome your elder's objections to discussing a will, it's time to start looking for solid legal assistance. How do you go about helping your parent find a good estate law or elder law attorney?

One good place to begin your search for information on attorneys specializing in elder law is the National Academy of Elder Law Attorneys. You can write to this organization at 1604 North Country Club Road, Tucson, AZ, 85716; or call 520-881-4005. They'll provide you with referrals to elder law specialists in your location. An attorney who specializes in estate law is another good option, although elder law specialists have a background in a broader range of the issues you and your parent will be facing, such as durable powers of attorney and guardianships.

Once you've gotten a few names, check credentials. Call your local bar association and inquire about your candidates' background and training. Solicit opinions from friends who have gone this route before you. Once you've got a few solid names to check out, share the information you've gathered with your elder—he's the one who ultimately has to be satisfied with the choice.

When you've whittled your list of prospective attorneys to just a couple of names, call for a preliminary appointment. Most law firms now make this first visit a free consultation, so you don't have to worry about running up huge fees while hunting for the right attorney (of course, you should not assume this—always ask first). There's no need to commit to any payments until your elder is certain you've found the right person to handle his legal needs.

Solutions for troubling emotional issues

Dealing with issues such as living wills, powers of attorney, and your parent's estate is emotionally difficult—for you, your siblings, *and* for your elder. It is inevitable that such discussions will bring other fears and insecurities out into the open, and that can lead to serious contention. Your parent may have trouble accepting the fact of his or her mortality and may simultaneously be trying to resolve old areas of conflict with you and your siblings. In addition, your brothers and sisters may be working out their insecurities and their own fears of losing a parent.

Bringing all these issues out into the open now will make it much easier to pull together as a family when your elder falls seriously ill and truly needs your support. Some of the more commonly reported fears that arise in this situation include these:

- The elder fears that by acknowledging the need for a will, he or she is somehow closer to death.

- The children fear that if they bring up the need for a will, the elder will think they're only after his or her money.

- The child who acts as primary caregiver worries that the other siblings will resent his or her influence over the parent.

Accepting mortality

It's not just your parent who has a hard time accepting his or her mortality. As we mentioned in earlier chapters, you and your siblings may also find it difficult to accept that the parent to whom you once turned for strength and support is now approaching his or her final years. Drawing up a will forces us to accept the inevitability of death, which is why it's so hard to actually buckle down and deal with the task.

It may help your elder—and *you*—to cope with these issues if you recast them in more life-affirming terms. You're not planning for your parent's death—you're laying the groundwork that will keep the surviving family strong and united by removing possible causes of confusion and contention. A will lets everyone know where they stand and reduces the likelihood of bitter resentments and bickering.

Dealing with the fear of seeming greedy

Your elder knows that he or she is getting older. The simple fact that you've brought up the idea of making a will need not trigger suspicions that you're only interested in your parent's money— as long as you exercise a little tact and consideration. Once again, it's helpful to stress the importance of a will in maintaining good relations among the siblings. And if you're careful to solicit your elder's preferences rather than trying to impose your own, you need not worry too much about giving a negative impression.

That last point is the key: You need to defer to your parent's choices, regardless of your own opinions or beliefs. You did not amass the estate in question—your elder did that over the course of a lifetime's hard work. Your elder expects and deserves your respect for his choices in how that estate is distributed.

Dealing with the fear of disapproving siblings

It is sometimes—though not all that often—the case that the primary caregiver expects either consciously or subconsciously that all the time and effort he or she puts into caring for the elder should somehow earn extra consideration when the time comes to draw up the will. Even when the caregiver has no such expectations, it's not unheard of for the less-involved siblings to fear that they'll be shut out or shortchanged in the will.

In the first instance, it's wisest not to assume anything about the relative size of shares in your elder's estate. Securing the lion's share of the estate should not be the reason you're caring for your elder in the first place. Your elder also may have his or her own reasons for dividing things up: It may be that you're the more financially settled, while younger brother John is still scratching at his first job and is in greater need of financial help. Or eldest son Joe got financial support for all those years in business school, and your elder now wants to balance the scales by giving the other siblings a little more in the will. Even if your parent's reasoning seems unfair to you, the decision as to how the estate will be divided is, as we've already stressed, your elder's alone.

The second issue—that your siblings may fear you have undue influence in your role as primary caregiver—is an easy one to address, if you're sensitive to their concerns. Simply involve them as much as possible in the day-to-day routine of your parent's life. For siblings who live far away, help them stay in touch with your elder—keep them posted about what's going on by letters and phone calls. For siblings who live nearby, take steps to keep them involved with your parent by inviting them for visits whenever possible. Fill them in when special problems arise, even if they're not in a position to assist you in caregiving. The more open you are with them, the less likely they will be to assume bad things about you and your relationship with your elder.

Just the facts

- It's best to sort out the legal aspect of medical and financial decision-making before your parent becomes incapacitated.

- Two legal instruments that confer decision-making rights upon a caregiver are the power of attorney and a court order of guardianship.

- Living wills and healthcare proxies are means by which your elder can make his wishes known on medical care if he becomes incapacitated by illness.

- It's important that your elder take the time while she is still in control of her faculties to set forth a last will and testament so that the division of her estate doesn't become a divisive issue among her children.

GET THE SCOOP ON...
The changing social role of elders ▪ Aging's
inevitability ▪ Eldercare, present and future ▪
Emotional costs—and benefits—of
caregiving

Eldercare, Your Elder, and You

B y now it should be clear that your role as a caregiver for your aging parent is an important one. You are the person upon whom your elder depends for help in maintaining his or her independence for as long as possible. You are the person to whom he or she has turned, or will someday turn, for help when independence is no longer an option. The responsibility is great, and at times the task can seem overwhelming, but the rewards can be extraordinary. In this final chapter, we review what aging has come to mean in American society. We then review the kinds of care you may be called upon to provide as your parent grows older, and we explore the social and emotional costs—and benefits—of a well-planned approach to the eldercare experience.

Aging in society

Aging and dealing with the elderly are universal issues. All societies have had to face the natural

Unofficially...
In traditional, preliterate societies, elders had extraordinary control over the life of society because only they knew all the rituals needed for younger members to pass through the various stages of life, from naming at birth, through initiation at puberty, through marriage, and finally, at death.

stratification in social groups that aging represents. In traditional, preliterate societies, this stratification has generally been one in which elders were perceived as wise and powerful. After all, they were the only ones with substantial accumulated experience (and relative wealth). In contrast, the young had relatively greater vigor, so a natural hierarchy arose: The younger adults provided the hard, day-to-day labor, while the elders acted as management and as ritual specialists. In this way, everyone contributed something important to the greater society—a society that was frequently small enough to consist of just a very few kin-based groups.

But this "natural" stratification has had less practical utility in industrial societies such as the United States. You don't need to be young and strong to handle a computer keyboard, and you needn't be a member of the gray-haired set to have access to the wisdom of previous generations. This may help explain why we have such difficulty developing a coherent set of policies and services for our elders. And it may go a long way to explaining, as well, our ambivalence about dealing with the elderly in our own families.

Longevity: the "inevitable and good"

We've long been able to ignore the demographic realities of modern society, perhaps because the elderly never before constituted a large segment of the general population. As the demographic data of Chapter 1, "The Growing Need for Eldercare," makes clear, it has only been in recent decades that the elderly population in America has attained numbers sufficiently great to make them a powerful voice in shaping political and economic policy. And this shift is worldwide in scope: Current demographic projections tell us that by 2050, one in five people will be over the age of 60; of that number, fully 25 percent will be over 80.

A number of observers have looked long and hard at this demographic trend and have drawn some compelling conclusions. For example, historian Theodore Roszak, author of 1968's *The Making of the Counterculture,* has recently published *America the Wise: The Longevity Revolution and the True Wealth of Nations* (Houghton Mifflin, 1999), a study of what some have termed "the graying of America." In it, he challenges old, negative stereotypes of aging and suggests that our new longevity is occasion for optimism: It is both "inevitable and good."

When youth confronts aging

Dr. Roszak's position notwithstanding, cultural prejudices change slowly. It is difficult to break down the perception that age and disability, and age and poverty, are inherently connected. The various media outlets in this society still seem fixated on catering to the youth market—implying, when not outright stating so, that its concerns, its tastes, and its trends, are at the very center of social life.

But this is perhaps a simple case of cultural inertia. After all, the demographic trends that show increasing longevity and a burgeoning population of the elderly also disclose that the younger generations, as a group, comprise a shrinking portion of society. This is because, along with trends toward better and more accessible healthcare, hygiene, and public policy, there have also come increased access to contraception and a greater acceptance for couples—and especially women—who choose to limit family size.

66

For age is opportunity no less/Than youth, though in another dress....
—Longfellow, *Morituri Salutamus*

99

This means that our elders are able, and encouraged, to continue to contribute to society in work and in play, in culture and in politics. This is perhaps best exemplified by their increased social and economic clout, as it is played out in the proliferation of services, policies, and consumer goods targeting the over-60 age group. After all, the American Association of Retired Persons claims a circulation rate of more than 20 million copies for its magazine, *Modern Maturity*. Where once elders may have felt that they were being shouldered out of the way, now many feel that they have every right to stand their ground and retain for as long as possible an active role in the life around them.

The inevitability factor

As American society and culture comes to grip with a burgeoning elderly population, it also confronts a long ignored truth: We are all potential elders. Older Americans are a much more highly visible population group than ever before, so aging and the effects of age become ever more present, visible, and acknowledged in our culture.

The message is unmistakable: How we treat our elders today will profoundly affect the way *we* will be treated tomorrow. That's not just by virtue of the example we set for our own children (although that is an important consideration), but it's also by virtue of the programs and policies aimed toward eldercare that we are willing to support. It may be tempting to think of, say, a local political initiative to provide quality control for assisted-living facilities in terms of their applicability to Mom and Dad's generation, but such legislation will also have an impact on what's available when our turn rolls around.

The boomer bubble goes gray

As the leading edge of the largest demographic bubble in this country's history—the baby boomers—now approaches the early years of what we call "old age," the presence—or lack—of viable eldercare alternatives becomes an issue of increasing immediacy and importance.

Dr. Roszak argues that these newest recruits to the ranks of the elderly have been, at every stage of their lifecycle, quick to confront the issues that most interest them, and they are unlikely to turn aside from their lifelong tradition of activism and social conscience. They will seek more and better ways to maintain their independence in daily life, even as they face the increasing physical frailty that comes with getting older. This presents some important challenges to society as a whole, as it confronts ageism in the workplace and in the community, and as it seeks to put in place mechanisms that will support the needs of the elderly and their primary caregivers.

Eldercare is a two-way street

Thus, it is likely that the current trend toward broadening eldercare options will continue and perhaps even increase in intensity. Today's caregivers recognize that they are the care-receivers of tomorrow. As they seek assistance for their elders, they learn firsthand what is—and what is not—available. As a result, they are making their voices heard by public, private, and governmental organizations that are in a position to improve the level and quality of eldercare.

But this is not to say that the boomer generation's involvement in improving eldercare options is wholly self-serving. Most of these same adult

children who are currently caretaking their elders
would cite factors of compassion and family duty as
important elements in their decision to serve as care
providers. Perhaps most of all, they will talk of the
tremendous rewards of caregiving—rewards that
come from having had the privilege to share in making a loved one's final years comfortable, fulfilling,
and peaceful.

We'll speak of these rewards later in the chapter.
For now, it's time to return to a review of the emotional issues and practical considerations you'll be
dealing with as you provide your elder with the care
and support he or she needs.

Elders have feelings, too

As your parent grows older, he or she is increasingly
faced with changes that may be difficult to accept,
such as an increasing loss of autonomy, decreased
mobility, and a diminished social circle as friends
and relations of a lifetime die. A poll conducted by
Genesis ElderCare, a for-profit corporation focusing
on the field of assisted-living facilities, identified
many of the issues that elders address. The study,
entitled "A Look at Aging In America," demonstrates how these concerns increase in immediacy
and importance as your parent gets older.

Aging's impact on self-perception

The Genesis poll makes it clear that elders are active
and engaged in life, and that they want to remain so
for as long as possible. Interests and activities that
engaged them in their younger years lose little of
their desirability over time. When asked about
aspects of self-image and personal preferences,
elders reported according to the data presented in
Table 14.1.

TABLE 14.1: POSITIVE FEELINGS ABOUT ONE'S SELF

	Total	ages 65–69	ages 70–74	ages 75–79	age 80+
I'm a practical person.	96%	97%	95%	97%	97%
I enjoy living independently.	93%	96%	91%	93%	89%
I look forward to each new day.	93%	94%	92%	95%	90%
I enjoy meeting new people.	91%	93%	93%	87%	90%
I'm a very trusting person.	91%	93%	90%	90%	87%
I enjoy keeping up with what's happening in the world.	89%	88%	91%	89%	86%
I'm more fortunate than most.	85%	87%	81%	87%	86%

Source: *The Genesis ElderCare™* Poll

Clearly, even as your elder achieves "very old" (over 80) status, he or she wants to be a vital, participating actor in life. Loss of interest isn't the issue behind an elder's gradual withdrawal from full activity—it's only when your elder loses particular capabilities or attributes that he or she is likely to pull back from active life. These losses are usually gradual, but the Genesis ElderCare poll points out that the effects of such losses are clear. As people age, they report a decline in pleasure for such activities as taking long trips, going to parties, or flying in airplanes—all of which can become increasingly uncomfortable as an individual loses mobility.

Missed pleasures

The Genesis poll also queried elders about the things they missed most as they got older. The two most significant losses elders reported were "losing family or friends" (with 58 percent reporting this in the 65–69 age range, increasing to 72 percent for those age 80 or older), and "not being able to get around as well (23 percent of those 65–69 reported this, while 61 percent of those 80 and older did so).

These findings are easily understood: They are responses to the natural process of aging. The older one gets, the more likely one is to see friends and loved ones pass on—many elders find themselves getting into the habit of checking the obituaries in the newspaper before even looking at the front page news. This isn't morbidity; it's facing facts. And the older one gets, the less easy it is to get around unassisted—a frustrating circumstance for anyone, not just elders.

Help where it's needed

As a primary eldercare provider, you're in large company: Studies by the Administration on Aging and by for-profit caregiving companies such as Genesis ElderCare and Fortis Long-Term Care agree that more than 60 percent of all of America's elderly receive some level of assistance from one or more family members. By far, the majority of the help required is emotional support, followed closely by help around the household—making minor repairs, for the most part. These needs remain consistent as your elder ages.

As we've stressed throughout this book, the particular constellation of caregiving needs you, as primary provider, must address will be unique to your elder's situation, preferences, and level of disability. One factor, of course, is the age of your elder—the number and intensity of needs for assistance will increase as your parent ages. But other factors affect the degree of care required as well. Your elder's general health makes a big difference in how much help he or she will need from you. All studies on this issue agree that your elder's income and available assets have a major impact on the caregiving demands that fall to family members.

The emotional center

As noted above, by far the single most important element of care your elder is likely to require is emotional support. Yet this is precisely the sort of assistance that is most difficult for many caregivers to provide. Your emotional response to the signs of aging in a loved one, and to the implications for your own mortality that those signs imply, can color your responses. In addition, the nature of the life-long relationship you have had with your elder can help—or hinder—your effectiveness in coping with your elder's emotional needs.

When the parent-child relationship is troubled

Sometimes it seems as if we can never escape the emotional baggage we first took on in childhood. Popular culture is rife with examples, usually (but not always) played for comedic effect, of the confrontation between adult children and their parents. Consider the many examples, from Hope's inability to hear anything except criticism from her mother in *Thirtysomething*, to Grace's embarrassment at her theatrical mom's flirtatiousness in *Will and Grace*, to Al Brooks' reversion to guilt and childishness when he moves back home in the film *Mother*. These scenarios work in TV and the movies because they resonate for all of us.

Watch Out!
Unexamined resentments— yours or your elder's—can make life miserable for all concerned. If you can communicate with your elder about them, do so. If you cannot, at least find some outlet for these feelings—a counselor, member of the clergy, relative, or close friend in whom you can confide. Don't let your resentments build—they *will* explode on you if you do.

When your elder needs your help, unfortunately, these kinds of conflicts don't go away by themselves. Mom is still going to do the "mom things" that make you crazy. Dad is more than likely to continue to believe that his way—not yours—is the best way to fix a washer, mow the lawn, drive into town, or anything else. These small things can become major irritants over time and can cloud our perceptions of the caregiving relationship (but see Chapter 5, "Strategies for Coping," for insights into these stresses and how to work through them).

Sometimes the stresses are much more profound. If you and your elder have had a strained— or even estranged—relationship, it can be difficult to find yourself later in life having to provide assistance for him or her. Old resentments die hard.

In some cases, it may be necessary to accept the fact that you simply are not suited to provide a certain kind or level of care. For example, if you and your parent are always up in arms against each other over every little detail of day-to-day life, you may not be able to have your parent stay with you in your home. But you can address your elder's needs for care in other ways—perhaps he or she would be happier living in an ALF, or would like to stay in his or her own home with a live-in companion. Quality of life—for both you and your elder—is an important issue, and there is little quality found in stressful, conflict-ridden relationships.

When the family fits

Most of us are fortunate enough to have relationships with our elders that are positive. Sure, there may be stresses, but the relationship bedrock is built on caring, not conflict. You, the caregiver, are capable of looking beyond the day-to-day inconveniences and irritants, and your elder fundamentally loves you, however critical he or she may sometimes seem to be.

In this situation, the emotional rewards of caring for your elder can be extraordinary. This can be a time when you grow closer to one another, sharing the things you've learned and experienced. Or, it may be a time when you can express your gratitude for all the things your elder did for you as you were growing up by caring for him or her during a final illness.

Even the irritants can be coped with more easily. Dad's outbursts of temper when you drive him to the doctor is understandable to you because you know it's based on a fear of the test results he's going to hear—or maybe it's because he's still not happy with having had to give up his right to drive himself. Mom's criticism of your bedside manner can be recognized for what it is—frustration that she can't be up and doing for herself.

So, yes, there is the opportunity for building a closer bond, and for expressing thanks to your parent. This can also be a rich time in other ways—if you make it so. Your parents had whole lives of their own, with childhood memories and coming-of-age adventures that they would probably share willingly, if anyone were interested in listening. This is a time when you can get to know your parent as a person— not just the adult who changed *your* diapers, sent *you* to school, and danced at *your* wedding. Like anyone else in this world, your elder has a unique story, but it's one that, as the child, you may never have really taken the time to learn. Now, for perhaps the first time, you can do that.

Functional assistance

While emotional support is the most frequently
cited need in surveys of the elderly, it is only to be
expected that a need for practical assistance is likely
to arise as well, and that such assistance will become
increasingly necessary over time. The types of assistance required, of course, will depend upon the specific functional loss an individual elder faces. To
review the information originally given in Chapter
2, "Who Needs Eldercare?," a partial list of such
assistance would include these issues:

- Transportation
- Shopping
- House- and yardwork
- Food preparation
- Financial assistance
- Money management
- Monitoring or dispensing medications

Your personal, emotional relationship with your
elder will have a great impact on your effectiveness
in personally providing assistance in these areas. So
also will the burden of other responsibilities you currently carry affect your response.

Whether you personally show up at Dad's house
to mow the lawn or cook Mom's special meals in
addition to the family dinner at your house, or
whether you help your parent screen the home-care
worker hired to provide these services, you are participating in the caregiving process. Once again, this
is an occasion in which you can deepen and
strengthen your relationship with your elder, an
opportunity that can enrich both your lives.

The trick is to find ways to assist that permit everyone concerned a chance to feel good about themselves. Consider this vignette: Ed had always lived an active life, and even well into his 70s, he showed no inclination of slowing down or giving up his independence. But recent episodes of shortness of breath had frightened him. Once, he even fainted, waking up on the floor of the living room disoriented and more than a little shaken. All his kids were grown, and although his son, Charles, lived in town and had offered to have Dad come stay with the family, Ed had said for years, "I'm not going to move in and become a burden to anybody!"

There was no changing Dad's mind on this, but everyone was rightly concerned about that fainting episode. So, father and son had a talk. Charles avoided direct reference to the fainting (Ed wouldn't tolerate talk about it), but he mentioned that since Dad's house was right on the route from Charles's home and his job, he really wouldn't mind having a place to stop off for a pre- and post-work cup of coffee. In fact, given how hectic his household was at those times of day, Dad would be doing him a favor by letting him have these two, regularly scheduled quiet moments in his day.

Ed was no less concerned about the fainting spell than the rest of the family—he was afraid that if it happened again, he wouldn't be able to get up or get help—but he couldn't admit to this fear. He heard Charles' request with great relief—it offered him a way to have someone come by regularly to check up on his well-being without having to admit he needed it. And during these regular visits, father and son shared stories, jokes, and political opinions. Charles told tales of his workplace, and Ed shared his plans for landscaping the backyard. Years later, both told the rest of the family that these were the occasions in which they became not just father and son, but true friends.

Not all elders are as prickly as Ed about accepting necessary assistance, but it happens often enough that the care provider needs to find a tactful way to get his or her elder to accept help. When you're successful, you can not only take care of a particular caregiving need, but you also can create an opening for forging new, deep connections with one another.

The importance of a proper plan

Sometimes it may seem as if your day-to-day round of caregiving tasks have come to consume your life. Perhaps the tasks and chores began small—a little periodic taxi-service duty and shopping once a week for Mom, or a few weekends spent at the old homestead refitting the bathroom with grab bars. But as time goes on, the number of occasions when assistance is needed is likely to increase—or, you may go along for quite a long time with no real problems, when a sudden accident or medical emergency changes everything overnight.

All the best will in the world won't do you much good if you find yourself handling every change in your elder's situation on an ad hoc basis—nor is this likely to contribute much to a calm and dignified experience for your elder. None of us are at our best when we cope by lurching from crisis to crisis. You cannot guard against all possible emergencies, but you can keep them from having the power to over-whelm you. You do this by planning ahead. Chapter 6, "Organizing Your Elder's Finances," and Chapter 7, "Organizing Your Elder's Medical Affairs," give you the information you need to get this process started. Chapter 12, "Managing Eldercare Costs," and Chapter 13, "Protecting Your Elder's Legal Rights," go into some detail about the financial and legal steps you can take to ensure that even in the most difficult situations you have some clear sense of direction.

Most important of all, every step of the way you want to involve your elder in any eldercare plan-ning, insofar as he or she is capable of participating. There are two equally important reasons for this. First, of course, is the fact that any decisions you make will materially affect your elder—his or her care, comfort, and contentment are in your hands. Second is protecting your *own* peace of mind. At times you, as primary caregiver, may be faced with extremely difficult choices, particularly if your elder is very sick or incapacitated. In the absence of a clear understanding of what your parent would want, you can find yourself stricken with doubt as to the right course of action to take. But if you have had the opportunity to work out with your elder what he or she truly would want done, you can carry out your responsibilities in full confidence that you are doing the right thing—no matter what the situ-ation you face.

Throughout the eldercare experience, and espe-cially at the very end, the finest gift you as caregiver can give is respect for your elder's deepest wishes. And the greatest reward that you yourself will attain during this time is the knowledge that you've done your best to ease your elder's later years.

Just the facts

- The new demographic reality is that the elderly have now become a major segment of the population, and their relative numbers are projected to continue to grow for several decades to come.

- Cultural prejudices that link aging with social obsolescence are breaking down as our aging population demonstrates a capacity for vigor and independence long after traditional retirement age.

- As elders assume a more visible role in society, all of us are forced to confront the natural truth: We are all potential elders, and how we treat our elders today has implications for the way we will be treated tomorrow.

- By far the most significant caregiving need cited by elders is a need for emotional support.

- The nature of your relationship with your elder, considered in conjunction with your elder's specific needs for assistance, are the two most important elements to consider in putting together a caregiving plan.

- A proper plan that takes into account your elder's own stated preferences for care and intervention is the best way to ensure that your elder's needs will be properly met, even in the face of emergency or crisis.

Glossary

activities of daily living (ADLs) Activities such as feeding, dressing, or grooming oneself that are necessary for day-to-day life but that may become difficult or impossible for a disabled person.

adult day center Private or non-profit programs that cater to elderly people with pronounced disabilities; some may specialize in providing services to elders with particular disabilities, such as Alzheimer's disease.

aging in place A term denoting the choice of many elders to remain in their home as long as possible, supplementing their eldercare needs when necessary with the periodic assistance of family members or outside agency services.

Alzheimer's disease A degenerative brain disease that strikes the elderly.

assisted-living facility A transitional form of housing for the elderly that combines largely independent living with onsite services such as transportation, meals, access to regular medical attention, asistance with personal care, and on-call emergency medical care.

baby boomer   The popular term for the generation born between 1946-1964. This generation makes up the largest single population segment in America.

caregiver   Anyone who provides medical, financial, personal, or emotional care to another.

community-based services   Eldercare assistance, ranging from senior centers to transportation to home-delivered meals, made available through local public and private not-for-profit organizations.

conservatorship   (also called *guardianship*) A court order granting one individual the right to act on behalf of another, sought when the latter individual is incapable of acting on his or her own behalf and when no other provision, such as a power of attorney, is in effect.

dementia   Impaired mental functioning resulting from a variety of illnesses, including Alzheimer's disease.

demographics   The numerical study of population statistics and trends.

durable power of attorney   A legal instrument that grants an individual specified rights to make decisions for or act on behalf of another in legal, financial, and/or medical matters; the instrument is not subject to a specified time period.

eldercare   The physical, psychological, financial, and other forms of assistance provided to people over the age of 65.

elder day services   Another term for *adult day centers* (see previous entry).

elderizing   Modifying or repairing a house or apartment to accommodate an elder's increasing physical frailties.

elder law   Law specifically geared to the issues and problems of the elderly.

elderly Anyone age 65 or older.

gerontology The study of the aging process.

guardianship See *conservatorship.*

healthcare proxy A document that specifies someone other than the elder as the legal decision-maker in medical matters once the elder can no longer make choices for him- or herself.

home care Non-medical services and assistance provided by outside agencies, both for-profit and not-for profit; services include housekeeping, meal preparation, and transportation.

home healthcare Health-related services provided by personnel who are recruited, trained, and paid by outside agencies, both for-profit and not-for-profit.

independent-living unit Any senior housing unit that provides no specialized service or staff intervention.

instrumental activities of daily living (IADLs) Activities such as meal preparation and heavy housework that may become difficult for an individual with a handicap. These are not essential for day-to-day survival but are important to maintaining a good quality of life.

living will A legal document in which an elder specifically indicates, in advance of any incapacitation, the kind of medical intervention desired—and rejected—should he or she become terminally ill.

longevity Life expectancy.

long-term care facility A residential facility that cares for the severely disabled or the elderly who require round-the-clock nursing care.

Medicaid A state-administered, federally mandated healthcare program aimed at providing access to medical care for low-income people (not just the elderly).

Medicare   Healthcare benefits earned during your working life, or available for a low fee, to cover costs of certain aspects of medical care for those over the age of 65.

Medigap insurance   Privately purchased insurance to cover the gap between medical costs and Medicare coverage.

nursing home   A full-service, 24-hour care facility for individuals who cannot care for themselves.

personal emergency device   A buzzer or switch that can summon emergency medical assistance when pressed.

power of attorney   The granting of certain rights to an individual to act in the name of another, subject to a specific end date after which the power of attorney lapses.

primary caregiver   The adult child of an aging parent who assumes primary responsibility for providing or coordinating that elder's assistance needs.

respite services   Short-term, limited services—from home care to healthcare—provided by outside agencies to provide the primary caregiver a break from the responsibilities of full-time eldercare.

senior centers   Community-run programs that cater to the needs of elders with minimal disabilities, offering such amenities as inexpensive hot meals, structured activities, exercise programs, and social events.

springing power of attorney   The legal instrument granting one individual the right to act in the name of another, but only once a triggering event (such as hospitalization of the principal) has occurred or a specified date has passed.

very elderly   An elderly person age 80 or older.

Resource Directory

National Organizations

ABLEDATA
8455 Colesville Road, Suite 935
Silver Spring, MD 20910
800-227-0216
www.abledata.com
Provides an informational database of more than
23,000 products used in assisted-living situations; the
Web site is searchable.

Alzheimer's Association
919 North Michigan Ave., Suite 1000
Chicago, IL 60611-1676
800-272-3900
National organization for people who suffer from
Alzheimer's disease and for their caregiving families. Contact this national organization to ask for the
local support group nearest you.

American Association for Retired Persons (AARP)
601 E St. NW
Washington, D.C. 20049
Phone: 1-800-424-3410
A national organization which offers information
and referral for the legal, medical, financial, and
social issues facing the elderly. Publisher of *Modern
Maturity* magazine.

American Association of Homes and Services for the
Aging
901 E St. NW, Suite 500
Washington, D.C. 20004-2037
202-783-2242
This umbrella organization represents not-for-profit
organizations dedicated to providing high-quality
healthcare, housing, and services to the nation's
elderly.

American Parkinson Disease Association
1250 Hylan Blvd., Suite 4B
Staten Island, NY 10305
718-981-8001
Hotline: 800-223-2732
Provides information for patients and families on
finances and research.

Arthritis Foundation
1314 Spring St. NW
Atlanta, GA 30309
404-872-7100
800-283-7800
Supports arthritis research and provides information on the condition.

Children of Aging Parents (CAPS)
1609 Woodburn Road, Suite 302A
Levittown, PA 19055
215-945-6900
800-227-7294
National organization for caregiving adult children, with support group chapters in most states. Provides pamphlets, information, and newsletters.

Children of Parkinsonians (COPS)
73-700 El Paseo, Suite 2
Palm Desert, CA 92260
760-773-5628
310-476-7030
National organization for adult children of parents with Parkinson's disease. Provides information, support, and a newsletter.

Department of Veterans' Affairs
810 Vermont Ave. NW
Washington, D.C. 20420
202-273-5700
800-827-1000
Federal agency that provides benefits to eligible service men and women and their dependents.

Eldercare Locator (phone number only)
Washington, D.C.
800-677-1116
Provides information on local resources nationwide to callers between 9 A.M. and 11 P.M. (Eastern standard time) Monday through Friday.

Gerontological Society of America
1275 K St. NW, Suite 350
Washington, D.C. 20005-4006
202-842-1275
www.geron.org
The Gerontological Society of America was established in 1945 to promote the scientific study of aging. The Society publishes several journals and holds an annual scientific meeting.

Lifeline Systems, Inc.
640 Memorial Dr.
Cambridge, MA 02139
800-543-3546
Offers personal emergency response systems, advises callers of nearest available resources, and researches aging and offers a database of information.

Medic Alert Foundation
P.O. Box 381009
Turlock, CA 95381-1009
209-668-3333
800-344-3226
Offers an emergency ID bracelet for people with a variety of medical problems.

National Aging Information Center
500 E St. SW, Suite 910
Washington, D.C. 20024
202-554-9800
www.aginfo.org
Established in 1995 by the Administration on Aging, this organization provides databases and information on a variety of aging issues.
National Association for Geriatric Care Managers

1604 N. Country Club Road
Tucson, AZ 85716
520-881-8008
Organization of professional care managers nation-wide.

National Association for Home Care
228 7th. St. SE
Washington, D.C. 20003
202-547-7424
Association that represents home healthcare services.

National Depressive and Manic Depressive
Association
730 North Franklin St., Suite 501
Chicago, IL 60610
800-826-3632
National DMDA is a not-for-profit organization
established to educate patients, families, professionals, and the general public about the nature and
management of depressive and manic depressive
illnesses.

National Family Caregivers Association
621 East Bexhill Dr.
Kensington, MD 20895-3104
301-942-6430
800-896-3650
National organization for family caregivers.

National Institute of Neurological Disorders and Stroke
P.O. Box 5801
Bethesda, MD 20824
800-352-9424
www.nih.gov/ninds/
Provides information on neurological disorders.

National Kidney and Urologic Diseases Information Clearinghouse
3 Information Way
Bethesda, MD 20892-3580
301-654-4415
Provides information on many of the most serious diseases affecting public health.

National Meals on Wheels Foundation
1621 Forty-Fourth St. SW, #300
Grand Rapids, MI 49509
800-999-6262
Provides local referrals to Meals on Wheels programs that offer delivered meals to homebound individuals.

National Osteoporosis Foundation
1150 17th. St. NW
Washington, D.C. 20036-4603
202-223-2226
800-223-9994
A national agency that provides information on osteoporosis, a disease that decreases bone density.

National Stroke Association
8480 East Orchard Road, Suite 1000
Englewood, CO 80111-5015
303-649-9299
www.stroke.org
Provides information for patients and family members about strokes.

Prostate Information Center
P.O. Box 9
Minneapolis, MN 55440
800-543-9632
Provides general information on diseases of the prostate and maintains a list of physicians who treat such illnesses in the caller's area.

Social Security Administration
800-772-1213 (phone number only)
Provides information on Medicare, SSI, and Social Security disability benefits.

Visiting Nurse Associations of America
3801 East Florida, Suite 900
Denver, CO 80210
303-753-0218
800-426-2547
Provides information on Visiting Nurse Associations, which provide healthcare and information to patients in their homes.

State Home Care Associations

These state associations are members of the National Association for Home Care in Washington, D.C. Check with them for information on home health agencies in your state. For an updated listing, see the National Association for Home Health Care Web site (www.nahc.org/).

Alabama
Alabama Association of Home Health Agencies
P.O. Box 230727
Montgomery, AL 36123-00727
334-277-2130
e-mail: AAHHA@aahha.org

Alaska
Alaska Home Care Association
c/o Hospice & Home Care of Juneau
3200 Hospital Dr., Suite 100
Juneau, AK 99801
907-463-3113

Arizona
Arizona Association for Home Care
2334 South McClintock
Tempe, AZ 85282
602-967-2524

Arkansas
Home Care Association of Arkansas
501 Woodlane, Suite 200
Little Rock, AR 72201
501-376-2273

California
Home Care and Hospice Association of California
4144 Winding Way
Sacramento, CA 95841
916-974-3522

Colorado
Home Care Association of Colorado
7853 East Arapahoe Road, Suite 2100
Englewood, CO 80112
303-694-4728
e-mail: hcac@assnoffice.com

Connecticut
Connecticut Association for Home Care, Inc.
110 Barnes Road
P.O. Box 90
Wallingford, CT 06492-0090
203-265-9931
e-mail: humphrey@chime.org

Delaware
Delaware Association of Home Care and
Community Care
P.O. Box 166
Montchanin, DE 19710
302-764-6155
e-mail: rphall@aol.com

District of Columbia
Capital Homecare Association
5151 Wisconsin Ave. NW, Suite 400
Washington, D.C. 20016-4124
202-686-8728

Florida
Associated Home Health Industries of Florida, Inc.
820 East Park Ave., Building H
Tallahassee, FL 32301-2600
850-222-8967
e-mail: gtischer@ahhif.org

Georgia
Georgia Association of Home Health Agencies, Inc.
320 Interstate N. Parkway, Suite 490
Atlanta, GA 30339-2203
770-984-9704
e-mail: gahomehealth@earthlink.net

Hawaii
Hawaii Association for Home Care
1471 Pule Place
Honolulu, HI 96816
808-735-2970

Idaho
Idaho Association of Home Health Agencies
2419 West State St., Suite 5
Boise, ID 83702
208-345-3072
e-mail: Csearles@compuserv.com

Illinois
Illinois Home Care Council
222 West Ontario, Suite 430
Chicago, IL 60610
312-335-9922
e-mail: mtkihcc@aol.com

Indiana
Indiana Association for Home Care, Inc.
8888 Keystone Crossing, Suite 1000
Indianapolis, IN 46240
317-844-6630
e-mail: iahcms@earthlink.net

Iowa
Iowa Association for Home Care
1520 High St., Suite 203-B
Des Moines, IA 50309
515-282-3965

Kansas
Kansas Home Care Association
1000 Monterey Way
Lawrence, KS 66049
913-841-8611
e-mail: exec@kshomecare.org

Kentucky
Kentucky Home Health Association
154 Patchen Dr., Suite 90
Lexington, KY 40517
606-268-2574
e-mail: kyhomehlth@aol.com

Louisiana
Home Care Association of Louisiana
3032 Old Forge Dr.
Baton Rouge, LA 70808
504-924-4144

Maine
Home Care Alliance of Maine
20 Middle St.
Augusta, ME 04841
207-623-0345

Maryland
Maryland Association for Home Care, Inc.
5820 Southwestern Blvd.
Baltimore, MD 21227
410-242-1973

Massachusetts
Home & Health Care Association of Massachusetts
20 Park Plaza, Suite 620
Boston, MA 02116
617-482-8830
e-mail: pkelleh@mass-homehealth.org

Michigan
Michigan Home Health Association
2140 University Park Dr., Suite 220
Okemos, MI 48864
517-349-9089
e-mail: mhhadck@aol.com

Minnesota
Minnesota HomeCare Association
1711 West County Road B, Suite 209N
St. Paul, MN 55113-4036
612-635-0607
e-mail: djkildahl@aol.com

Mississippi
Mississippi Association for Home Care
P.O. Box 68681
Jackson, MS 39286
601-355-8900
e-mail: mahc@teclink.net

Missouri
Missouri Alliance for Home Care
2420 Hyde Park Road, Suite A
Jefferson City, MO 65109
314-634-7772
e-mail: mahc@computerland.net

Montana
Montana Association of Home Health Agencies
P.O. Box 39
Polson, MT 59860
406-883-7300
e-mail: maggied@netrix.net

Nebraska
Nebraska Association of Home and Community
Agencies
P.O. Box 22234
Lincoln, NE 68502
(No telephone)

Nevada
Home Health Care Association of Nevada
P.O. Box 12190
Reno, NV 89510-2190
702-323-6003

New Hampshire
Home Care Association of New Hampshire
8 Green St.
Concord, NH 03301
603-225-5597
e-mail: susan@hcanh.mv.com

New Jersey
Home Health Assembly of New Jersey, Inc.
14 Washington Road, Suite 211
Princeton Junction, NJ 08550-1030
609-275-6100
e-mail: HHANJ@homecarenj.org

New Mexico
New Mexico Association for Home Care
3200 Carlisle Blvd. NE, Suite 115
Albuquerque, NM 87110
505-889-4556
e-mail: joieg@earthlink.net

New York
Home Care Association of New York State, Inc.
21 Elk St.
Albany, NY 12207
518-426-8764
e-mail:crodat@earthlink.net

North Carolina
North Carolina Association of Home Care, Inc.
1005 Dresser Court
Raleigh, NC 27609
919-878-0500
e-mail: nchacl@interpath.com

North Dakota
North Dakota Association for Home Care
P.O. Box 2175
Bismarck, ND 58502-2175
701-224-1815

Ohio
Ohio Council for Home Care
6230 Busch Blvd., Suite 460
Columbus, OH 43229-1826
614-885-0434
e-mail: ochc@aol.com

Oklahoma
Oklahoma Association for Home Care
6303 North Portland, Suite 205
Oklahoma City, OK 73112-1411
405-943-6242
e-mail: request@oahc.com

Oregon
Oregon Association for Home Care
147 Southeast 102nd Ave.
Portland, OR 97216
503-253-9237

Pennsylvania
Pennsylvania Association of Home Health Agencies
20 Erford Road, Suite 115
Lemoyne, PA 17043
717-975-9448
e-mail: starkl@igateway.com

Rhode Island
Rhode Island Partnership for Home Care, Inc.
P.O. Box 603309
Providence, RI 02906
401-751-2487

South Carolina
South Carolina Home Care Association
P.O. Box 1763
Columbia, SC 29202
803-254-7355

South Dakota
South Dakota Home Health Association
P.O. Box 751
Watertown, SD 57201-0751
605-353-6271

Tennessee
Tennessee Association for Home Care, Inc.
131 Donelson Pike
Nashville, TN 37214-2901
615-885-3399

Texas
Texas Association for Home Care
3737 Executive Center Dr., Suite 151
Austin, TX 78731
512-338-9293
e-mail: anita@tahc.org

Utah
Utah Association of Home Health Agencies
6075 South Highland Dr.
Salt Lake City, UT 84171-0348
801-277-7084

Vermont
Vermont Assembly of Home Health Agencies
52 State St.
Montpelier, VT 05602
802-229-0579
e-mail: vahha@plainfield.bypass.com

Virginia
Virginia Association for Home Care
5407 Patterson Ave., Suite 200B
Richmond, VA 23226
804-285-8636
e-mail: vahc@erols.com

Washington
Home Care Association of Washington
23607 Highway 99, Suite 2C
P.O. Box C-2016
Edmonds, WA 98026
425-775-8120
e-mail: HomeCareWA@aol.com

West Virginia
West Virginia Council of Home Health Agencies,
Inc.
2567 University Ave., Suite 5011
Morgantown, WV 26505
304-292-5826
e-mail: wvchha@access.mountain.net

Wisconsin
Wisconsin Homecare Organization
5610 Medical Circle, Suite 33
Madison, WI 53719
608-278-1115
e-mail: WIShomecare@earthlink.net

Wyoming
Home Health Care Alliance of Wyoming
2600 East 18th St.
Cheyenne, WY 82001
307-778-5616

State Long-Term Care Ombudsmen

These individuals will hear and investigate your complaints about nursing homes and adult care homes. For an uypdated listing, see the Administration on Aging Web site (www.aoa. dhhs.gov).

Alabama
Marie Tomlin
State LTC Ombudsman
Commission on Aging
770 Washington Ave.
RSA Plaza, Suite 470
Montgomery, AL 36130
334-242-5743

Alaska
Frances Purdy
State LTC Ombudsman
Older Alaskans Commission
State LTC Ombudsman Office
3601 C St., Suite 260
Anchorage, AK 99503-5209
907-563-6393
e-mail: fran_purdy@admin.statc.ak.us

Arkansas
Raymon Harvey
State LTC Ombudsman
Division of Aging & Adult Services
State LTC Ombudsman Office
P.O. Box 1437
Donaghey Plaza South, Slot 1412
Little Rock, AR 72203-1437
501-682-2441

Arizona
Rosalind Webster
State LTC Ombudsman
Aging & Adult Administration
1789 West Jefferson 950A
Phoenix, AZ 85007
602-542-4446

California
Phyllis Heath
State LTC Ombudsman
California Department of Aging
1600 K St.
Sacramento, CA 95814
916-323-6681

Colorado
Virginia Fraser
State LTC Ombudsman
The Legal Center
455 Sherman St., Suite 130
Denver, CO 80203
303-722-0300

Connecticut
Barbara Frank
State LTC Ombudsman
Connecticut Dept. on Aging
Department of Social Services
25 Sigourney St., 10th floor
Hartford, CT 06106-5033
860-424-5200

Delaware
Maxine Nichols
State LTC Ombudsman
Division of Health and Social Services
Services for the Aging & Disabled
New Castle Country
256 Chapman Road
Oxford Building, Suite 200
Newark, DE 19702
302-453-3820

Florida
Gwen Schaper
State LTC Ombudsman
State LTC Ombudsman Council
Carlton Building, Office of the Governor
501 South Calhoun St.
Tallahassee, FL 32399-0001
904-488-6190
e-mail: floms@aol.com

Georgia
Becky Kurtz
LTC State Ombudsman
Division of Aging Services
2 Peachtree St. NW, Suite 36-233
Atlanta, GA 30303-3156
404-657-5319
e-mail: bkurtz@mail.doas.state.ga.us

Hawaii
Michael Ragddale
State LTC Ombudsman
Office of the Governor
Executive Office on Aging
250 South Hotel St., Suite 107
Honolulu, HI 96813-2831
808-586-0100

Idaho
Cathy Hart
State LTC Ombudsman
Idaho Office on Aging
P.O. Box 83720
Statehouse, Room 108
Boise, ID 83720-0007
208-334-3033

Illinois
Beverly Rowley/Nyena Johnson
State LTC Ombudsmen
Illinois Department on Aging
421 East Capitol Ave., Suite 100
Springfield, IL 62701-1789
217-785-3143

Indiana
Arlene Franklin
State LTC Ombudsman
Division of Aging & Rehab. Services
P.O. Box 7083 MS 21
402 West Washington St.
Indianapolis, IN 46207-7083
317-232-7134

Iowa
Carl M. McPherson
State LTC Ombudsman
Iowa Department of Elder Affairs
Clemens Building
200 10th St., 3rd floor
Des Moines, IA 50309-3609
515-281-4656

Kansas
Matthew Hickam
State LTC Ombudsman
Office of the State Long-Term Care Ombudsman
610 SW 10th Avenue, 2nd Floor
Topeka, KS 66612-1616
785-296-3017

Kentucky
Gary R. Hammonds
State LTC Ombudsman
Division of Aging Services
State LTC Ombudsman Office
275 E. Main St., 5th Floor West
Frankfort, KY 40621
502-564-6930

Louisiana
Linda Sadden
State LTC Ombudsman
Governor's Office of Elderly Affairs
State LTC Ombudsman Office
412 N. 4th St., 3rd floor
Baton Rouge, LA 70802
504-342-7100

Maine
Brenda Gallant
State LTC Ombudsman
State LTC Ombudsman Program
21 Bangor St.
P.O. Box 126
Augusta, ME 04332-0126
207-621-1079
Toll-free instate: 800-499-0229

Maryland
Patricia Bayliss
State LTC Ombudsman
Maryland Office on Aging
301 W. Preston St., Room 1004
Baltimore, MD 21201
410-225-1074

Massachusetts
Mary McKenna
State LTC Ombudsman
Executive Office of Elder Affairs
1 Ashburton Place, 5th floor
Boston, MA 02108-1518
617-727-7750

Michigan
Hollis Turnham
State LTC Ombudsman
Citizens for Better Care
State LTC Ombudsman Office
416 N. Homer St., Suite 101
Lansing, MI 48912-4700
517-336-6753

Minnesota
Sharon Zoesch
State LTC Ombudsman
Office of Ombudsman
444 Lafayette Road, 4th floor
St. Paul, MN 55155-3843
612-296-0382

Mississippi
Anniece McLemore
State LTC Ombudsman
Division of Aging & Adult Services
750 North State St.
Jackson, MS 39202
601-359-4929

Missouri
Carol Scott
State LTC Ombudsman
Missouri Division of Aging
Department of Social Services
P.O. Box 1337
Jefferson City, MO 65102-1337
573-526-0727

Montana
Doug Blakley
State LTC Ombudsman
Senior and Long-Term Care Division
Department of Public Health and Human Services
P.O. Box 8005
Helena, MT 59604-8005
406-444-5900

Nebraska
Geri Tucker
State LTC Ombudsman
Nebraska Department on Aging
301 Centennial Mall South
P.O. Box 95044
Lincoln, NE 68509-5044
402-471-2306

Nevada
Bruce McAnnany
State LTC Ombudsman
Compliance Investigator
Department of Human Resources
340 N. 11th St., Suite 203
Las Vegas, NV 89101
702-486-3545

New Hampshire
Judith Griffin
Acting State LTC Ombudsman
Division of Elderly & Adult Services
State LTC Ombudsman Office
6 Hazen Dr.
Concord, NH 03301-6505
603-271-4375
Toll-free instate: 800-443-5640

New Jersey
Bonnie Kelly
State LTC Ombudsman
Ombudsman Office
101 S. Broad St., 6th floor
Trenton, NJ 08625-0808
609-984-7831

New Mexico
Tim Covell
State LTC Ombudsman
State Agency on Aging
State LTC Ombudsman Office
228 E. Palace Ave., Suite A
Santa Fe, NM 87501
505-827-7663

New York
Faith Fish
State LTC Ombudsman
NYS Office for the Aging
2 Empire State Plaza
Albany, NY 12223-0001
518-474-0108

North Carolina
Michael McCann
State LTC Ombudsman
Division of Aging
693 Palmer Dr.
Caller Box Number 29531
Raleigh, NC 27626-0531
919-733-3983

North Dakota
Helen Funk
State LTC Ombudsman
AGING SERVICES DIVISION, DHS
600 South 2nd. St., Suite 1C
Bismarck, ND 58504-5729
701-328-8989
88funh@state.nd.us

Ohio
Beverley Laubert
State LTC Ombudsman
Ohio Dept. of Aging
50 W. Broad St., 9th floor
Columbus, OH 43215-5928
614-466-7922

Oklahoma
Esther Houser
State LTC Ombudsman
Aging Services Division
Oklahoma Department of Human Services
312 NE 28 St.
Oklahoma City, OK 73105
405-521-6734

Oregon
Meredith A. Cote
State LTC Ombudsman
Office of the LTC Ombudsman
3855 Wolverne NE, Suite 6
Salem, OR 97310
503-378-6533

Pennsylvania
Joyce O'Brien
State LTC Ombudsman
Pennsylvania Department of Aging
LTC Ombudsman Program
400 Market St., 6th floor
Harrisburg, PA 17101-2301
717-783-7247

Rhode Island
Denise Medeiros
State LTC Ombudsman
Department of Elderly Affairs
160 Pine St.
Providence, RI 02903-3708
401-277-2858

South Carolina
Mary B. Fagan
State LTC Ombudsman
Division on Aging
202 Arbor Lake Dr., Suite 301
Columbia, SC 29223-7501
803-737-7500

South Dakota
Jeff Askew
State LTC Ombudsman
Office of Adult Services & Aging
Department of Social Services
700 Governors Dr.
Pierre, SD 57501-2291
605 773-3656

Tennessee
Adrian Wheeler
State LTC Ombudsman
Tennessee Commission on Aging
Andrew Jackson Building, 9th floor
500 Deaderick St.
Nashville, TN 37243-0860
615-741-2056

Texas
John F. Willis
State LTC Ombudsman
Texas Department on Aging
State LTC Ombudsman Office
4900 North Lamar Blvd.
Austin, TX 78751-2316
512-424-6840
800-252-2412

Utah
Carol Bloswick
State LTC Ombudsman
Department of Human Services
Division of Aging & Adult Services
120 North 200 West, Room 401
Salt Lake City, UT 84103
801-538-3910

Vermont
Jacqueline Majoros
State LTC Ombudsman
Vermont Legal Aid, Inc.
264 North Winooski
P.O. Box 1367
Burlington, VT 05402
802-863-5620

Virginia
Mark Miller
State LTC Ombudsman Program
Virginia Association of Area Agencies on Aging
530 East Main St., Suite 428
Richmond, VA 23219-2327
804-644-2923

Washington
Kary W. Hyre
State LTC Ombudsman
S. King County Multi-Service Center
State LTC Ombudsman Office
1200 South 336th St.
Federal Way, WA 98003-7452
206-838-6810

West Virginia
Carolyn S. Riffle
DHHR Specialist
West Virginia Commission on Aging
State LTC Ombudsman Office
1900 Kanawaha Blvd. East
Charleston, WV 25305-0160
304-558-3317

Wisconsin
George F. Potaracke
State LTC Ombudsman
Board on Aging & Long-Term Care
214 North Hamilton St.
Madison, WI 53703-2118
608-266-8944
e-mail: gportarac@mail.state.wi.us

Wyoming
Deborah Alden
State LTC Ombudsman
Wyoming Senior Citizens, Inc.
756 Gilchrist
P.O. Box 94
Wheatland, WY 82201
307-322-5553

Web site Directory

Aging and eldercare— General

Administration on Aging (AoA)

www.aoa.dhhs.gov/

This site includes information designed for older Americans and their families, including information on the Older Americans Act.

American Association of Retired Persons (AARP)

www.aarp.org/

AARP is the nation's leading organization for people age 50 and older. The Web site includes information on eldercare-related research, volunteer and community programs, and advocacy issues.

The American Society on Aging

www.healthanswers.com/sponsor_directory/asa/
    index.htm

This site provides information similar to that at the AoA site.

The Caregiver's Handbook

www.acsu.buffalo.edu/~drstall/hndbk0.html

This full online handbook covers all aspects of caregiving.

EldercareWeb

www.elderweb.com/about.htm

This Web site provides links to financial, legal, social, health, and other informational sources.

ElderWeb
www.elderweb.com/
This award-winning online sourcebook includes links to articles about eldercare topics, sites where you can search for services by state, information about how to apply for Medicaid in various states, and much more.

Interactive Aging Network
www.ianet.org/
This site includes links to senior resources, research on aging, and advocacy and fundraising sites.

National Association of Area Agencies on Aging
www.n4a.org/
This Web site includes the Network News and a Legislative Update for members containing late-breaking news on aging policies in Washington, D.C.

National Institute on Aging
www.nih.gov/nia/
This site includes updates on the latest research on aging and an online ordering form for publications on health and aging topics for health professionals and the public.

Senior Options
www.senioroptions.com/
This site helps identify your local options for senior living facilities and provides local options for senior insurance, healthcare discount cards, and other frequently needed health and professional services.

Senior Resource
www.seniorresource.com/
This site provides information on health, finances, insurance, and housing.

ThirdAge
www.thirdage.com/
This is a general Web site for older Americans, including tips on finances, sex, romance, health, and family care.

Health
Alzheimer's Association
www.alz.org/
This site includes news updates, facts, and the latest research on Alzheimer's disease.

Alzheimer's Disease Education and Referral Center
www.alzheimers.org/
This site includes links to articles from *Connections*, an Alzheimer's publication, as well as Alzheimer's research, clinical trials, and referrals.

Alzheimer's Disease Review
www.coa.uky.edu/ADReview/
This site provides information on the latest advances in research on Alzheimer's disease and related disorders.

American Academy of Opthalmology
www.eyenet.org/
Includes information on glaucoma, cataracts, and other vision problems.

American Cancer Society
www.cancer.org/
This site includes the latest cancer research and information.

American Heart Association
www.americanheart.org/
This site includes information on the causes and prevention of heart disease and stroke, as well as general health information.

American Stroke Association
www.americanheart.org/Stroke/index.html
This division of the American Heart Association includes information on the risk factors and warning signs of stroke.

Arthritis Foundation
www.arthritis.org/
This site includes information and research on arthritis.

Health Answers
www.healthanswers.com/
The Aging section of this site includes links to information on health, nutrition, fitness, sexuality, and other subjects tailored to seniors.

Health Net
www.health-net.com/seniors.htm
The Senior's Health section of this site includes information on heart disease, weight control, vaccination, and other medical topics of interest to seniors.

Mayo Clinic
www.mayo.edu/geriatricsrst/2.GeriPage.html
The Geriatrics page includes health topics of importance to the elderly.

Mental Health Net
www.cmhcsys.com/guide/aging.htm
The Aging section of this site includes links to sites of interest to seniors, including Alzheimer's sites, eldercare and senior sites, and newsgroups and mailing lists.

Novartis Foundation for Gerontological Research
www.healthandage.com/fpatient.htm
Includes links to information on healthy nutrition and exercise, as well as specific conditions such as diabetes, stroke, and depression.

Prostate Health
www.prostatehealth.com/

USA Today
www.usatoday.com/life/health/seniors/lhsen000.htm
The Senior's Health section of this online publication offers links to articles on senior health.

Advocacy and Eldercare Law
Commission on Legal Problems of the Elderly
www.abanet.org/elderly/home.html
The CLPE Web site includes updates on recent legal initiatives in elder law.

Court TV Elder Law Center
www.courttv.com/legalhelp/elder/
This site includes links to legal organizations, information on Medicare and Medigap, wills and estates, pensions and retirement plans, and more.

Flying Solo
www.flyingsolo.com/
The Elderly and Disabled section of this site includes information on Medicaid qualification, patient's rights, discharge and transfer issues, estate planning, retirement planning, healthcare planning, special needs trusts, protecting assets, and more.

Kansas Elder Law Network
www.ink.org/public/keln/
This site provides access to primary and secondary materials pertaining to elder law.

Leading American Attorneys
www.lawlead.com/
This site includes a searchable database of lawyers who specialize in elder law.

National Consumer Law Center
www.consumerlaw.org/
The Free Consumer Information section of this site includes articles on avoiding telemarketing fraud, avoiding second mortgage fraud, the latest on Social Security and SSI payments, and more.

National Senior Citizens Law Center

www.nsclc.org/

This site includes information on Medicare, Social Security, age discrimination issues, nursing homes, and other subjects of interest to the elderly.

Senior Law Home Page

www.seniorlaw.com/

Established by the law firm of Goldfarb & Abrandt (a New York City-based firm that focuses on elder law), this site includes information about elder law (Elderlaw), Medicare, Medicaid, estate planning, trusts, and the rights of the elderly and disabled.

Eldercare Living options

AAAA Senior Housing and Service Referrals

www.aaaalliance.org/

This site offers assistance to making decisions about senior housing care.

American Association of Homes and Services for the Aging

www.aahsa.org/

Members of AAHSA receive updates on legislative, regulatory, and management issues; reports from AAHSA newsletters; and deals on insurance, financing, technology, and other products and services.

Eldercare Locator

www.ageinfo.org/elderloc/elderdb.html.

This site includes an online database to help you quickly find the available eldercare options in your area.

Extended Care Information Network
www.elderconnect.com/Eldercare/public/main.
html
ECIN provides a searchable database of more than
35,000 care providers in the United States, as well as
information on how to assess your needs.

Family Caregivers Alliance Resource Center
www.caregiver.org/resource.html
This site offers practical, hands-on information for
caregivers to assist in care, planning, stress relief,
and locating and using community resources such
as in-home or daycare services.

Homecare Online
www.nahc.org/
This site includes a home care and hospice agency
locator, as well as information on home care.

Hospice Web
www.teleport.com/~hospice/
This site includes a listing of hospice organizations
by state, as well as general information on hospices.

The National Center for Assisted Living
www.ncal.org/
This site provides general information on assisted
living, including statistics, consumer information,
and a regulatory review.

Nursing Home Info
www.nursinghomeinfo.com/
This site offers a searchable database with basic contact information for more than 17,000 long-term
care facilities.

The Retirement Net
www.retirenet.com
This site offers a directory of housing options in and
outside of the United States.

Senior Alternatives for Living
www.senioralternatives.com/
This site offers a free referral service to those communities that meet a specified location and level of
care criteria. It also contains information on nursing
homes, retirement communities, hospice care, and
care for those with Alzheimer's disease and provides
a list of elder law attorneys by state.

Senior Living
www.seniorliving.com/Directory.HTML
This site offers information on the leading retirement communities in 13 states.

Visiting Nurse Association of America
www.vnaa.org/Home.htm
This site includes links to home care resources and
caregiver information.

Further Readings

Adamec, Christine. *How to Live with a Mentally Ill Person: A Handbook of Day-to-Day Strategies.* New York: John Wiley & Sons, 1996.

Albert, Steven M., Ph.D., and Elaine M. Brody, M.S.W. "When Elder Care is Viewed as Child Care: Significance of Elders' Cognitive Impairment and Caregiver Burden." *The American Journal of Geriatric Psychiatry* 4, no. 2 (Spring 1996): 121–130.

"Alzheimer's Found in a Third of Aged Driver Fatalities." *The Brown University Long-Term Care Quality Advisor* 9, no. 12 (June 23, 1997): 3.

Barton, Linda J. "A Shoulder to Lean On: Assisted Living in the U.S." *American Demographics* 19, no. 7 (July 1997): 45–52.

Bruck, Laura. "Welcome to Eden." *Nursing Homes* 46, no. 1 (January 1997): 28–32.

Campbell, A. John, et. al. "Randomised Controlled Trial of a General Practice Programme of Home Based Exercise to Prevent Falls in Elderly Women." *British Medical Journal* 315, no. 7115 (October 25, 1997): 1065–1070.

Appendix C

Clarke, Sally C. "Advance Report of Final Marriage Statistics, 1989 and 1990." *Monthly Vital Statistics Report* 43, no. 12 (July 14, 1995): supplement.

Cox, Barbara J., and Lois Lord Walter. *Bridging the Communication Gap with the Elderly: Practical Strategies for Caregivers.* Chicago: American Hospital Association, 1991.

Cummings, Jeffrey. "Dementia: The Failing Brain." *The Lancet* 345, no. 8963 (June 10, 1995): 1481–1485.

Curran, Julie, S.M. "The Impact of Day Care on People with Dementia." *International Journal of Geriatric Psychiatry* 11, no. 9 (1996): 813–817.

"Employee-Caregivers Cost U.S. Firms $11 Billion Annually in Lost Productivity." *BNA Employment Policy and Law Daily* (June 19, 1997).

Faught, Leslie. "At Eddie Bauer You Can Work and Have a Life." *Workforce* 76, no. 4 (April 1997): 83–88.

Greider, Katharine, and Jill Neimark. "Making Our Minds Last a Lifetime." *Psychology Today* 29, no. 6 (November-December 1996): 42–47.

Hamel, Glen. "A Freestanding Nursing Home Tackles Diversification." *Nursing Homes* (October 1996): 56–57.

Happ, Mary Beth, et. al. "Factors Contributing to Rehospitalization of Elderly Patients with Heart Failure." *Journal of Cardiovascular Nursing* 11, no. 4 (July 1997): 75–83.

"How to Talk to Someone Who Keeps Forgetting Things." *The Brown University Long-Term Quality Advisor* 9, no. 17 (September 8, 1997): 51.

"Integrating Assisted Living with Independent Living." *Nursing Homes* 46, no. 8 (September 1997): 53–54.

Katherine, Anne. *Boundaries: Where You End and I Begin.* New York: Fireside/Parkside, 1991.

Lee, Michele Y., M.A., and Karen D. Novielli, M.D. "A Nutritional Assessment of Homebound Elderly in a Physician-Monitored Population." *Journal of Nutrition for the Elderly* 15, no. 3 (1996): 1–13.

Levine, Susan. "Nursing Home Movement Stresses Quality of Life." *Washington Post* (November 21, 1997): A1.

Levy, David T., et. al. "Relationship Between Driver's License Renewal Policies and Fatal Crashes Involving Drivers 70 Years or Older." *JAMA* 274, no. 13 (October 4, 1995): 1026–1030.

Matthews, Joseph. *Beat the Nursing Home Trap: A Consumer's Guide to Choosing & Financing Long-Term Care.* Berkeley, CA: Nolo Press, 1995.

McDaniel, Janet L., Ph.D., R.N., and Brenda G. Via, B.S., R.N., COHN-S. "Aging Issues in the Workplace." *AAOHN Journal* 45, no. 5 (May 1997): 261–272.

McKinlay, John B., Ph.D, et. al. "The Everyday Impacts of Providing Informal Care to Dependent Elders and Their Consequences for the Care Recipients." *Journal of Aging and Health* 7, no. 4 (November 1995): 497–527.

"Medicaid—Who Gets What." *State Legislatures* 23, no. 2 (February 1997): 5.

Meyer, Harris. "Home Care Goes Corporate." *Hospitals & Health Networks* 71, no. 10 (May 5, 1997): 20–25.

Mollica, Robert L. "Assisted Living and State Reimbursement Policy." Published by the *National Academy for State Health Policy.* (October 1997).

"More Workers Say Family Concerns Restrain Job Moves, Survey Finds." *BNA Pensions & Benefits Daily* (October 28, 1996).

Murphy, Barbara, et. al. "Women with Multiple Roles: The Emotional Impact of Caring for Aging Parents." *Ageing and Society* 17 (1997): 277–291.

Phillips, Charels D., Ph.D., M.P.H, et. al. "Effects of Residence in Alzheimer Disease Special Care Units on Functional Outcomes." *JAMA* 278, no. 16 (October 22-29, 1997): 1340–1344.

Rappaport, Judith B. "Unburden the Trust Officer: Employ a Private Care Manager." *Trusts & Estates* 135, no. 2 (February 1996): 46–53.

Razzi, Elizabeth. "Finding the Right Caregiver." *Kiplinger's Personal Finance Magazine* 50, no. 5 (May 1996): 67–71.

Schiffman, Susan, Ph.D. "Taste and Smell Losses in Normal Aging and Disease." *JAMA* 278, no. 16 (October 22-29, 1997): 1357–1362.

Singleton, Judy. "The Impact of Family Caregiving to the Elderly on the American Workplace: Who Is Affected and What Is Being Done?" A dissertation for the Department of Sociology. University of Cincinnati: 1996.

The State Bar of Georgia Younger Lawyers Section Elder Law Committee. *Senior Citizens*

Handbook. Athens, GA: The Institute of Continuing Legal Education, revised August 1997.

Stephen, Mary Ann Parris, and Aloen L. Townsend. "Stress of Parent Care: Positive and Negative Effects of Women's Other Roles." *Psychology and Aging* 12, no. 2 (1997): 376–386.

Strauss, Peter J., and Nancy M. Lederman. *The Elder Law Handbook: A Legal and Financial Guide for Caregivers and Seniors.* New York: Facts on File, Inc., 1996.

Taccino, Kenn B. "Life-Care Communities: What They Are—And Aren't." *Accounting Today* 11, no. 2 (January 20, 1997): 8–9.

Thompson, Mark. "Fatal Neglect." *Time* 150, no. 17 (October 27, 1997): 34–39.

Tsuji, Ichiro, M.D., Sarah Whalen, B.S., and Thomas E. Finucane, M.D. "Predictors of Nursing Home Placement in Community-Based Long-Term Care." *Journal of the American Geriatrics Society* 43, no. 7: 761–766.

Uhlenberg, Peter. "Replacing the Nursing Home." *The Public Interest* 128 (Summer 1997): 73–85.

Wagner, Donna L., Ph.D. *Comparative Analysis of Caregiver Data for Caregivers to the Elderly, 1987 and 1997.* Published by the National Alliance for Caregiving. Bethesda, MD: June 1997.

"Work and Family Benefits Provided by Major U.S. Employers in 1996: Based on Practices of 1,050 Employers." Lincolnshire, IL: Hewitt Associates, 1997.

Important Documents

On the pages that follow, you'll find useful forms, checklists, and documents to help you assess your elder's needs and plan an optimal eldercare experience.

Gathering your elder's financial and legal information

Name

Social Security #

Accountant _____   Phone:_____

Attorney   _____   Phone:_____

Financial planner _____   Phone:_____

Insurance agent _____   Phone:_____

PERSONAL PAPERS   **LOCATION**

Birth certificate   _____

Children's birth certificates _____

Passport   _____

Adoption papers   _____

Naturalization papers   _____

Marriage certificates   _____

Divorce decree(s)   _____

Military records   _____

House deed(s)   _____

Auto title(s)   _____

Social Security card   _____

Insurance ID cards   _____

Location of and access to

safety deposit box   _____

DOCUMENT	**ACCOUNT #** **(IF APPLICABLE)**	**LOCATION**
Will	_____	_____
Living will	_____	_____
Power of attorney		
Finances	_____	_____
Health decisions	_____	_____
Pension	_____	_____
Checking account(s):		

_____

_____

_____

Saving accounts:

_____

_____

_____

Mortgages and notes:

_____

_____

_____

Tax records: _____

Canceled checks: _____

Credit cards:

_____

_____

_____

Certificate(s) of deposit:

_____

_____

_____

Checkbook: _____

Bonds: _____

Mutual fund shares: _____

Annuities: _____

IRA(s): _____

Records of payment
    Medical bills   _____
    Utility bills   _____
    Telephone bills   _____
    Tax bills   _____
    Other   _____

Insurance
    Life   _____
    Property   _____
    Liability   _____
    Medical   _____
    Dental   _____
    Homeowners   _____
    Automobile   _____
    Medigap   _____
    Long-term care   _____
    Pre-need contract_____
    Other   _____

Reprinted courtesy of AdultCare, Inc., a Fortis Company.

Getting your elder's medications in order

GENERAL MEDICATION SURVEY

Condition	Name of medication	Dose/How often?
Sleeping		
Arthritis		
Pain killers		
High blood pressure		
Diuretics		
Cardiac		
Chest pain		
Blood thinners		
Insulin		
Diabetes		
Depression		
Stress/Nerves		
Anti-inflammatory		
Antibiotics		
Vitamins		
Eye drops		
Thyroid		
Cold/flu		
Stomach		
Cholesterol		

Do you self-administer your drugs?

_____ Yes _____ No

If not, who does?_____

Do you routinely use:

    Laxatives?   _____ Yes _____No

    Antacids?   _____ Yes _____No

Do you take medications as prescribed?

_____ Yes _____No

Do you ever skip doses?

_____ Yes _____No

Reprinted courtesy of AdultCare, Inc., a Fortis Company.

The Patient's Bill of Rights
Introduction

The American Hospital Association presents *A Patient's Bill of Rights* with the expectation that observance of these rights will contribute to more effective patient care and greater satisfaction for the patient, his physician, and the hospital organization. Further, the Association presents these rights in the expectation that they will be supported by the hospital on behalf of its patients, as an integral part of the healing process. It is recognized that a personal relationship between the physician and the patient is essential for the provision of proper medical care. The traditional physician-patient relationship takes on a new dimension when care is rendered within an organizational structure. Legal precedent has established that the institution itself also has a responsibility to the patient. It is in recognition of these factors that these rights are affirmed.

1. The patient has the right to considerate and respectful care.

2. The patient has the right to obtain from his physician complete current information concerning his diagnosis, treatment, and prognosis in terms the patient can be reasonably expected to understand. When it is not medically advisable to give such information to the patient, the information should be made available to an appropriate person in his behalf. He has the right to know, by name, the physician responsible for coordinating his care.

(Reprinted with permission of the American Hospital Association, ©1992.)

3. The patient has the right to receive from his physician information necessary to give informed consent prior to the start of any procedure and/or treatment. Except in emergencies, such information for informed consent should include but not necessarily be limited to the specific procedure and/or treatment, the medically-significant risks involved, and the probable duration of incapacitation. Where medically-significant alternatives for care or treatment exist, or when the patient requests information concerning medical alternatives, the patient has the right to such information. The patient also has the right to know the name of the person responsible for the procedures and/or treatment.

4. The patient has the right to refuse treatment to the extent permitted by law and to be informed of the medical consequences of this action.

5. The patient has the right to every consideration of his privacy concerning his own medical care program. Case discussion, consultation, examination, and treatment are confidential and should be conducted discretely. Those not directly involved in his care must have the permission of the patient to be present.

6. The patient has the right to expect that all communications and records pertaining to his care should be treated as confidential.

7. The patient has the right to expect that, within its capacity, a hospital must make reasonable response to the request of a patient for services. The hospital must provide evaluation, service, and/or referral as indicated by the urgency of

the case. When medically permissible, a patient may be transferred to another facility only after he has received complete information and explanation concerning the needs for and alternatives to such a transfer. The institution to which the patient is to be transferred must first have accepted the patient for transfer.

8. The patient has the right to obtain information as to any relationship of his hospital to other healthcare and educational institutions insofar as his care is concerned. The patient has the right to obtain information as to the existence of any professional relationships among individuals, by name, who are treating him.

9. The patient has the right to be advised if the hospital proposes to engage in or perform human experimentation affecting his care or treatment. The patient has the right to refuse to participate in such research projects.

10. The patient has the right to expect reasonable continuity of care. He has the right to know, in advance, what appointment times and physicians are available and where. The patient has the right to expect that the hospital will provide a mechanism whereby he is informed by his physician or a delegate of the physician of the patient's continuing healthcare requirements following discharge.

11. The patient has the right to examine and receive an explanation of his bill, regardless of source of payment.

12. The patient has the right to know what hospital rules and regulations apply to his conduct as a patient.

Conclusion

No catalog of rights can guarantee for the patient the kind of treatment he has a right to expect. A hospital has many functions to perform, including the prevention and treatment of disease, the education of both health professionals and patients, and the conduct of clinical research. All these activities must be conducted with an overriding concern for the patient and, above all, the recognition of his dignity as a human being. Success in achieving this recognition assures success in the defense of the rights of the patient.

Sample Durable Power of Attorney

Be it known that _____ the undersigned Grantor, does hereby grant a durable power of attorney to _____ as my attorney-in-fact.

My attorney-in-fact shall have full powers and authority to do and undertake all acts on my behalf that I could do personally, including but not limited to the right to sell, deed, buy, trade, lease, mortgage, assign, rent, or dispose of any real or personal property; the right to execute, accept, undertake, and perform all contracts in my name; the right to deposit, endorse, or withdraw funds to or from any of my bank accounts or safe deposit box; the right to borrow, collect, lend, invest, or reinvest funds; the right to initiate, defend, commence, or settle legal actions on my behalf; the right to vote (in person or by proxy) any shares or beneficial interest in any entity; and the right to retain any accountant, attorney, or other advisor deemed necessary to protect my interests relative to any foregoing unlimited power. My attorney-in-fact shall have full power to execute, deliver, and accept all documents and undertake all acts consistent with the foregoing.

This power of attorney shall become effective upon and remain in effect only during such periods as I may be mentally or physically incapacitated and unable to care for my own needs or make competent decisions as are necessary to protect my interests or conduct my affairs.

My attorney-in-fact hereby accepts this appointment subject to its terms and agrees to act and perform in said fiduciary capacity consistent with my best interests as my attorney-in-fact as his/her best discretion deems advisable, and I affirm and ratify all acts so undertaken.

This power of attorney may be revoked by me at any time and shall automatically be revoked upon my death, provided any person relying on this power of attorney shall have full rights to accept the authority of my attorney-in-fact until in receipt of actual notice of revocation.

Signed under seal this _____ day of _____ 20_____

STATE OF _____

COUNTY OF _____

on _____ before me, _____, personally appeared _____, personally known to me (or proved to me on the basis of satisfactory evidence) to be the person(s) whose name(s) is/are subscribed to the within instrument and acknowledged to me that he/she/they executed the same in his/her/their authorized capacity(ies), and that by his/her/their signature(s) on the instrument the person(s), or the entity upon behalf of which the person(s) acted, executed the instrument.

WITNESS my hand and official seal,

Signature _____

Affiant _____ Known

_____ Unknown _____

ID Produced _____

NURSING HOME EVALUATION CHECKLIST

☐ Does the nursing home have a current state license on display?

☐ Does the administrator have an up-to-date state license?

☐ Does the facility have a history of serious violations? (Check with your state ombudsman or ask the home for a copy of its latest survey report.)

☐ Is the nursing home certified for Medicare or Medicaid? (Even if these problems are not important to you now, they may be in the future.)

☐ Do the residents seem happy?

☐ Is the location convenient to family and friends?

☐ Is the location convenient to the patient's physician?

☐ Is the facility near a hospital?

☐ Is a Patients' Bill of Rights posted in plain sight?

☐ Are there handrails in the hallways, grab bars in the bathrooms, and other features aimed at accident prevention? Are toilet facilities raised and doors designed to accommodate residents in wheelchairs? Are wheelchair ramps provided indoors as well as outdoors?

☐ Are the hallways wide enough to permit two wheelchairs to pass with ease?

☐ Are there clearly marked exits and unobstructed paths to these exits?

☐ Are there fire extinguishers, automatic sprinklers, and smoke detectors throughout? Are they checked annually? Have they recently been checked?

☐ Is there emergency lighting in rooms and halls?

☐ Is the furniture sturdy?

☐ Is a physician available at all times for emergencies?

☐ Is there security personnel to prevent confused residents from wandering away from the building?

☐ Is the facility clean, well-maintained, and odor-free?

☐ Is a licensed dietitian on the premises often enough to provide adequate supervision of planning and preparation of meals? (Ask to see the kitchen area in order to observe cleanliness.)

☐ Is a weekly menu plan available? Are the meals nutritious and tasty?

☐ Does the staff assist residents who have difficulty feeding themselves?

☐ Is the staff friendly, available, caring, and accommodating to residents and visitors?

☐ Is there an activity room where residents can read, do crafts, play games, or socialize?

☐ Are physical therapy and rehabilitative services available?

☐ Is a list of references available?

☐ Would this nursing home provide the best possible care for your loved one?

This checklist was reproduced with permission from the MetLife Consumer Education Center.

A

The *Unofficial Guide*™ Reader Questionnaire

If you would like to express your opinion about eldercare or this guide, please complete this questionnaire and mail it to:

The *Unofficial Guide*™ Reader Questionnaire
Macmillan Lifestyle Group
1633 Broadway, floor 7
New York, NY 10019-6785

Gender: ___ M ___ F

Age: ___ Under 30 ___ 31–40 ___ 41–50
___ Over 50

Education: ___ High school ___ College
___ Graduate/Professional

What is your occupation?

_____

How did you hear about this guide?
___ Friend or relative
___ Newspaper, magazine, or Internet
___ Radio or TV
___ Recommended at bookstore
___ Recommended by librarian
___ Picked it up on my own
___ Familiar with the *Unofficial Guide*™ travel series

Did you go to the bookstore specifically for a book on eldercare? Yes ___ No ___

Have you used any other *Unofficial Guides*™ ?
Yes ___ No ___

If Yes, which ones?

_____
_____
_____

What other book(s) on eldercare have you purchased?

_____

_____

_____

Was this book:
___ more helpful than other(s)
___ less helpful than other(s)

Do you think this book was worth its price?
Yes ___   No ___

Did this book cover all topics related to eldercare adequately?
Yes ___   No ___

Please explain your answer:

_____

_____

_____

Were there any specific sections in this book that were of particular help to you?   Yes ___   No ___

Please explain your answer:

_____

_____

_____

On a scale of 1 to 10, with 10 being the best rating, how would you rate this guide? ___

What other titles would you like to see published in the _Unofficial Guide_™ series?

_____

_____

Are _Unofficial Guides_™ readily available in your area?   Yes ___   No ___

Other comments:

_____

_____

_____

_____

Get the inside scoop...with the Unofficial Guides™!

The Unofficial Guide to Acing the Interview
ISBN: 0-02-862924-8 Price: $15.95

The Unofficial Guide to Alternative Medicine
ISBN: 0-02-862526-9 Price: $15.95

The Unofficial Guide to Buying or Leasing a Car
ISBN: 0-02-862524-2 Price: $15.95

The Unofficial Guide to Buying a Home
ISBN: 0-02-862461-0 Price: $15.95

The Unofficial Guide to Casino Gambling
ISBN: 0-02-862917-5 Price: $15.95

The Unofficial Guide to Childcare
ISBN: 0-02-862457-2 Price: $15.95

The Unofficial Guide to Conquering Impotence
ISBN: 0-02-862870-5 Price: $15.95

The Unofficial Guide to Coping with Menopause
ISBN: 0-02-862694-X Price: $15.95

The Unofficial Guide to Cosmetic Surgery
ISBN: 0-02-862522-6 Price: $15.95

The Unofficial Guide to Dating Again
ISBN: 0-02-862454-8 Price: $15.95

The Unofficial Guide to Dieting Safely
ISBN: 0-02-862521-8 Price: $15.95

The Unofficial Guide to Divorce
ISBN: 0-02-862455-6 Price: $15.95

The Unofficial Guide to Earning What You Deserve
ISBN: 0-02-862716-4 Price: $15.95

The Unofficial Guide to Having a Baby
ISBN: 0-02-862695-8 Price: $15.95

The Unofficial Guide to Hiring and Firing People
ISBN: 0-02-862523-4 Price: $15.95

The Unofficial Guide to Hiring Contractors
ISBN: 0-02-862460-2 Price: $15.95

The Unofficial Guide to Investing
ISBN: 0-02-862458-0 Price: $15.95

The Unofficial Guide to Investing in Mutual Funds
    ISBN: 0-02-862920-5 Price: $15.95
The Unofficial Guide to Living with Diabetes
    ISBN: 0-02-862919-1 Price: $15.95
The Unofficial Guide to Managing Your Personal Finances
    ISBN: 0-02-862921-3 Price: $15.95
The Unofficial Guide to Overcoming Arthritis
    ISBN: 0-02-862714-8 Price: $15.95
The Unofficial Guide to Overcoming Infertility
    ISBN: 0-02-862921-3 Price: $15.95
The Unofficial Guide to Planning Your Wedding
    ISBN: 0-02-862459-9 Price: $15.95

All books in the *Unofficial Guide*™ series are available at your local bookseller, or by calling 1-800-428-5331.

About the Author

Christine Adamec is a freelance writer who has written ten books and more than eight hundred feature articles in her nearly twenty-year writing career. Adamec is also a retired Air Force Major who served on active duty and in the Air Force Reserves.
Christine first became interested in elders when she wrote about older citizens who volunteered their services to the Jacksonville, Florida Sheriff's Department in the mid-1980s. Since then she has written many features about elders.